Autism: A Holistic Approach

In Memory of Hans Müller-Wiedemann

Autism

A Holistic Approach

Bob Woodward
and Dr Marga Hogenboom

Floris Books

First published in 2000 by Floris Books
Second edition 2002

British Library CIP Data available

ISBN 0–86315–378-X

Printed in Great Britain
by J.W. Arrowsmith Ltd, Bristol

Contents

Foreword

Helping Autism with Knowledge of Human Nature

Infants and autistic children remind us how subtle the natural beginning state of mental life is, and how it depends on human sympathy. What is this consciousness, emotion and sympathy for human company which an infant can show?

After thirty years work as an infant *psychobiologist* I am sure that our fundamental motives require a profound revision of scientific explanations accepted by mainstream psychology over the past century. I am, therefore, willing to listen to alternative accounts that claim to be comprehensive. I am especially interested if they also claim to have useful applications in the education of the young, or in therapeutic work with persons of any age who are emotionally disturbed and handicapped in thinking, learning and communicating with other persons.

What prevents experts from grasping essential motive principles in the naive? What kind of approach would be more successful? Must it be scientific, and if so in what way? Scientists have to concentrate on one line of enquiry, paying close attention to the often very delicate and difficult methods they use to get evidence. Their notions or *models* of reality deliberately reduce their view, in order to see their subject clearly and have some predictable influence over it.

Common sense can readily find shortcomings in the more contrived explanations, which often seem only able to see what a person can acquire by education or through the conventions of social institutions, art, literature, technology, logic and science. Sympathy and compassion, which are so important in the actual experience of family and life in a close community, in caring for the sick and in teaching, are intuitive and spontaneous. They are not easily explained in terms of external facts and information understood. The understanding mind in itself has moral impulses that have to be accepted without reasoned explanation.

Infants are inarticulate, unskilled and unsophisticated. They have no authority and no justifiable beliefs or opinions. However, as the research of the past few decades has brought to light, they do have purposes, interests and moral emotions. They perceive other persons' actions and imitate. They perceive their mother's voice from before birth and attend to the musicality and narrative impulse of human talk and songs before they can see well. They engage purposefully with objects and events in the world around them and explore the effects of their body moving. They soon attend closely to interests and tasks that can be shared, seeking to grasp the meaning of the shared world. All this is achieved in the first year, much in the first few months, long before language and independent walking (Trevarthen 1987).

Many, perhaps most, academic authorities, including leading developmental psychologists, represent the infant as an impressionable learner, who, with little mental activity at first, has to acquire awareness of a self with a body and consciousness. Who has to learn to perceive the independent life of other persons with their bodies and consciousness. This psychology conceives the newborn as a scarcely conscious being whose emotions are crude states of agitation or arousal within the physiology of the brain and body, and are undifferentiated with regard to the reactions and identities of other persons. More and more, this rational constructivist position, which sees the body as innate but the mind as learned, has had to revise its models. It has had to grant greater intuitive psychological powers to the infant, even from the moment of birth, and thus, inevitably, from before birth too.

True, the rapid growth of a child's consciousness and skill that occurs in the first years of life obviously occurs with amazing speed. From day to day the baby becomes more aware and productive in response to its family and society, and then the toddler picks up the words that name the things and actions that are most interesting in the talk around them. However, this learner is from the start an active one, seeking companionship from persons who accept his or her own vitality, curiosity and emotional enthusiasm. Learning to be clever in human society takes a human effort in the learner, and only a human child can contribute this active interest.

The autistic child has lost some of this natural vitality of mind, some of the intricate proficiency of acting and attending, of sensing the body and the world. As infancy passes there are higher hurdles to climb and a confusion of awareness, which the autistic toddler has to overcome in achieving confidence in his or her feelings of self, and finding the right methods of communication to make others understand and share (Hobson 1993). The main task is to attract sufficiently patient, supportive and receptive attention from those who would give care and teach.

In this book, Bob Woodward has brought together a valuable fund of wisdom from members of the Camphill movement who have many years experience in therapeutic communities. In these residential settings they guide autistic youngsters to come to terms with their bodies and with a world that is more incomprehensible than it should be, and especially baffling in that essential human element on which meaningful learning depends.

The authors present a very readable account of the special features of an autistic child, which I find to be accurate and comprehensive. Case reports clearly illustrate how the principles of anthroposophy are applied in practice. The lectures and articles by Dr. Hans Müller-Wiedemann trace the development of a child through stages of mastery in engagement with an elusive reality and in communication. They also follow how an autistic youngster develops in spite of disjointed senses and incoherent or compulsive impulses to act, which themselves form a distorting barrier between the child and the world. Dr. Marga Hogenboom brings her medical training to confront the problems autistic children have inside their bodies, and the possible effects of diet on their psychological life.

As with many who use a sympathetic intuition and direct experience to guide their therapeutic work, these authors are suspicious of, or sceptical about, brain-based explanations. Clearly they believe that reference to current brain science is reductive, and likely to miss psychological events that can be experienced and worked with. But all the links and dependencies that they so carefully record — between the digestive system and the mind; between bodily feelings and imagination or learning; between self-knowledge and sensitivity for other person's intentions, interests and feelings — are mediated by the brain, if we but knew how. And brain science is changing. At least some of those who are concerned with the richness of normal consciousness, or with the changes brought on by brain injury, neural disease, or developmental disorder, are clear that some unifying principle operates and that emotions are integral to its operation (Damasio 1999).

Those of us who have filmed and analyzed how infants come to the human condition with such eager anticipation and sensitivity are convinced that there is a coherent intentionality and intersubjectivity, or sense of 'self-with-other,' from birth and before. The challenge is to understand how it gains in strength, discrimination, knowledge, skill and moral astuteness, while remaining whole and in sympathetic resonance with other human beings.

The authors of this book refer to evidence that an autistic youngster has been missing something from the start, and that this lack gradually becomes more obvious and worrying to parents and others, including peers, in the early years, especially the second and third years. As I have indicated, I do not believe we should take this account, with which I concur, as evidence that the human mind is incoherent at birth. Although subtle signs of detachment and turning inward can be discovered in retrospect in the life record of an autistic child, it remains unlikely that autism will ever be reliably diagnosed in early infancy. And that beginning of an active human spirit gives us hope.

Why take the emergence of a child's strength, skill and discrimination to be signs of construction of the mind from ground zero? Perhaps this idea reflects a weakness, a vanity in our whole culture's sense of the human condition, which is evident in psychological science and medicine. I believe it comes from too much faith and admiration for the training or instruction intended to make us accomplished citizens — skilled in movement, rational, articulate, literate and prosperous in a worldly sense. What is it to be humanly spiritual? Is it not to be biologically, essentially human — to be unsophisticated yet powerful in natural terms? I see all infants, including those becoming autistic, as being like this. In that I believe I am at one with the authors of this book.

Science does change our view of reality, and cognitive science and brain science are actively doing that now, but there is a price to pay for new expertise, dependent as it is on worlds that are technically strange, and remote from ordinary experience and common sense. The Western world changed after Darwin and Copernicus. Philosophers, too, also change our ways of living, and the post-classical philosophers of education in particular — including Comenius, Rousseau, Froebel and Steiner — upheld the human needs of children against projects of utilitarian instruction that may push them too hard or too early, into a conventional mould.

With all the influences of our education, we remain both constrained and inspired by natural motives, and the motives of children are astonishingly strong. They are strong, too, when they are unusual, as in the case of children who become isolated and obsessional in their toddlerhood, and remain distant from the activities of their peers. They remain cut off in a world that becomes increasingly their own unless others are sensitive to the need for companionship that they still possess, and that they greatly enjoy when the opportunity arises. This chance depends on sympathetic, playful and imitative approaches by persons whose consciousness has gone through many stages of education, but who can still forgo levels of skill and sophistication to share the fundamental human impulses of what anthroposophy calls the 'spirit.'

Having recently reviewed treatments, therapies and educative regimes for autistic children, I would say this (Trevarthen, Aitken, Papoudi and

Robarts, 1998). Those methods that work best set out to meet the individual child's motivations and enthusiasms, such as they are, directly. They accept the expressions and actions of the child with all their puzzling incoherence and fixations, emotional frailty and weak empathy, but also perceive their times of spontaneous ebullience, courage and affectionate appreciation of sympathetic care and fun. They realize that if there are to be beneficial changes in the child, changes have to come about in the responsiveness of parents, siblings, therapists and teachers — changes that will foster interest, enjoyment and learning. I see that accepting a 'holistic' or inclusive attitude to humanity in all the children, as well as respect for their individualities, brings improvements. I contrast this with the academic identification of specific deficiencies at a higher, more educated level of mental functioning, which are all measurable by controlled pre-structured tests. While these tests, models and theories certainly illuminate puzzles that arise in the exploration of pathological effects that develop in the psychology of different groups of children, they have remarkably little practical use in helping these children. Every technique of intervention that does help has made direct engagement with the motives of the child for noticing things, feeling with people, and striving to have consistent effects in action, however weakened these motives may be. There is always a vitality that can be engaged. That is where one must begin.

Steiner's 'inner spiritual resources' are not *hidden* or *slumbering* in the infant. Nor are they lost in our purposeful rational selves. They remain efficiently active beneath the surface of all practicality, productive co-operation and explicit language. The moving body needs to be made to work as a whole, mechanically pacing and ordering the dynamic forces of mass and inertia of its parts harmoniously, co-operatively and economically, with little error or waste energy. The intelligence that understands what is perceived and that deploys special senses at the right moment and to the right place, is an agent of the impulse that moves the body, and that emotionally evaluates the risks and benefits of every intended action. All these are manifestations of the spirit of a person's living.

The coherence in time and space of these outputs of the mind — of the brain in its body — challenges the ambitions of human sciences, be they behavioural, psychological, cognitive, linguistic, physiological, biochemical or 'brain science.' Increasingly, all these different disciplines have, in a sense, had to become less disciplined, less confined within special paradigms and models, and more ready to take in evidence from the wide field of human natural history, the arts and common experience. Human minds have general emotional and emotive powers which are both spiritual and intelligent (Donaldson, 1992).

This book has taught me that the philosophical approach of anthroposophy, aiming to be guided by a comprehensive 'knowledge of the nature of man' clearly does inspire carers and teachers. It helps them take human concern for the life difficulties of a child who feels unsure in his or her body, is out of firm touch with earthly reality, disorganized in senses, especially the sense of shared meaning, and unable to conceive of the sympathy and companionship extended by parents, peers and teachers. They find the human spirit in the child, in the sense of a unified purpose and consciousness, and identify in what ways it is frustrated by unclear representations of how to intend and what to expect of the world.

I admire this approach and am impressed with what I hear about achievements in the Camphill therapeutic communities, where staff, parents and companions of autistic teenagers enter into communication at many levels besides the rational and pragmatic.

Colwyn Trevarthen
Professor (Emeritus) of Child Psychology and Psychobiology
The University of Edinburgh

References:

Damasio, A., *The feeling of what happens: Body, Emotion and the Making of Consciousness,* Heinemann, 1999.

Donaldson, M., *Human Minds,* Penguin, 1992.

Hobson, P., *Autism and the Development of Mind,* Hove/Hillsdale: Erlbaum, 1993.

Trevarthen, C., 'Infancy, mind in,' in Gregory, R.L., and Zangwill, O.L. (Eds.), *Oxford Companion to the Mind,* Oxford University Press, 1987.

Trevarthen, C., Aitken, K.J., Papoudi, D. and Robarts, J.Z., *Children with Autism: Diagnosis and Interventions to meet their Needs,* Jessica Kingsley, 1998.

Preface

Autism is one of the most intriguing conditions of our time. It is unsettling to meet children and adults with such outstanding problems of social interaction. It puzzles us because it challenges the essential core of every human being — how to relate to our fellows.

For the last forty years, work has been continuing with autistic children and adults, in residential settings based on curative education and social therapy. These places have developed their work according to the holistic knowledge of the human being, as originally described by Rudolf Steiner (1861–1925) in his science of anthroposophy. However, this perspective has not been sufficiently visible, and, until now, no book has been published in the English language on the anthroposophical approach to autism. This book has therefore been published to address the need to present a holistic and spiritually deepened view of autism.

We would like to dedicate *Autism: A Holistic Approach* to Dr Hans Müller-Wiedemann, who died in December 1997, and was an outstanding pioneer in the field of autism research based on his comprehensive understanding of anthroposophy. His work was published mainly in German, and has remained mostly unknown to the English reader.

Dr Müller-Wiedemann spent many years of his life living with autistic children and young people, in several therapeutic communities belonging to the worldwide Camphill movement. I met him for the last time in 1996, at a medical conference in Switzerland, where the sensory experience of the autistic child was discussed. Dr Müller-Wiedemann was already frail and only able to attend part of the conference. However, he still managed to make an inspiring contribution regarding the lack of secure bodily experience in children with autism, and how to remedy this.

The authors hope that this book will stimulate the open-minded reader, whether a person with autism, a parent or a professional, to consider a new point of view. Autism is a relatively newly described condition, and research is continuing to develop further insights into this disorder.

This book does not claim to provide all the answers, but hopes to contribute to this research in the field of autism.

Dr Marga Hogenboom

Acknowledgments

The authors would like to thank Johannes M. Surkamp MBE. for his translations from the original German of the four articles by the late Dr Hans Müller-Wiedemann (see Part IV). The authors are grateful to Verlag Freies Geistesleben, Stuttgart, Germany for permission to publish translated versions of three articles (Chapters 11, 12 and 13), previously published in *Der frühkindliche Autismus als Entwicklungsstörung* (1981). Chapter 14 originally appeared as 'Neue Aspekte der Förderung Autistischen Kinder,' in *Autismus Heute Band 2,* Verlag Modernes Lernen, Dortmund (1990). Again the authors are grateful for permission to reproduce a translated version of the text.

My own contributions have largely been selected from my 1997 M.Phil. thesis entitled *Autism in the Light of Anthroposophy.*

Thanks also to the two boys described in the case studies, and to their parents for permission to refer to the boys' developmental histories and my work with them. I am also grateful to my colleagues at the Sheiling School, Camphill community who fully supported this new research project.

Finally, thanks to Hazel Townsley for her professional skills on the word processor.

Bob Woodward

Contributors

BOB WOODWARD, MEd, MPhil.

Since 1970, Bob Woodward has lived with, and taught, children with severe learning difficulties, including children with autism, at The Sheiling School Camphill community, in Thornbury, Gloucestershire. Over the past ten years, he has taken a special interest, in trying to come to a better understanding of autism on the basis of Steiner's holistic *Image of Man*.

DR MARGA HOGENBOOM, MRCGP (Utrecht)

Dr Hogenboom lives and works at the Camphill Rudolf Steiner Schools near Aberdeen, and specializes in working with children and adults with special needs. She is a member of the Editorial Group of *The Journal of Curative Education and Social Therapy,* and is also a regular contributor to this quarterly publication.

DR HANS MÜLLER-WIEDEMANN, MD, PhD.

During the 1960s, Dr Karl König, the founder of the Camphill movement, asked Hans Müller-Wiedemann specifically to develop an anthroposophical understanding of the autistic child, and to investigate how to help these children become socially integrated. Dr Müller-Wiedemann took up this task in earnest over some thirty years, and became an acknowledged and respected authority in this field. He published various books and articles about his work, as well as poetry. He died in 1997.

JOHANNES M. SURKAMP, MBE.

For many years Johannes Surkamp was the Principal of Ochil Tower, a Camphill Rudolf Steiner school for children with special needs in Perthshire, Scotland. He has been a co-worker in the Camphill movement for over forty years, and was awarded the MBE. in 1995 for his services to education.

I

Background and Medical Research

The phrase 'Image of Man,' used in reference to Steiner's holistic understanding of the human being, is intended to include both masculine and feminine genders, in the same sense as mankind.

Throughout the text, the male gender has been used inclusively to acknowledge the fact that the ratio of autistic boys to girls is approximately three or four to one.

The Editor

1. What is Autism?

During the last half-century, since Leo Kanner's (1943) first description of the syndrome which he termed *Early Infantile Autism,* many people have sought to explain the symptomatology of autism. This search has given rise to important observations and investigations of autistic children, made at biological, psychological, and behavioural levels (Happé 1994). This data has in turn generated a divergency of theoretical interpretations of causation, but as Baron-Cohen and Bolton (1993) point out, there is still no clear-cut answer as to the cause, or perhaps causes, of autism. The focus in this chapter will be on the phenomenology which enables us to suspect or recognize that a child is autistic, and will then examine the key criteria for gaining a formal diagnosis.

Phenomenology

Biographical accounts written by parents of autistic children provide telling first-hand descriptions of the typical features of the condition (Lovell 1978, Park 1983, Hocking 1990, Kaufman 1976). These features are listed on pages 23–24, and appear during the first three years of life. They are evident in the marked indifference and aloofness of these children towards other people. The following examples, from these four biographies, illustrate this important and central autistic characteristic.

Simon was about nine months old, and apparently physically *perfect*, when his mother, who was pregnant with her second child, began to feel anxious about her first-born son. These anxieties arose through observing Simon's rate of development and that of a friend's little girl who was of the same age. In comparison Simon seemed much slower and too placid and '... seemed to take no interest in the world around him' (Lovell 1978, 4).

Moreover, he did not make eye contact with others. By the time he was twenty-one months old, Simon showed a marked indifference towards his peers, and also towards his new baby sister. When he was three and a half years old Simon was seen by a paediatrician at the local hospital, and, after observation and tests, the mother was told that 'Simon is autistic.' (Lovell 1978, 18)

Elly the fourth child of Clara Park, smiled at seven weeks, later made eye contact, and reached out for objects at the usual time. She sat at nine months and only learned to walk when about two years old. However, it was not late motor milestones which concerned her parents, but rather Elly's marked lack of response to their spoken requests during her second year. Physically nothing seemed to be amiss, but the beautiful two-year-old child took no notice of other people. Describing a seaside holiday, Park writes that Elly was:

> ... a bronzed, gold baby of unusual beauty walking along the sand. She might have walked straight ahead, deliberately swerving to avoid an occasional collision, without a backward look, forever, so little did she need of human contact. (Park 1983, 5)

Sam was the first child of a mother who, during and after pregnancy, was often anxious and stressful. He smiled at five weeks and physically seemed to be developing normally. However, Sam did not look at his mother, nor did he reach out for things later on. By ten months he could sit, but it was impossible to catch his attention person to person. Towards the end of his second year, Sam did not respond to anything his mother said, and appeared unable to understand language. He rarely looked at anyone, or only with an indirect glance. In the course of his third year, medical advice was sought by his parents from Dr Elizabeth Newson, an expert on autism. After observing Sam and interviewing his parents, she remarked that: ' ... he does present as a rather classically autistic child.' (Hocking 1990, 37)

Raun, the third child of Barry and Suzi Kaufman, appeared as being perfectly healthy at birth, and was given an Apgar rating of ten.*

---

* APGAR RATING: a method of assessing the general state of a baby immediately after birth. A maximum of two points is given for each of the following signs — breathing, heart rate, colour, muscle tone and response to stimuli. Thus a baby scoring ten points sixty minutes after birth would be in optimum condition. When the score is low, the test is repeated at intervals as a guide to progress.

However, during the first month at home he cried day and night and was unresponsive when held or fed. He developed a severe ear infection which needed antibiotics, which resulted in dehydration and urgent hospitalization in intensive care. Fortunately, Raun recovered well and during his first year, was a beautiful baby who smiled, laughed and played.

However, from one year of age Raun became more and more aloof, and by eighteen months eschewed human contact and communication.

> When Raun turned to you, he turned through you as if you
> were transparent. (Kaufman 1976, 23)

An interview with medical and psychiatric professionals confirmed that Raun was showing 'autistic behaviour patterns.'

Typical characteristics

An overview of the four biographies quoted above reveals the following autistic features:

— Aloofness and indifference towards others, including parents and peers.
— Looks *through* other people.
— Avoids eye contact.
— Treats others like an object or tool.
— Lacks communicative intent via sound, speech or gesture.
— When speech is present appears to lack comprehension.
— Shows a marked preference for sameness and routine.
— Engages in repetitive and obsessional actions.
— Lacks interest to reach out and explore the surroundings.
— Shows fascination for inanimate objects to be manipulated or put in order.
— Has no overt imaginative play.
— Shows little, if any, normal imitation.
— Displays unusual reactions to sensory stimuli.
— Is not deaf.
— Often musical.

— Good rote-memory.
— Able with jigsaw puzzles and has good visual-spatial skills.
— Physically good-looking, even beautiful, and often demonstrates
    co-ordinated and skilful movements.

All these typical features, as movingly described by the children's parents, are also confirmed in Wing 1996, Chapter 4. It is clear that autistic children appear either soon after birth, or at least by their third year of life, to be withdrawn and cut-off from their closest human surroundings. However, although their typical features are well known, historically the formal diagnosis of autism has not been entirely straightforward.

Diagnosing autism

The Kanner criteria

In the United States, Leo Kanner (1943) was the first person to describe autism when he identified eleven children as a distinct diagnostic group, who showed strikingly similar behavioural symptoms. Foremost among their symptoms was their '... inability to relate themselves in the ordinary way to people and situations from the beginning of life.' (Kanner 1943, 242)

Kanner chose to label the cluster of behaviours which united these eleven children as Early Infantile Autism, and concluded that:

> We must, then, assume that these children have come into the
> world with innate inability to form the usual, biologically
> provided affective contact with people, just as other children
> come into the world with innate physical or intellectual
> handicaps. (Kanner 1943, 250)

Although Kanner's original paper (1943) lists ten diagnostic points, in a later, joint paper with his colleague, Eisenberg, they were reduced to the following five features:

1. Extreme detachment from human relationships.
2. Failure to use language for the purpose of communication.
3. Anxiously obsessive desire for the maintenance of sameness, resulting in a marked limitation in the variety of spontaneous activity.
4. Fascination for objects; handled with skill in fine motor movements.
5. Good cognitive potentialities. (Furneaux and Roberts 1979, 41)

By 1955, when they had seen more than one hundred and twenty such children, Kanner and Eisenberg isolated just two primary diagnostic features for autism.

1. Extreme self-isolation (or aloneness), and
2. Obsessive insistence on the preservation of sameness.

However, since then, there has been considerable further debate.

Post-Kanner

In England in 1960, a committee chaired by Dr Mildred Creak, was convened to examine diagnostic criteria. They listed nine points describing the condition of childhood schizophrenia which at that time, was a term which included 'childhood psychoses' and early infantile autism (Schreibman, 1988, p.29). The first of the Creak points was:

Aloneness and apparent lack of any social skills. (Furneaux and Roberts 1979, 24)

While this was considered essential to a diagnosis of autism, views differed about the key relevance of the other eight features. In any event it was rare that all nine features would be seen in children said to be *autistic*. Notably, and in contrast to Kanner, the Creak committee acknowledged impairments in the intellectual functioning of these children. However, autistic individuals differ in their degree of intellectual impairment as well as in the severity and combination of their other symptoms.

Schreibman points out the historical vicissitudes that have accompanied the diagnosis of autism:

> A major result of the evolutionary process of diagnosis, of
> the appearance of different sets of diagnostic criteria, and of
> differing motivations for diagnosis (*e.g.* research, education,
> economic considerations), is that diagnosis is not applied in a
> consistent manner. This has resulted in a tremendously het-
> erogeneous population of autistic children. (Schreibman
> 1988, 33)

This very heterogeneity has led professionals to refer to a *contin-uum*, or *spectrum*, of autistic disorders (Wing 1993 & 1996), with Kanner's classical autism seen as a sub-group. Clearly, however, if the diagnostic goalposts are moved at different times and for different reasons, there will be more or less autistic children identified, and as Wing points out, epidemiological studies of the prevalence of such children do in fact give widely differing figures.

> A few studies have strictly applied Kanner's criteria of
> severe lack of affective contact (social aloofness) and insis-
> tence on elaborate repetitive routines, and they found 4 to 5
> children in every 10,000. (Wing 1996, 61)

However, in 1991, Swedish research raised the grand total of all autistic spectrum disorders to at least fifty-eight per ten thousand, that is, almost six in every thousand. What then are the currently accepted core criteria for diagnosing autism?

The triad of impairments

Since 1978, two well-documented and internationally-accepted medical diagnostic systems have been in use. These are:

1. The World Health Organization's International Classification of Diseases, now in its tenth version (ICD-10),
   and,

2. The American Psychiatric Association's Diagnostic and
Statistical Manual, in its fourth edition (DSM-IV).

Since 1980, both of these systems have included the notion of the
Triad of Impairments, which is regarded as common to autistic individuals across the continuum. For example, in ICD-10:

> Childhood autism (F84.0):
> Impaired or abnormal development must be present *before*
> three years of age, manifesting the *full* triad of impairments
> in:
> 1. reciprocal social interaction;
> 2. in communication; and
> 3. in restricted, stereotyped, repetitive behaviour.
> (Trevarthen *et al* 1996, 11)

Today, it is this triad which is regarded as the defining core feature
of autistic continuum disorders. However, in practice, definitive diagnosis requires considerable experience and expertise, for as Wing
points out:

> Diagnostic problems arise because the triad can be shown in
> many different ways. Unless the diagnostician is fully aware
> of the triad of impairments underlying autistic conditions,
> s/he may be confused by a whole series of variables that
> affect the outward manifestations ... (Wing 1993, 5)

Moreover, the triad could appear to be a very broad and relatively
imprecise instrument which might, in inexperienced hands, result in
the incorrect diagnosis of some children. There are, for example, some
constitutionally over-sensitive children (with Fragile X syndrome),
who often find it very difficult to meet people directly and to enter into
reciprocal social interactions and communication. Nevertheless, they
are actually very interested in, and often deeply concerned for, others
despite showing some superficially autistic features (Luxford 1994,
Rutter *et al* 1994).

Writing of the necessity for careful *differential diagnosis* when autism
is associated with any other physical or psychological disabilities, Wing

(1993) emphasizes the importance of obtaining a detailed, early developmental history for each child. It is also important to have descriptions of the child's behaviour and responses in a variety of different settings, not just in the doctor's or psychologist's clinic. For a diagnosis of an autistic continuum disorder to be made, the full Triad of Impairments must have been evident from early childhood. Even though, according to Wing (1996), the precise age of onset of autistic behaviours may not be an essential criterion for diagnosis, the Triad is typically manifest by the second or third year. The tremendous developmental significance of the first three years of life will be highlighted later, when we interpret autism on the basis of anthroposophy. Meantime, it is noteworthy that for autistic children:

> It is significant that their insensitivity to other persons' feelings, purposes and experiences appears before the child is three years old, and after an early infancy that was apparently almost normal.(Trevarthen *et al* 1996, 24)

The central problem

As Kanner originally observed, it is precisely the inability of autistic children to relate socially with other people that remains the most pervasive and definitive feature of autism, and in a recent and thorough survey it was concluded that:

> The diagnostic or descriptive systems that we have reviewed affirm that autistic children have a primary inability to perceive others as people and to conceive what they may communicate. (Trevarthen *et al* 1996, 24)

This conclusion, pointing as it does to a fundamental perceptual and conceptual inability and difficulty, is confirmed by the anthroposophical theory of autism presented in Chapter 8. This is particularly relevant in relation to the development and functioning of the child's higher senses of ego and thought, seen against a background of the incarnation processes of soul and spirit during the formative first three years. In Chapter 8 it will also become clear that disturbances in the typical steps leading to the experience of self-identity in the young child, vis-à-vis its surroundings, should also be recognized as central to the autistic condition, and the evident lack of social awareness and reciprocity.

Whereas the autistic child's inability to make affective contact and relationships with others has long been acknowledged, the role of the child's own self-experience has probably not yet been fully appreciated.

In order to gain this appreciation it is not only necessary to view the question of What is Autism? on biological and psychological levels (Happé 1994), but also to include the spiritual level on which each autistic child's essential being is to be found intact. In other words, we must aim for a holistic view which encompasses body, soul and spirit.

2. Causes and Alleviation

Historical perspectives

According to Kanner (1943) autism is a condition, precipitated by the over-intellectual, emotionally inadequate and frigid characteristics of the child's parents. In 1956, Eisenberg and Kanner spoke of how:

> Emotional refrigeration has been the common lot of autistic children. (Bettelheim 1967, 389)

However, Kanner himself did not claim that *refrigerator* parents were the sole cause of autism. Rather he believed that the pathology was present from birth, and was either a result of organic factors or, as Schreibman expressed it, of 'the interaction of organic predispositions with specific environmental events.' (Schreibman 1988, 49)

Nevertheless, *environmental* and *psychogenic* factors were strongly advocated during the 1960s by the psychoanalyst, Bruno Bettelheim. He wrote that:

> Wherever infantile autism is viewed as an inborn impair-
> ment, of whatever variety, the resultant attitudes towards
> treatment will be defeatist. (Bettelheim 1967, 405)

These views express the polarization which existed between advocates of the organic versus the psychogenic and the environmental schools of primary causation.

While Bettelheim did not accept the hypothesis that autism was due to an original organic defect, he did not however rule out the possibility of its later appearance.

Actually, I believe that in earliest development, soma and psyche are so little differentiated that to a more enlightened time the entire controversy between organic and psychogenic hypotheses at that age may appear moot. (Bettelheim 1967, 403)

However, he still recommended the removal of autistic children from their parents, in order to provide them with a more supportive environment in which they could be helped to recover from their withdrawn and traumatized state (Baron-Cohen & Bolton 1993).

Recent approaches

A review of recent literature from the past five years, leaves us in no doubt that organic pathology is now believed to lie at the root of autism. Most commonly, it is held to be an impairment and/or dysfunction of the brain. Although the precise neurological site of this presumed *in-child* problem has not yet been clearly located, fairly definitive statements have appeared, as illustrated below:

We now know that autism is a type of mental handicap due to abnormalities of brain development. (Frith 1989, 186)

It seems very likely that brain damage or dysfunction is present in autism in all its manifestations.
(Aarons & Gittens 1992, 20)

The fact that the autistic spectrum comprises disorders of development due to physical dysfunctions of the brain is now generally accepted ... (Wing 1996, 11)

Autism is the consequence of a complex disorder of brain development affecting many functions.
(Trevarthen *et al* 1996, 5)

However, the current focus on brain pathology needs to be qualified in the light of hard evidence. So far, whilst most brain-imaging studies have shown a heterogeneous range of abnormalities in some autistic individuals, there is no consistent pattern, and it seems there is also no understandable, clinical meaning with regard to the diagnosis or treatment of autism (Rutter *et al* 1994, 319). Furthermore, we know that there are many brain-damaged children who do not become autistic. A child's identified brain pathology may render them severely physically disabled and unable to speak, and yet they can establish, and clearly want, warm affective contact and communication with others (Scotson 1985).

Probably the most influential reason for suspecting, or assuming, that autism has a biological root, is its co-occurrence, in some children, with other known clinical conditions, such as epilepsy (Baron-Cohen & Bolton 1993, Chapter 4). Additionally, it is recognized that certain physical illnesses which affect the brain, such as tuberose sclerosis, encephalitis, and untreated phenylketonuria, can also be associated with autistic disorders. However, despite the inclusion of these instances, the rate of known medical conditions in autism is not, it seems, more than ten per cent, and these are least common in Kanner's Autism (Rutter *et al* 1994, 315). Therefore, although much of the recent literature asserts that the evidence is now 'overwhelmingly in favour of a biological cause for autism,' there may still be grounds to look for psychogenic causes, at least for some forms of autism (Happé 1994, 3).

This latter view is adopted by Frances Tustin, a respected and open-minded psychotherapist.

> I have come to realise that autism may arise in several different situations : for example, organic autism can be a reaction to brain damage or sensory defect, whereas psychogenic autism is the reaction to a delusory traumatic situation which seems to threaten life and limb. (Tustin 1992, 11)

Certainly in children who display Kanner's Autism, (that is, classic or pure autism), there is as yet no proven physical or psychological cause to account for their unusual state of being, in which they appear to exist in 'a world apart,' divorced from active interpersonal and affective relationships.

An anthroposophical interpretation of pure, or primary, autism offers another explanation for the core autistic symptoms. This view recognizes the intact spiritual being of each child, which is *hidden* behind any other psychological or organic factors. It is important that investigations into possible causative factors for autism should be conducted on different levels (organic, psychological *and* spiritual), which co-exist and interact in the total human being. However, the reality of the child's essential spiritual nature should not be denied due to a one-sided focus on physical organic problems. Rudolf Steiner (1990b) often pointed out that an incomplete knowledge, in which the spiritual element was omitted, would inevitably lead to an erroneous view of material-physical processes.

A cure

According to recent literature, there is no known cure for autism (Schreibman 1988; Ellis 1990; Baron-Cohen & Bolton 1993; Happé 1994). In most cases it is a pervasive and life-long, developmental disorder (Wing,1993; Trevarthen *et al* 1996). There are, it is true, isolated examples of remarkable recoveries from infantile autism (Kaufman 1976; Stehli 1991; Barron 1993), and there are even some impressive autobiographical descriptions written by exceptional autistic people (Grandin 1986; Miedzianik 1986; Williams 1992, 1994).* Nevertheless, these outstanding successes are rare and few (Trevarthen *et al* 1996).

Since it is a developmental disorder, autism manifests itself in a differentiated way in the course of time, and according to an individual's own unique biography.

> So, while a single glance may suffice for clinical diagnosis,
> if we hope to understand the autistic individual nothing less
> than a total biography will do. (Sacks 1994)

Many autistic children never learn to speak during infancy, and remain mute. Unless children have acquired some useful, pragmatic speech by five years of age, their future prognosis is usually much less

* For a critical review of such autobiographical accounts *see* Happé in Frith (Ed.) 1991, 207–42.

favourable in comparison to verbal autistic children (Aarons & Gittens 1992). Beyond childhood, and after adolescence and the demands of early adult life, there appears to be a tendency for any challenging behaviours to lessen, and for co-operativeness to increase (Wing 1990). However, irrespective of progress made or skills acquired, it appears that autistic young people continue to be socially handicapped (Elliot 1990).

Some contrasting interventions

Education

In the 1960s, the importance of education for autistic children had already been recognized by some professionals. In 1967, Michael Rutter stated that:

> In our present state of knowledge education probably constitutes the most important aspect of treatment and it is to school in one form or another that we must look for the greatest hope of bringing about achievement in the autistic child. (Furneaux & Roberts 1979, 57)

Boucher and Scarth (1977) outline three different approaches to teaching autistic children:

1. The psychodynamic;
2. Behaviour modification;
3. Environmental.

However, they point out that the structured, environmental approach, involving adult and task-directed activities, may also include elements of the more relationship-centred psychodynamic and/or the behaviourist methods. Since that time, the special learning difficulties shown by autistic children,and the development of different teaching methods and attitudes, have continued to be acknowledged and addressed (Elgar & Wing 1981; Jordan & Powell 1990 & 1996).

A particular, behaviourist approach, developed by Erich Schopler, is known as the *TEACCH Program.* (TEACCH stands for **T**reatment and **E**ducation of **A**utistic and related **C**ommunication-handicapped **CH**ildren.) It relies on a highly structured environment, and individually-planned programmes of work (Sanderson & Fraley 1994).

Another behavioural intervention described by Rutter and Howlin (1989) recognized the need to involve the parents of autistic children, as partners and participants in the implementation of home-based treatments.

However, in marked contrast to TEACCH and other behavioural methods, the Linwood Method for reaching 'the hidden child,' has an emphasis on psychodynamic insights and interrelationships, in which:

> The focus is on educating the total child in an environment
> designed to make all experiences therapeutic.
> (Simons & Oishi 1987, 26)

Such a holistic educational and therapeutic approach is also practised in the Camphill and Steiner special schools, but there it is underpinned by anthroposophy's developmental *Image of Man* (Woodward 1985).

Other therapies and treatments

The Option Method or *Process* which was developed by Barry and Suzi Kaufman to help their autistic son, Raun Kahlil, is an example of early, pre-school intervention. They started with this before he was two years old. At the core of the method is a complete acceptance of where the child is, and a willingness to try to enter into his autistic world. This might, for example, involve spinning objects with the child, perhaps for hours on end.

> We started to imitate him ... We wanted to use his cues as a
> basis of communicating. (Kaufman 1976, 62)

The child's being is respected through this gentle, non-invasive attempt to build bridges of contact and communication. However, this is in stark contrast to the *Holding Therapy* developed by Martha Welch, which is based on the notion that autism is caused by faulty bonding between mother and child. In this therapy the mother faces and forcefully holds her autistic child until, at the end of an inevitable battle it is claimed that:

> ... the child relaxes, moulds to her body, clings, gazes into her eyes, explores her face lovingly and gently, and eventually talks. (Tinbergen & Tinbergen 1983, 326)

Some examples of this method with young, pre-school children are given in the Tinbergens' (1983) book.

Facilitated Communication (FC) is a technique in which the autistic child is given direct physical support by an adult facilitator, to either point to individual letters or words, or to type them on the keyboard of a typewriter or word processor. While the method is not claimed to be a cure for autism, its enthusiasts regard it as an important means of enabling communication to take place. The major point of contention here is, who is actually doing the communicating — the autist or the facilitator? (Howlin 1994).

A book typed by means of FC, originally in German, describes the profound experiences and inner conflicts of Birger Sellin, and has received recent publicity (Sellin 1995; Holtzapfel 1993). Although such writings via FC can be impressive in content, one acclaimed American researcher recommends scepticism:

> It is now my considered opinion, after 35 years of experience [with FC] that what is being described as facilitated communication is invariably (unless proven otherwise) fraudulent. (Rimland 1996)

In each specific case it seems likely that much depends on the integrity and the intention of the facilitator.

The method of *Auditory Integration Training (AIT)* addresses the unusual, and often over-sensitive hearing perceptions of autistic children. The Berard version of this approach employs systematic desensitization or habituation of the child to particular, individually-assessed frequencies of sound, that have been a source of distress. Another version of AIT, known as *The Tomatis Method,* aims to develop the active listening ability of the child.

Berard's AIT received considerable impetus through the successful recovery from severe autism of Georgie, the daughter of Annabel Stehli (Stehli 1991). However, in common with other therapies which have relieved autism in some children, AIT still requires monitoring and controlled assessment to determine its efficacy for other autistic children (P & J Richardson 1994).

To date, the variety of special methods and treatments that have been offered to autistic children is considerable. Summaries of these can be found in recent literature (Baron-Cohen & Bolton 1993; Trevarthen *et al* 1996; Autism Research Unit 1991). For some people, biochemical approaches are a current source of optimism (Autism Research Review 1995). However, the father of one autistic child gives a sober reflection on the changing therapeutic scenario.

> They come up with a new 'miracle' every four years — first
> it was elimination diets, then magnesium and vitamin B6,
> then forced-holding, then operant conditioning and behaviour
> modification — now all the excitement is about auditory
> desensitisation and FC. (Sacks 1994)

Perhaps in fairness to all these contrasting interventions, we must admit that what may be helpful for one child — whether it be TEACCH, Linwood Method, Option Process, Holding Therapy, Facilitated Communication, Auditory Integration Therapy, or Biochemical Treatments — may not work well for another autistic child.

The real nature of autism

In the continued search for effective interventions there remains a pressing need to find a deepened and extended understanding of the real nature of this pervasive developmental disorder. In particular I will argue that the current, predominantly in-child (organic) view of autism is inadequate to meet the challenge of developing effective therapeutic relationships with these children. While we do have to accept that there is no known cure for autism, this does not mean that we cannot make significant strides towards its alleviation. To do this is however dependent upon the understanding we have towards the autistic child. This in turn must be based on our understanding of human nature, and especially of early child development. Chapter 8 presents anthroposophy's holistic Image of Man as a foundation for seeing autism in a new light.

3. Autism:
A Metabolic Disorder?

In the twenty-first century scientists are now striving to find a common cause, gene or pathway, which might explain autism. In his foreword to this book, Colin Trevarthen sums up the challenges, which scientists encounter when trying to understand consciousness and grasp the innate drive in human being to communicate.

The understanding of autism is closely linked to these challenges. In general autism is now firmly viewed as a *neurodevelopmental* disorder with a genetic basis. It is clear that autism is a complex disorder and that no single cause is likely to be found.

This chapter gives a brief summary of the main areas of biologically-orientated research, with a special emphasis on one of the latest hypotheses; that autism could be a metabolic disorder.

Genetics

According to the newspapers genetics will soon be able to explain all human behaviour. The headlines speak about a gene for obesity and schizophrenia. This is, of course, an over-simplification. There is no direct relation between our genes and our behaviour, but it is clear that autism does have a genetic component. This has been found through twin and family studies. There are families with two autistic children, or families where a parent has Asperger's syndrome and a child has autism.

Kanner's autism, or classical autism, seems especially to have a genetic component. One of the indications for this is from research with twins. Identical twins share the same genetic make-up, and there is a high risk of both twins having autism as opposed to non-identical twins. The risk of both identical twins having autism varies from thirty-six per cent to ninety-one per cent. This was found in three epidemiological studies (Folstein and Rutter 1977 and 1988; Le Couteur, Bailey and Rutter 1989; Steffenbergetal 1989, in Harris 1995).

I knew two young ladies, identical twins both with classical autism, who had limited speech, hardly made eye contact and particularly enjoyed rocking backwards and forwards. However, they had completely different personalities — one was out-going and sanguine, and the other more serious and melancholic; they were completely different characters.

The genetic link is also visible in certain genetic syndromes, such as Rett's syndrome and tuberose sclerosis, in which there is a high incidence of autism. In these instances, the risk of having a second child with autism is higher than originally thought, and could be between three and five per cent, which is important for families to know (Connor and Ferguson-Smith 1997). In addition, the higher incidence of communication problems in non-autistic siblings of children with autism also points to a genetic component.

However, science is unclear how a genetic predisposition might cause autism, and the search is still on to find a specific gene, although it is most likely that various genes are involved (International Molecular Genetic Study of Autism Consortium 2000).

Brain research

Another area of great interest at the moment is the function of the brain. As autism can be seen as a brain dysfunction, are the brains of people with autism different from those of non-autistic people?

Research shows that the area of our brain that relates to emotions (the limbic system) is affected in some people with autism. This could have happened already during the embryonic period, but becomes visible around the age of two to three years.

Another part of the brain where abnormalities are often found in autistic people is the cerebellum, the smaller part of our brain relating to co-ordination of movement and the co-ordination of sense impressions (Courchesne 1991; Raymond, Bauman and Kemper 1989, in Harris 1995).

Despite finding these different brain abnormalities, no consistent change in brain structure has been found in people with autism. The emphasis is now veering towards research into brain function, which has been tested with modern imaging techniques. Some reports show that there is less co-ordination between the different regions of the brain in people with autism than in other people.

But what does this tell us? Although autism is regarded as a neuro-developmental disorder what is the cause of different neurological development? Brain development occurs primarily during the embryonic period and the first two years of life, and takes place through the multiplication and migration of nerve cells, although selective cell death is also important. However, this process of normal brain development can be disturbed.

From an anthroposophical point of view, the ego-organization of a child is engaged in the development of the brain — or, in other words, our experiences and activities help to shape the brain. Therefore it is understandable that the natural development of the brain is affected if the ego is not properly integrated. In this book we work with the assumption that autism is an ego-integration problem. Thus the spiritual-soul being of the child can't sufficiently direct the bodily, sensory, emotional and intellectual development of the child.

Some children clearly have previous, or existing, brain damage, and their lack of ego-integration can be caused by the difficulties of the ego in making use of the damaged instrument, as is the case in some secondary autisms (see Chapters 2 and 9).

Neurochemistry

There are different chemicals, called neurotransmitters — such as serotonin, dopamine, adrenaline and endogenous opiates — that affect brain function by passing neural impulses between different cells. Is autism caused by an abnormality in the function of one of the neurotransmitters?

Serotonin abnormalities have been found to play a role in autism, but there is no consistent abnormality found in all people with autism. Endogenous opiates (also known as *endorphins)* can play a role in all this, as they could influence all the neurotransmitters (Knivsberg 1997).

Metabolic aspect

Metabolism relates to the intake and digestion of our food. We are mostly unaware of these processes, but the moment we are aware of them we experience discomfort, cramps, reflux or constipation.

Our digestive process starts the moment we smell or see food. We produce saliva, our gastric juices are stimulated and we feel hungry. During chewing the breakdown of carbohydrates starts in the mouth itself (Smith 1995). On swallowing, the digestion of proteins and fats commences in the stomach. After a couple of hours the food is passed on to the small intestine, two important organs secrete digestive juices into the duodenum — the first part of the small intestine. The liver, on the right side of our body below the diaphragm, produces bile, which is a waste product of blood metabolism but also helps with the digestion of fats. The pancreas is situated behind the stomach and produces digestive juices, which help with the breakdown of protein and carbohydrate. The small intestine itself also produces enzymes that are involved in the digestion of sugars and protein.

When the food is properly broken down it is absorbed through the wall of the intestines into the bloodstream.

How does this digestive process relate to autism?

Many parents of autistic children with autism noted that their children had not digested their food properly, and often had smelly bowel movements. Some children suffered from chronic constipation or diarrhoea. The parents mentioned it to their doctor, a stool sample was taken but a diagnosis was never made.

Other parents realized that their autistic children reacted strongly to different foods. Parents experimented with diets and noticed that their children calmed down when milk, bread or other foods were excluded.

All these observations indicated that something in the digestive process might be disturbed.

Those experiences stimulated research into the effect of diets and the digestive process in people with autism. In 1966, Dohan, indicated a possible connection between food and mental health, and published his results in an article entitled 'Cereals and Schizophrenia: Data and Hypothesis.' A Norwegian scientist, Reichelt. and his co-workers found an increased level of peptides (the breakdown product of protein) in urine collected over twenty-four hours, from people with autism and schizophrenia. These peptides were in part breakdown products derived from gluten (found in wheat, barley, rye and oats) and casein (milk products).

Paul Shattock, a biochemist and the father of an autistic child, did extensive research in this area together with Paul Whiteley and others (Whiteley *et al* 1999). They focused their research on the digestive problems and developed a method to examine the morning urine of people with autism. An increased concentration of certain peptides was found. What did this mean? Based on these observations a hypothesis was developed — *autism as a metabolic disorder.*

Despite exciting research theories, there is no overall explanation for brain abnormalities or the neurochemistry findings, and there is no explanation for the fact that some children seem to develop normally until eighteen months to two years of age, when suddenly their development stops and they even regress. I see many children who have followed this pattern.

It appears that something is primarily wrong with the digestive process in the gut. Food substances, especially proteins are not properly broken down. Consequently, peptides permeate the gut, enter the bloodstream and even pass the blood/brain barrier. (This is a fine barrier of blood vessels that protects our brain by trying to keep toxic substances out). These peptides manage to enter the brain where they then act as a neurotransmitter and have the same affect as endorphins (or opiates). Endorphins, which are substances with opiate-like effects, are produced by our body and, in our brain, help to create a feeling of well-being. However, if the level of opiate activity is raised due to other opiate-like substances then they make us high, restless, or spaced out, with a poor ability to concentrate. They can also alter our sensory perceptions; we would see colours differently and our perception of our body would alter. Many of these symptoms can be found in people with autism. They are hyperactive, have a high pain threshold, and we now know, from many personal descriptions, that their sensory impressions are fragmented.

Excess peptides in the blood are excreted by the kidneys and can be found in urine. Research has confirmed that people with autism can have different peptides in their urine compared with other people (Whiteley *et al* 1999).

Why are these peptides absorbed in a higher concentration by autistic people? This can be due to many reasons. In the gut there is a fine balance among the different enzymes, acidity and bacteria, which together maintain the health of the gut.

These peptides derive especially from milk products (casein) as well as from wheat, barley, rye and oats (gluten), and are seemingly not properly digested or broken down in certain people with autism. It is interesting that gluten is broken down to gluteomorphine and casein to casein morphine, which are peptides with opiate-like effects.

The intestinal balance can be disturbed for different reasons:

1. There are not enough peptidase enzymes (which break down proteins), the acidity in the stomach is too low or there is a lack of vitamins and minerals.
2. The gut wall itself is too permeable through inflammation, caused by excess antibiotic use or candida infections. Vaccines can also cause this damage. A specialist in gastroenterology, Dr Wakefield, noticed that the intestines of many autistic children with digestive problems showed inflammation and irritation when examined with an endoscope — an instrument with which a doctor can look into the stomach or intestine of a patient (Wakefield 1998).
3. The blood/brain barrier could be less effective because of a viral or bacterial infection or trauma.

The following children showed some of the problems discussed above.

EXAMPLE 1

Jamie was the second child, and seemed to develop normally until the age of eighteen months. He used some words, had good social interaction with his family, but then suddenly within a week he withdrew into autistic behaviour. He suffered frequently from ear infections that required treatment with antibiotics. When he arrived at our school at the age of six he was in total control of his bodily functions, and would pass water twice a day, but only opened his bowels when he was at home with his parents and wearing a nappy.

EXAMPLE 2

Brian was the second child in his family. His brother has Asperger's syndrome. His development appeared normal until he was about 14 months old. Overnight, he changed into a restless, aggressive boy who lost all his speech. He now has severe sleeping problems.

Whatever the reason for the metabolic disturbance in children, if the hypothesis is correct, there will be an elevated level of opiate activity in the brain, which will affect the perceptions, mood, behaviour and emotions of that person. The elevated opiate level in the brain could also affect brain development in a young child. During embryonic development and the first two years, there are many connections formed between different nerve cells in the brain. If this process is prevented or altered, brain dysfunction will arise.

I have discussed the effect of metabolic problems on the well-being and behaviour of the autistic child through the effect of the endorphins, but as a parent, carer and doctor it is vitally important to be aware of the possible pain and discomfort that gastro-intestinal problems can cause. For example, constipation can be quite distressing for a child and cause discomfort, sleeping problems and aggression.

A researcher investigated thirty-six autistic children with gastro-intestinal problems (chronic diarrhoea, flatulence and abdominal discomfort and distension) by means of gastro-intestinal gastroscopy. It was found that twenty-five children had reflux, whereby food from the stomach enters and irritates the gullet; fifteen had chronic gastritis (an irritation of the lining of the stomach); and fifteen children had chronic duodenitis (Howard *et al* 1999). This illustrates the point that we must be aware of medical problems in the gastro-intestinal tract of children with autism.

Therapies

Different approaches to remedy the metabolic, intestinal problem have been developed. Donna Williams, a woman with autism who has written extensively about her experiences, believes she is able to function properly thanks to a very restricted diet (Williams 1996).

Therefore, exclusion diets are one approach, and often mean the exclusion of gluten and casein. In the past few decades this approach has been studied scientifically on a small scale with convincing results. One study compared parents' observations of twenty children with urinary peptide abnormalities. Ten children followed a special diet and ten children did not. After one year, there was a significant reduction of autistic behaviour in the children on the diet, and no change of autistic behaviour in the control group. The different research projects are summarized in the article 'A survey in dietary intervention in autism' (Knivsberg, A.M., Reichelt, K.L., Nodland, M. 1999).

If possible, a good way to start an exclusion diet is to first send a morning sample of urine for testing. The only place where this is possible in Britain at the moment is the University of Sunderland. If gluten and casein are a problem, then the urine will clearly show elevated levels of the peptides, which relate to casein and gluten. It is very important to have a clear record of the child's behaviour before and after the diet. After a year on the diet another urine test can be done, which should show normalization of the peptide excretion. A blood test can support the diagnostic procedure. Higher levels of antibodies to casein and gluten are found in twenty per cent of the cases.

It is best to start a diet before a child is ten years old, as increased awareness of the diet can create tension. Also a diet should not be started light-heartedly, as it can be necessary for some children to continue with this diet for their whole lives. Some children react very negatively to the reintroduction of gluten or casein in their diet.

In Britain Paul Shattock and Paul Whiteley from the University of Sunderland have developed a protocol — known as *The Sunderland Protocol* — to give some guidance with exclusion diets (Shattock and Whiteley 2000). Their advice is to first remove casein from the diet for a three-week trial. In young children any change is usually visible in a few days, whereas in adults changes are seen after ten to fourteen days. The withdrawal effects are mostly short-lived, but can be severe in young children.

After three weeks gluten removal can be tried, which means the removal of wheat, barley, oats and rye from the diet. Gluten seems to need longer to leave the body so the effects are not so dramatic, and it takes up to four weeks to see any difference. Shattock and Whiteley suggest trying the diet for three months and then re-evaluating the situation. The withdrawal effects with gluten are milder but can last longer.

It is possible that other foods or additives could be the problem. Whiteley and Shattock recommend keeping a food diary to see if any particular food leads to a change in mood, sleeping or performance. To prevent nutritional deficiencies the support of a dietician during this process is also a good idea.

The protocol also discusses whether a particular yeast in the gut could be a problem because it may make the gut more permeable to certain foods. Shattock and Whiteley mention that some parents remove yeast from the diet, or treat the child with nystatin, an anti-yeast drug (this has to be prescribed by a GP).

All in all the area of food exclusion and possible supplements is not an easy issue and asks for a huge commitment and close observation of the child from parents.

It may be that the person is over-sensitive to some food substances. However, the reaction to gluten and casein is not an over-sensitivity but a *toxic reaction*. This can be difficult to prove but an exclusion diet seems the most useful to determine this. A problem with exclusion diets is that people can become sensitive to foods that are used to replace the gluten or casein. If this happens, then after initial progress, a regression in behaviour is seen.

This seemed to be the case with Martin, a tense, restless but gentle twenty-five-year-old man with autism. At certain moments he would become very aggressive and difficult, but really improved after the introduction of gluten and dairy-free diet. He was calmer; more concentrated and had fewer outbursts. This suddenly changed after one year, and he became quite unsettled and aggressive. His diet had not changed, so there was the suggestion that he had become over-sensitive to corn, which was used to replace the gluten in his bread.

Another problem is that any exclusion diet can be very antisocial and can result in a preoccupation with food and the person's diet. This was also a problem for Martin; he started to resent his diet and this created a lot of tension.

It is, of course, much simpler with young children who are not so aware of the food they receive on their plate. In some families everybody sticks to the diet to make it easier for the person with autism.

Understanding and Implementing Special Diets by Lisa Lewis is a practical book, which helps people to start this complicated diet and also provides recipes. Another more recently-published title, *Diet Intervention and Autism* by Marilyn le Breton, offers another straightforward guide to this kind of diet (Lewis 1998; Le Breton 2001). There are other possible approaches with diets. Low sugar and low carbohydrate diets combined with anti-fungal treatment are used to treat the problems of candida (a fungal infection) in the gut, which is caused by repeated antibiotic use. Supplements with minerals and vitamins are another approach; the most commonly used are vitamin B6 and magnesium.

Developments are very rapid in this field, and it is best to acquire the most current knowledge. The AiA (Allergy induced Autism, a charitable organization) can provide this information or will be able to direct you to a source of information. The address can be found in Appendix 3.

The real problem is to know which autistic child or adult can benefit from a diet, supplements or the use of medicines, such as secretin. The guidelines for the diet are clear as described above, but there are no clear guidelines for other interventions as yet.

Possible indications for a metabolic approach could be:

1. Problems with digestion, such as constipation or diarrhoea, or a diagnosis of a bowel illness;
2. Regression into autism after normal development;
3. An increase in the urinary excretion of certain peptides, are related to gluten or casein;
4. Strong family history of sensitivity to gluten;
5. Negative reaction to certain foods;
6. History of severe colic as a baby;
7. Black rings around the eyes.

Despite writing this chapter not many children in the special needs school where I work are on the diet. This is mainly due to the fact that, ideally, it should be initiated by parents. Also, we have not been totally convinced that the diet is always helpful.

Secretin

A new discovery is the remarkable effect of secretin. This is a hormone, formed in the mucosa of the duodenum, which is produced when the acid level in the stomach increases. Secretin stimulates the release of pancreatic enzymes and bicarbonate. The bicarbonate helps to regulate the acid level in the intestine, and the enzymes help to break down fat and proteins. Secretin has to be injected in the bloodstream, which is not always easy for children with autism, and there has been some concern about the long-term effect of this treatment.

At this moment more than two thousand children have received this treatment, with, according to parents, a positive response in eighty per cent of them. The children need repeat injections every five or six weeks.

An article was published in the *New England Journal of Medicine* in 1999 that questioned the effect of secretin. Thirty children were treated with an infusion of secretin, and thirty children were given an infusion of salt water. Parents did not know which treatment their children had received. After one month, there was no clear difference between the two groups. This poses the question of whether secretin is at all effective. Further research is needed to find out which children might benefit specifically from secretin.

MMR and Autism

Every parent with young children is aware of the discussion on the possible relationship between the MMR (measles, mumps and rubella) vaccine and autism. There are two strong sides to this argument.

On one hand there are the parents, who observed that their children changed after receiving the MMR immunization, sometimes overnight as in the case of Brian. His mother noticed that he had a fever after the MMR and underwent a dramatic change.

Dr Andrew Wakefield, a gastro-enterologist, investigated the bowels of a small group of autistic children and found inflammation in the bowels of most of them. This led him to question whether it was advisable to give three live vaccines simultaneously. He published his findings in *The Lancet* in 1998, thus initiating the discussion and subsequent controversy over the MMR vaccine.

The opponents, on the other hand, are health officials concerned with possible outbreaks of measles and the health of the child population as a whole. As a result of Dr Wakefield's publication, and the enormous amount of subsequent media attention, the immunization rates for MMR have dropped, so that there is now a very real danger of a possible measles outbreak. Measles still has the potential to cause death in one or two of every thousand cases.

The hypothesis is that there is a *new variant autism* where developmental regression is reported to follow shortly after the MMR vaccination, accompanied typically by bowel problems. Epidemiological studies have been designed to investigate such a causal association. They have not found any connection between MMR uptake and the incidence of autism, nor any evidence of behavioural disturbance, including regression, shortly after vaccination (Taylor *et al* 2002). However, it has been stated that the onset of *MMR-induced regressive autism* may occur after a prolonged interval, and would require other factors to be present: for example, an infection at the time of vaccination; a history of atopy (eczema, asthma or other allergies); a strong family history of auto-immune disease; or the immunization of the mother with MMR or Rubella shortly before or during pregnancy.

A recently-published article in the *British Medical Journal,* looked at the link between MMR and autism (Taylor *et al* 2002). The MMR vaccination was introduced in 1988, yet the proportion of children with developmental regression (25% overall) or bowel symptoms (17%) did not change significantly over twenty years from 1979. Also, children who were *not* immunized during that period had the same levels of regressive autism and bowel problems.

The research did find a possible relation between non-specific bowel problems and regression in children with autism but this was not related to the MMR vaccination.

Interestingly, in the 2002 Spring issue of the *Journal of Molecular Pathology* an article was published that found that among ninety-one children with the variant form of bowel disease seventy-five had the measles virus in their guts. However, it was only found in five out of seventy healthy children studied. More boys than girls were affected.

These results are evidence of a possible relationship between disturbed interaction between brain and gut, but the role of MMR in this is unclear, as the study did not look at whether the children had been vaccinated with the MMR vaccine.

The conclusion appears to be that what is visible in individual children — according to parents' observations and the presence of the measles virus in the gut — is not reflected in epidemiological studies. It is possible that a small sub-group of susceptible children respond to the triple MMR vaccine with autism. At the time of writing new research is being published every week, and it is hoped that the future will bring about some answers to the confusion. However, in my personal opinion, the rise in incidence of autism will not be explained solely by the MMR vaccination.

Anthroposophical understanding

How, therefore, does this all relate to insights derived from anthroposophy? Ego-integration is a real problem for autism (see Chapters 8 and 9). It is clear that failed ego-integration will be noticeable on all levels of the human being; on the level of sensory integration; in difficulties developing empathy; and, in problems with communication, social interaction and imagination.

One of the consequences of unsuccessful ego-integration is that digestion does not function properly. It is the task of the ego to break down food substances, which is done with the help of digestive enzymes.

Rudolf Steiner describes this process in a book he wrote with Dr Ita Wegman entitled *The Fundamentals of Therapy*. In Chapter 9 'The Role of Protein in the Human Body and Proteinuria,' he describes how protein is a living substance, made up of oxygen, nitrogen, hydrogen and carbon, and is full of life giving forces.

When we eat we absorb protein. The digestive process starts in the stomach and is aided by pancreatic juice. Protein is an alien substance for our body, because it contains etheric life forces of another living being, namely, from a plant or an animal. The protein is broken down into peptides and amino acids, absorbed and used by the body to form our own protein. During this process, the life forces from the other organism are removed and the protein is integrated in the etheric forces of our own body.

Therefore, the protein has to be transformed in the digestive tract so that there are no alien etheric forces left. The protein has to become inorganic and lifeless so we can make it our own. The ego-organization does this with the help of the pancreatic juice. A person needs an ego-organization that is strong enough to digest protein and to re-integrate it in our etheric body. If not, then the protein will contain too much foreign ether from a foreign organism. The consequence is that the protein is excreted. This is a way of describing an allergy or intoxication caused by protein.

According to Steiner, healing results from the strengthening of the activity of the ego-organization in the pancreatic juice. Steiner wrote this in 1924, and it is, therefore, fascinating in the light of recent research, which clearly shows that people with autism excrete certain peptides. The latest experiences with secretin could indicate the importance of the pancreas.

Steiner clearly put a lot of emphasis on the proper digestion of proteins. In 1924 he also gave lectures to co-workers who started to work with special needs children (Steiner 1998).

Here, he discusses the importance of the relationship of chemical substances in protein and the profound effect they can have on the behaviour of children. He describes what happens if the metabolic limb system of a child is too weakly developed, and the albumen substance of the human organism is prevented from containing the right amount of sulphur. The consequence, according to Steiner, is that the child will have fixed ideas, starting from early childhood.

Recent research by Waring points to the possible importance of sulphurization in autism (Waring 2000). The indications are that in autistic children there is a deficiency of the enzyme, *phenol suphur transferase*. This enzyme has two functions. Firstly, it ensures that mucous membranes are coated with mucous to protect them. Secondly, it helps to *hydrolate* toxins from the body — that is, surround toxins with extra water molecules. If a person does not have enough of this enzyme toxins build up and the gut can become permeable to undigested proteins. In this instance, parents can add bath salts containing magnesium sulphate to their child's bath, which has had seemingly good results. It is interesting to note that, in 1924, Steiner highlighted a link between sulphur deficiency and obsessive behaviour.

Anthroposophical treatment

The challenge for Anthroposophy is to translate these insights into an anthroposophical medical treatment. The whole idea of exclusion diets is to remove foods that could cause problems for a child. However, ideally we would like to strengthen the digestive system of the child, so that it can cope better and digest different foods.

In curative education the input from anthroposophically-trained doctors has always played a central role in the education and treatment of the child. Doctors working in the same field have used remedies to help the autistic child with sensory integration, the development of emotional life (König 1953), or to help the child's ego become more incarnated (Klimm 1981).

The treatment of different metabolic organs has always played an important role in the treatment of autistic children. Potentized remedies have been used to stimulate the ego-organization to incarnate in the metabolic system. Another approach has been to give compresses or specific massages to different organs.

The aim of these treatments is to strengthen the working of the ego-organization in its digestive activity. This can be done through strengthening liver function, stimulating pancreatic activity, and harmonizing the activity of the gut.

So how can anthroposophical medications and therapies strengthen the activity of ego-organization in the metabolic tract? Some doctors have made careful attempts to treat the pancreas, digestive tract and liver with anthroposophical remedies. The children have responded positively to the treatment. There is often a rapid response with regard to bowel movement, and a consistent, subsequent improvement in social interaction according to personal statements from colleagues. The following example illustrates the response:

Craig is a four-year-old boy with autism. He has severe diarrhoea, which is smelly, and acidic. This was investigated but no diagnosis was made. He was started on a treatment of anthroposophical medication, and received Digestodoron tablets, which harmonize the bowel function. He also received other remedies directed at activating the pancreas. He responded well, and his bowel movement improved. His behaviour also changed; he became less hyperactive, his eye contact improved, and after three months of treatment, he speaks in sentences (he had already some words) and said 'Mummy, look at the clouds.' This shows a wish to share observations; an activity which is so often lacking in children with autism.

Development in this area is happening very quickly. I expect that our approach to autism and understanding of autism will progress in the coming years, especially with regard to the role of the metabolism in autism.

Conclusion

I have tried to show that the concept of autism as a metabolic disorder does not contradict the concept of autism as failed ego-integration. Research indicates that, in certain children, autism could be caused by a disruption of the normal levels of endorphins. Insufficiently broken-down proteins can cause this disruption by having a disturbing effect on the development and activity of the brain.

If the ego is not fully integrated, it has profound effects on the developing child at all levels, and also on the working of the organs in the digestive tract. If the organs involved in the metabolism do not work properly, then food cannot be properly digested.

Exclusion diets and the administration of secretin are approaches which have been developed in the 1990s with some success, to address this metabolic disturbance.

Anthroposophical medicine can support the activity of the metabolic organs with appropriate remedies, and so enable the ego to connect better with the metabolic system. It is important to know that this approach is just one aspect of the anthroposophical medical approach to autism. More research is needed to evaluate this approach.

II

Interventions and Case Studies

4. Curative Educational Interventions and Autism

The context for curative education

The term 'curative education' is a translation of *'Heilpädagogik;'* a word commonly used in German-speaking countries, which clearly links the educational process with a healing impulse.

> Curative education is that science which ... seeks predominantly paedagogical means for the treatment of intellectual and sensory defects, of nervous and emotional disturbances in children and adolescents. (Asperger 1956)

However, in its widest aspect, curative education is not only a science, not only a practical art, but also a human attitude.

> Only the help from man to man — the encounter of ego with ego —the becoming aware of the other man's individuality without enquiring into his creed, world conception or political affiliations, but simply the meeting, I to I, of two persons, creates that curative education which counters, in a healing way, the threat to our innermost humanity. This, however, can only be effective if with it a fundamental recognition is taken into consideration, a recognition which has to come out of the heart. (König in Pietzner 1990, 26)

This fundamental heart knowledge arises from the warmth of genuine interest, compassion and sympathy for the situation of the other human being.

Over the past fifty-six years, the Camphill organization, or move-ment, has established therapeutic school and college communities, as well as village communities with adults (Pietzner 1990). Altogether, these Camphill centres now number more than seventy, and are dis-tributed over eighteen countries.

Curative education has been implemented in other anthroposophi-cal residential and day centres for many years (Roggenkamp & Fischer 1974). The total number of centres worldwide, including Camphill places, is around three hundred. In a therapeutic community such as a Camphill school, autistic children are integrated with other children with special needs, as well as with staff children and adult co-workers; including experienced curative educators *(i.e.* teachers, house parents, therapists, doctors, etc.). Curative education, in this context, becomes a conscious way of life, which permeates equally the triad of: home life; school; and therapies.

Autistic children become members of their house community and their class of peers, as well as of the total community. The relation-ships between the different children are very important, and can often be a major curative influence. For example, a sociable, outgoing child with Downs syndrome, may be happy to include a withdrawn autistic child into some game or fantasy, without being at all put off, or offended, by their friend's autistic aloofness. The social and therapeu-tic value of educating children of mixed abilities, and with a variety of special needs, has always been acknowledged and practised in Cam-phill and other curative centres.

A rich cultural life, with the non-denominational celebrations of the main Christian festivals through music, art, drama, speech and song, is a common feature of all anthroposophical centres. For all children with special needs the rhythmic pattern of the years, colourfully marked by regularly recurring Christian festivals, becomes a familiar and culturally-enlivened framework which supports their social exis-tence. Meaning, purpose, and clear structures permeate every aspect of life in a curative environment, and this, in turn, may indeed help the autistic child to also experience a greater sense and meaning in their own life (Hansmann 1992; Luxford 1994). Particularly the child's own sense of life as an existential sensory experience, can be strengthened and fostered in a setting where daily, weekly and yearly rhythms are consciously cultivated, so creating a health-giving way of life. It is in such a holistic, and thoroughly human context, that special curative educational interventions and exercises can best be practised.

> Therefore it can also, in the education of autistic children, be considered to be the most important aim — besides all special measures — to enable these children to live as people, as free as possible, albeit handicapped, with other people in community. (Müller-Wiedemann *et al* 1988, 182)

Survey of anthroposophical interventions

The following interventions are all compatible with the anthroposophical model presented in Chapters 8 and 9, and are strongly suggested, or generated, by that model. We can summarize these intervention areas as:

1. Inter-human attitudes
2. Imitation, rhythmic activities, and play
3. Sensory-perceptual development
4. School curriculum
5. Crafts and work
6. Specific therapies and medical treatments

Inter-human attitudes

The power of empathy must be the foundation of all genuine (also non-anthroposophical) intervention attempts. This power can be developed by the educator, whether they are a teacher, house parent or therapist. Steiner indicated precisely how this could be done when, in the second of the twelve lectures on curative education, he described the *Pedagogical Law* which intimately links both educator and child (Steiner 1972, 39). This fundamental relationship is indicated in Table 1.

This means that the educator's ego has a direct influence on the astral body of the child, their astral body on the child's etheric body, and their etheric body on the child's physical body. Steiner indicated how educators must be willing to consciously develop, and work

Educator ⟶	Child
Ego	Astral Body
Astral Body	Etheric Body
Etheric Body	Physical body

Table 1. The inner relationship between educator and child.

upon, their own being and bodily sheaths, in order to bring healthy and vitalizing influences to the child's bodily constitution. For example,

> By ridding himself of every trace of subjective reaction the teacher educates his own astral body. (Steiner 1972, 40)

This is then able to extend positive, and corrective, effects on a child's inner etheric organization.

Following a moral path of self-development and genuine self-knowledge, was considered by Steiner to be essential for a curative teacher.

> For you have no idea how unimportant is all that the teacher says or does not say on the surface, and how important what he himself is, as teacher. (Steiner 1972, 41)

Therefore we see that to develop human interrelationships consciously, informed by anthroposophy's differentiated Image of Man, is at the heart of curative education. It is necessary to build up a relationship which engenders mutual trust and confidence. An autistic child is in many ways insecure and anxious, and possibly at times, terrified. Since the child has not yet achieved a centred self-consciousness, an indirect, non-invasive approach should generally be adopted.

> This therapeutic attitude entails never confronting the child directly. We should never attempt to look into his eyes and

address him as we would another person. Rather it is necessary to learn to see that the autistic child is not truly 'in himself,' and that we can reach him if we address ourselves to
his 'peripheral self,' to that which is not centred. (Weihs
1984, 92)

This indirect attitude is the opposite of the confrontational approach
of Holding Therapy as developed by Martha Welch (see Chapter 2).
We often, deliberately leave a *space* for the child to enter into when he
feels able and ready to do so. This space can be a *soul* space, created
through our empathy, and sometimes also a *physical* space. Some
autistic children react with distress if expected to enter a room with
many other people, such as a dining room. However, the same child
may manage well if allowed to be the first to go into an empty room,
and only then be joined by others.

Again, the opportunity to be outdoors, in wide natural surroundings, can often provide observable relief for such children. As a general rule, genuine enthusiasm should not lead an eductaor to be
over-demanding or ask too much of autistic children. Compulsive and
ritualistic behaviours may largely be accepted and allowed provided
that they do not seriously interfere with others. If the child feels properly understood and accepted such behaviours may relax or even dis-
appear of their own accord.

Imitation, rhythmic activities and play

These three areas are interrelated and can support each other. In the
1960s, König was clear that in order to help the autistic child the child
needed to learn to imitate and play (König 1960 & 1989). How to do
this of course depends on the individual child, and the creativity of the
educator.

Normally, a young child naturally imitates what is going on in his
surroundings, including the work of adults. However, as this usually
does not come about spontaneously with the autistic child, the imitation of actions needs to be taught as a conscious intervention. This can
include rhythmic to and fro activities, turn-taking activities and simple play. For example, when building a tower with toy bricks, the adult

can first show the child how it is done, and then try to engage them one brick at a time. This can be accompanied by simple speech, 'I place a brick, you place a brick,' and so on. Starting perhaps from sitting behind the child, the adult can then sit next to and finally, opposite the child.

Depending on the age of the child, a variety of games can also be used to establish interrelationships.

> These can be ball or ring games, or simple dances connected with songs and rhymes. For children not ready to enter into a game situation, however simple, clapping exercises between child and therapist, crosswise and parallel, can be helpful or even more rudimentary measures, such as infant games with fingers and toes. (Weihs 1984, 95)

It may be quite possible to slowly involve the autistic child in traditional ring games with a group of peers, in which the children first stand, take hands and form a circle (Opie 1988). A child who will not initially join in may do so in time if a space is left for them to enter into, when they themselves feel able and ready to join. These singing and ring games, such as, *Here we go round the mulberry bush, / Water, water wallflower, / Poor Jenny a-weeping,* have definite therapeutic benefits, which can help children to develop their learning abilities and also their self and social awareness (Heider 1995).

Eurythmy movements corresponding to the sounds of speech can also be done on an individual basis or with others (Raffe *et al* 1974; Steiner 1967). If the child is perhaps first physically helped to perform such gestures from behind, then they may, through their own sense of movement, begin to experience some joy in the gestures and, eventually start to imitate them spontaneously.

Play with various materials such as sand, water, beeswax, clay or other objects can be fostered as a reciprocal activity between adult and child, and perhaps later with peers. By doing so the child's repetitive, bizarre or ritualized behaviours can be led into the inter-human realm.

Sensory-perceptual development

As the anthroposophical model emphasizes, the proper functioning of the child's four lower senses is of existential importance. It also provides the foundation for the proper development of the higher, social senses. Müller-Wiedemann (1990) has shown that disorders of the lower, or body, senses often appear as:

1. a disturbed relationship with organic substances, with nutritional and digestive problems (sense of life);
2. stereotypic and bizarre movement patterns (sense of movement);
3. the avoidance of experiences and exploration through touch and, often, in the child's inappropriate touching of others (sense of touch);
4. in the realm of gravity a compulsive dependency on spatial positioning; walking on tiptoes; making roundabout turns; spinning of objects or own body; placid muscle tone (sense of balance).

It is interesting to note that autistic children often appear to be very able in terms of balance and movement. However, as Engel (1968) described, both exceptional abilities in these areas and abnormal movement patterns can be understood as the lack of ego-integration within these two lower senses, and the resulting preponderance of instinctive, astral soul activity.

Some curative educational interventions, directed to the lower senses are given below. All such interventions aim to stimulate the child's own motivation and, through this, to individualize the field of the lower senses.

The sense of life

Over the course of time, the child can learn to accept varied kinds of food in regular daily meals, when only small portions of those foods, which the child has an aversion to, are given initially (autistic children often have compulsive food fads). Care may be needed to provide an eating environment where other sensory impressions are reduced — a peaceful instead of a noisy dining room, mellow lighting etc.

A rhythmic pattern, and predictability in the child's daily life is of special significance for the development of the sense of life. This is consciously created in holistic community living in Camphill and other centres and,through this, the autistic child is embedded and supported by definite *life rhythms.* We have already emphasized the special disturbance of the sense of life in autistic children (see Chapter 9). Their often unusual reactions to circumstances that would normally cause bodily pain, sometimes even severe pain, can be clearly understood as directly symptomatic of the immature development of this sense.

The child is helped to better perceive their state of bodily health through nutritional and rhythmic interventions such as those described above. Anthroposophical medicines and special baths can also help to stimulate and order the metabolic processes.

The sense of movement

Although eurythmy movements have special value here, all forms of co-ordinated movement exercises can be attempted and practised. Müller-Wiedemann (1982) recommended that the child be helped to make *slow* movements as autistic children tend to do things quickly, as if they have no time. Again, many children show a tendency towards symmetry. Here, laterality and dominance exercises are important, such as catching and throwing a rod with the dominant hand. With older pupils *aim* exercises with a bow and arrow, or fencing, have proved helpful (Weihs 1984).

Form or *dynamic drawing,* applied curatively, stimulates ego-integration and bodily self-experience through the sense of movement, and also through the senses of balance and life (Niederhäuser & Frohlich 1974; and Kirchner 1977). Such exercises involving the rhythmical drawing of curved or straight-line forms, have been used helpfully with some autistic children. Forms which require the child to cross over lines, when drawing lemniscates for example, can help to strengthen the child's inner self-awareness.

The sense of touch

This can be developed by activities in which the child is helped to discriminate between the *feel* of contrasting surfaces and objects. First, the educator takes the initiative to stimulate the child's tactile perceptions, for example, by touching exposed skin areas such as the face, neck, arms, lower legs and feet with a variety of materials. Brushes of different textures, can also be used effectively. Later, children can be led into explorative touching, also without visual input if objects are hidden in sand or beneath a cloth. Importantly the child can be guided to touch, identify and explore their own body. Clearly the aim of such exercises is to establish the child's own body boundaries — and thereby his self-experience — with regard to the surroundings. Both the separation and distance between *self* and *world* is thereby strengthened.

The sense of balance

This sense is stimulated by the child coming to terms with the force of gravity through resistance exercises, and by experiencing weight. For example, the autistic child is asked and shown how to carry heavy objects across a room. This can be performed as a turn-taking exercise with the educator/therapist. Medicine ball games, exercises with hand weights, balancing, walking with lead-weighted anklets in order to enhance the experience of gravity, and partner resistance exercises can be used.

Another effective intervention consists of the child standing on the feet of the therapist — both in bare feet — and walking across the room whilst holding on to each other. This can first be done with the child's back towards the therapist, and then facing them. According to Müller-Wiedemann (1982), this exercise enables the child to literally 'creep into your own lower senses,' and through this to freshly experience the gravity space.

Success with lower sense exercises can be clearly indicated by increased eye contact, social smiling, a lessening of obsessional behaviours, greater relaxation, increased muscle tone, a widened diet, and improved sleeping-waking patterns. In effect, these are all indicators of better ego-integration.

The autistic child is often overwhelmed by meaningless percepts, and is unable to integrate them into personal coherent experiences. Therefore, in general, care must be taken to protect the child from too much sensory stimulation and exposure. Without this care, the child can only withdraw, perhaps into ritualistic behaviours, as a form of defence strategy. Two other senses will be considered here, namely hearing and warmth, with examples of some of the interventions for autistic children as described by Müller-Wiedemann (1990).

The sense of hearing

Curative education interventions which develop the active usage of the sense of hearing, (the first of the higher social senses), aim especially to increase the child's listening capacities. Exercises are done to further, or newly develop, the connection between listening and movement organization, that is, muscle tone as the basis of perceptional interest and the processing of auditory percepts (see Appendix 1). The stereotypic fixation of a child's movements, and also slack muscle tone, are both outer signs of insufficient sensory ego-integration. They can lead to a high degree of avoidance within the acoustic realm, including speech, and sometimes appear as an over sensitivity to certain tones or sounds. Therefore, interventions are used which involve both movement and listening; such as tone eurythmy in which the child is guided to make specific eurythmy gestures corresponding to specific heard tones.

Improvised musical conversations, where the therapist speaks to the child with tone phrases on the lyre and the child is encouraged to answer freely on their lyre, also provide a means of communication. Such tone conversations have the power to undo the *talking to themselves* of some children, which can become a pathological habit preventing spontaneous communication, due to the preponderance of rigid memories. As such, the value of music with autistic children has long been acknowledged (Weihs 1984; Alvin & Warwick 1992). Some of these musical interventions take the form of specialized therapies.

The sense of warmth

This middle or soul sense has a quite particular significance in the *twelvefoldness* of the sensory organism (see Appendix 1),

> It is the archetypal sense, which has a primary presence in all other senses. (Soesman 1990, 97)

In terms of the human soul, it enables a warm interest and responsiveness to take place between child and world, including the social world. Some autistic children show hyposensitive reactions to both heat and cold.

Pyrogenic baths, in which the temperature is raised by one or two degrees Centigrade above the usual body temperature for each child, have been used successfully with autistic children. According to Müller-Wiedemann:

> During and after such applications the children make better
> eye contact; in speaking children their speech is activated,
> and one can better communicate with simple games and with
> imitation. (Müller-Wiedemann 1990)

Similar positive effects also result from using warm foot baths in the morning and then rubbing until the feet become pink. Foot baths given in the evening, help children in going to sleep. Through warmth interventions of this kind, ego-integration is facilitated and soul expression and responsiveness stimulated. It should however be emphasized that therapeutic measures such as pyrogenic baths, require the recommendation of a qualified medical practitioner, as well as the expertise of trained curative educators.

School curriculum

In curative education the use of the Rudolf Steiner, or Waldorf, school curriculum has a major role to play (Woodward 1985; Hansmann 1992). However, the effectiveness of the curriculum, both with autistic and other children with special needs, depends centrally on the empathetic relationships which the teachers develop with their particular classes and individual pupils (Weihs 1975, 103). Both in mainstream Waldorf schools and in curative schools, having the same class teacher — ideally from the age of six to fourteen — is of unique importance. This allows time for relationships to grow and mature, and is also a challenge for the educator's path of self-knowledge.

The Waldorf curriculum, which was outlined by Steiner in his many educational lecture cycles, is based on the anthroposophical understanding of child development, and the typical stages of ego-integration. When this is applied pedagogically to a class of children with special needs and diverse abilities, as has been practised for more than forty years in Camphill schools, it is found that:

> The Waldorf syllabus, as part of our overall curriculum, furthers and restores harmony between body, mind, and spirit, and is the strongest educational healing element we can apply. (Hansmann 1992, 83)

When one or more autistic children are integrated socially with their peers into a class, and taught according to the Waldorf curriculum, they are fully recognized and respected as human beings in the process of becoming. The age appropriateness of the subjects and activities in the curriculum always aim to foster the sense of dignity and self-esteem in each child. As one curative school expressed it:

> The Waldorf Curriculum, adapted to the child's ability to understand, is one of the most powerful tools to help autistic people to find themselves and their place in the world.

Even if a child with autism does not outwardly appear to be taking-in much of what is brought to the class, it is an unjustified assumption to think that he is not aware of what is happening in the class. The inner attitude of the teacher, and their awareness of the child's being, is of prime importance in what are often very subtle processes of interaction. With autistic children, where an indirect approach is usually called for, their *peripheric consciousness,* and sensitivity to their surroundings, must be acknowledged.

The clear form, structure and predictability of much of the school day and week provide important support to the autistic child. However, if a child appears to have a secondary autism, due to a primary aphasia, then the presentation of some curriculum contents needs to be communicated differently than with an ordinary class of mixed ability, special needs children. An aphasic autistic pupil may respond better in a class specially for aphasic children.

> The aphasic class provides a highly specialised programme of visually and practically presented lesson contents and therapeutic exercises for those children with primary difficulties in word understanding and speech. The pupils all have additional handicaps, often including autistic or psychotic tendencies, being a developmental reaction secondary to their ability to understand words or even gestures. (Hansmann 1992, 157)

Crafts and work

For the autistic child, and more particularly for the autistic adolescent, these two areas of learning can often be of very great help and support. Crafts, which are also an essential part of the Waldorf curriculum, can include: weaving, basketry, woodwork, pottery, candle making, metalwork and bookbinding. Work can take the form of helping with daily household tasks, such as sweeping the floor, laying the table, or washing and drying-up, etc. Land work and gardening have often proved effective with older pupils, especially heavy tasks such as pushing a loaded wheelbarrow. Log sawing provides a good, rhythmic and interactive activity with a partner.

The variety of craft and work activities belong in the sphere of holistic curative education, in which it is the growing relationships and attitudes between educator and pupils that is central. Through these interactions, and the educator's empathetic attitudes, even a mundane daily task such as drying the dishes, can become a valuable curative exercise. Often such tasks also serve as a medium for social integration, communication and gradual participation with others. Writing on the theme of youth guidance in curative education, Luxford remarks that:

> Craft work and other kinds of practical activities should play
> a larger part in the education of the youngster and particu-
> larly that of the student with special needs. A new area of
> self-recognition can be gained in the encounter with craft and
> practical activities. Crafts are particularly important because
> through these, skill training, observation, judgements and
> social motivation unite in the forming of a bowl, the weaving
> of a basket, or the dipping of a candle. (Luxford 1994, 97)

From my own experience, weaving has proved to be of particular
benefit for autistic adolescents, who seem to find security, order and
peace in this essentially rhythmic activity, and communication and
conversation can sometimes occur whilst the youngster weaves.

Work and crafts which have clearly visible end results, can help to
provide meaning and sense to an autistic person. This can be wit-
nessed particularly in the purposeful integration of autistic adults in
the life of sheltered village communities (Farrants 1988; Pietzner
1990; Christie 1989; Frankland 1995).

Specific therapies

These particular forms of curative educational interventions are prescribed, on a purely individual basis, during the internal reviews, or
clinics, held for pupils in the school, or centre, he attends, and the centre's anthroposophical medical adviser is always present. Clinics take
place once or twice a year for each child, though they can be called
more often if needed.

Specific therapies require the expertise of curative educators who
have received some training in the particular therapy concerned. However, as with the lower sense exercises described earlier in this chapter, they do not necessarily require a specially qualified therapist.

As there is no one therapy for autism, it is always necessary to see
which therapy can best meet an individual child's needs at that time,
from the range of therapies which are available in any centre. All that
can be done is to identify those therapies which have proved helpful
for some autistic children (Hansmann 1992; Müller-Wiedemann 1990;
Weihs 1984. See also Appendix 2). Ideally, a specific therapy will take

place three (or more) times a week with the same child, and continue for at least several months. Again it must be emphasized that the inter-relationships between therapist and child are of key importance. Anthroposophical therapists will realize that they are also continually learning and developing through the acknowledgment of the child's spiritual soul being and their special situation in the world. The work must always involve a dynamic, two-way process on a number of different, but connected, levels of involvement.

Medical treatments

The use of anthroposophical, potentized remedies and medicines, is very important in the totality of curative education, and is clearly the prerogative of a qualified doctor. However, the doctor's diagnosis, and subsequent treatments, are arrived at partly by listening to the descriptions given in the review meeting, by those curative educators who know the child well. Treatment must be based on a thorough knowledge of the fourfold human constitution and the threefold organic systems (see Chapter 8). The doctor's insights and observations help the educator to see exactly how these are related, and functioning, in a particular child.

Anthroposophical medicines aim to treat, or remedy, the illness or disorder, and not merely eliminate symptoms. The specific therapies, outlined in the Appendix, should be viewed as an integral part of holistic treatments for, and with, autistic children.

The college meeting

Interpersonal, interdependent relationships and empathy are at the centre of curative education. These are highlighted when a college meeting is held in a school community. At this special meeting, centred on a particular child, all the educators are present who teach, live and work with that child. Through listening to an account of the child's early history, and their progress and difficulties since coming to the centre, they endeavour to gain a deeper insight into, and recognition of, the child's being, and perhaps something of the child's personal karma.

Although the child is not physically present at this event, a college meeting can help to positively change and develop the interrelationships between the child and his educators as a result of a new anthroposophical understanding of his situation. However, for developmental reasons and out of respect for the individual's dignity and freedom, a college meeting is not usually held for pupils after their fourteenth year of age.

Autism should not merely be seen as an in-child problem, such as it appears when viewed on the purely organic level of causation. Rather it should be viewed as a challenge to our own willingness to build genuine human relationships, despite the obvious difficulties which autistic reactions present us with. The college meeting is therefore an important and central intervention event in curative education.

5. Results of Individualized Interventions

In this section we shall look at the development of my interrelationships with two autistic boys, together with the implementation of specific interventions and curative attitudes. The anthroposophical model of autism gives the clear, underlying basis for all of this. The two boys, James and Roger, with whom I worked were both residential pupils in a Camphill community school, therefore it is important to keep in mind the holistic context for curative education, described at the beginning of Chapter 4. There are many differentiated areas for positive interventions, through which autistic children can gradually integrate into the triad of home life, school and therapies, and become members of the school community. They include many opportunities for the development of interrelationships, both among children of different ages and abilities, and between children and their educators.

As I am not trained as a specialist therapist (such as a curative eurythmist or art therapist), the therapeutic measures which I practised with the boys were derived from the first three intervention areas, described at length in Chapter 4 and specified on page 76. This interventional work was a further continuation of research, in which I had already been engaged for several years.

The aims

1. To develop the interrelationship between myself and each of the boys in order to alleviate the degrees of autism which they usually showed;

2. To construct and implement an individual programme of intervention exercises on the basis of the anthroposophical model, in order to alleviate the autism;

3. To evaluate the effectiveness of the first two aims as:

— perceived by myself;
— by others in the school community;
— by the child's parents.

The pupils: a brief background

The information given below on each of the boys over the crucial first three years was derived from their case files. Firstly, I consulted the recordings of the initial interviews which took place prior to the children being admitted to their Camphill community school. In these interviews the school's medical adviser met the children and their parent(s), and an early developmental history was verbally obtained and recorded immediately. Secondly, these interview records were then carefully cross-checked with educational, psychological and medical records, and also with each child's *statement of special educational needs*. These comparisons were essential to ensure the reliability of the information which is presented below. However, the names of the children have been changed and their birth dates are not given, in order to preserve confidentiality.

James: Features of Early Development

Pre-& Post Natal & Birth

Third child. Mother was 26 years old. James' conception occurred only six months after the birth of his sister.

Although the child was planned the mother felt unhappy throughout her pregnancy. Otherwise the pregnancy was normal except for slightly raised blood pressure and an unspecified *fall* or blow at full term.

Apparently no significant hereditary or congenital diseases in either family.

Labour took five hours, and the birth was described as easy and diffi-
cult! Birth weight 7lb 2oz.
Baby did not cry at once. Jaundiced for three days. Had a very low
Apgar score at birth. Given oxygen.

FIRST YEAR
A restless baby, quite 'whingy,' and didn't show affection to mother.
Did not look at mother. Smiled late.
One and a half months. Admitted to hospital for observation; had a
cough. First immunization (not whooping cough).
Five months. Breastfed for 4–5 months. Fed well and gained weight.
Seven months. Sat unaided. Never crawled.
Ten months. Teething occurred.

SECOND YEAR
Sixteen months. Mother made him walk by standing him against the
wall.
Eighteen months. Walked by himself.
Twenty months. Did not point. Did not look at people. Lined up toys.
Repetitive patterns of behaviour. No speech development. Did
not respond to noise, sounds, voices.

THIRD YEAR
Did not speak.
Diagnosed as 'a little boy with autism.'

In a personal telephone conversation which I had with James' mother,
she informed me that James was 'freezing cold' when he was born in
the middle of the night, in the summer. Moreover, his skin looked
almost 'black,' and he just 'hung.' Altogether his appearance at birth
was 'a great shock.' Seemingly, James did speak a few single words at
around thirty months, but without any further progress thereafter.
    In the written records, James was initially described by his mother
as a 'restless baby,' later he became a 'very placid child,' who became
more affectionate with his close family. He tolerated other children,
but did not interact with them. When younger (age unspecified) he
was prone to viruses, and was seen by an ear, nose and throat (ENT)
specialist and fitted with grommets. He also saw an eye specialist for

his squint. According to his mother, James had various tests — 'too many to remember' — and was seen by 'lots of psychologists' over the years. A psychological update when he was seven years old, described him as:

> a profoundly autistic little boy whose difficulties in learning
> are severe and complex.

James attended a special unit in a mainstream day school for four years. As a 5/6-year-old he was said to have 'poor bodily awareness.' When he was eight years old he came to his present Camphill community school, as a termly residential pupil who was not yet toilet-trained. The school's medical adviser confirmed James' diagnosis as a 'deeply autistic boy.'

Finally, and perhaps significantly, it should be noted that his mother commented:

> I have also thought that James somewhere along the line made
> a choice not to speak. (If that doesn't sound a bit strange.)

Whether or not James did make such a choice, we should always take such intuitive impressions seriously, as a mother has a special connection towards the real being of her child.

Roger: Features of Early Development

Pre-& Post Natal & Birth

Second child. Mother was 31 years old. Child was planned. Normal
    pregnancy. Labour 4 hours at most.
Birth was easy and no instruments or special treatments were required.
Probably cried at once. Was jaundiced, a little, for about 3 days.
    Birth weight 7lbs.
Breastfed for 11 months.
Family history: his maternal grandfather suffered from depression
    from age 54, and his maternal great aunt was epileptic in her
    teens, as well as diabetic. (Roger has had no fits.) He seemed to
    be a normal baby.

FIRST YEAR

A passive baby. Did not pass a motion until the eighth day.

One month. First smile. Did not stretch his arms out. Slightly floppy.

Two and a half months. First triple injection (including whooping cough).

Seven and a half months. Teething began. Lacked early 'joint attention' behaviours.

Eleven months. Stopped breast feeding.

SECOND YEAR

Thirteen months. Sat unaided.

Twenty-one months. Differences from 'normal' noted, *e.g.* didn't show normal affection.

Twenty-four months. Walked unaided. Did not point. Did not look at people. Lined up toys. Repetitive patterns of behaviour. No speech development. Did not respond to noise, sounds, voices.

THIRD YEAR

Had words, but lost them.

Lacked motivation to communicate.

Roger's history shows late motor development and though he was said to have spoken at the normal age, he then lost the words and thereafter was described as not using speech but 'understanding everything.' As he grew older he remained an 'aloof' child, seemingly indifferent to others.

Roger attended a specialist unit at a local mainstream school from age four until nine. He underwent a course of Doman-Delacato therapy for eighteen months, though it was not specified when this began. This therapy is based on the repetition and patterning of developmental motor functions that any particular child omitted to achieve at a younger age. It aims to reinforce the child's sensory development and nervous system organization.

At the age of eight, after he was diagnosed as autistic, he went to the Higashi School in Boston, USA, for two years. This school practises *Daily Life Therapy,* in which children with autism are put through intensive physical activities according to a highly regimented schedule.

Sometime after this Roger attended a special unit at a local secondary school, and from there was eventually admitted to the Camphill school, aged fifteen. His parents describe Roger as:

> An intelligent and good-natured boy who was adored wherever he went. He lacks language and self-motivation, but with the help of a 'facilitator' he can communicate via a qwerty keyboard. He can ride a bike, roller and ice skate, and is quite capable physically to do most tasks put to him. We have been communicating via his keyboard for about a year and are most impressed by his knowledge and wisdom.

Diagnosis

Both James and Roger had received definite diagnoses of autism. However, whereas James was diagnosed in his third year, Roger's diagnosis was only made when he was eight years old. Nevertheless, both boys had shown autistic symptoms within the first three years' life.

Although both had been jaundiced for three days after birth, James had required some special treatment (*e.g.* oxygen) and was, from an early age, prone to viruses.

In terms of differential diagnosis it seems possible that Roger may have presented a more classic (Kanner's type) autism, whilst with his early health problems, low Apgar score and ENT investigations, James' autism might have been a secondary reaction to other primary difficulties. In James' case, there has been no sign of any speech development even up to the present day. Interestingly, both boys have largish heads, as did five of Kanner's original sample of eleven children (see Chapter 9).

Principles of the interventions

The three areas from which individually designed programmes of intervention exercises were constructed were:
   1. Inter-human attitudes;
   2. Imitation, rhythmic activities and play;
   3. Sensory-perceptual development.

Within the third of these areas the realm of the lower senses was specifically addressed, in order to facilitate the process of ego-integration, and the increased usage of each child's higher social senses for interpersonal contact and communication. As we have seen, a fundamental principle of all anthroposophical interventions is that of mutual changes and developments in both pupil and educator. Participants are therefore interdependent. This principle acknowledges that the degree of autism is not only an in-child condition but also, and possibly equally, an environmental issue.

Procedure and implementation

The individual sessions with the two boys took place during the school year 1998/99, and within the Autumn and Spring terms, beginning in September 1998 and concluding in March 1999. Each term had a half-term holiday of two weeks in the Autumn and one week in the Spring, when the boys went back to their homes. The three-week Christmas holiday separated the two terms from each other. Effectively then, our sessions took place over three clear periods as shown in Table 2. Whereas I had previous experience in implementing individualized interventions with autistic children, one special feature of the work

	Autumn Term Sep – Oct	Autumn Term Nov – Dec	Spring Term Jan – March
Frequency per week	4	4	3
No. of sessions with James	24	15	20
No. of sessions with Roger	22	15	22

Table 2. Distribution of sessions.

with James and Roger was the increased frequency of the interventional input. Namely, with each boy, sessions of around forty minutes,
on a frequency of four times a week during the Autumn term, and
three times weekly in the Spring term. On this basis a total of fifty-
nine sessions took place with each child. (A single, follow up session
— the sixtieth — took place in the Summer term.)

In each case the sessions took place in the same physical surroundings, the school's large movement hall, and at the same time in the
morning for each of the boys, thus providing a predictable and consistent rhythm to each school week.

The second special feature of my work with James and Roger was
that it had been agreed with the school that no other special measures,
whether in the form of therapies or remedies, would be given during
the period of my interventions.

The third special feature which should be emphasized, and kept in
mind throughout, was that the individualized intervention programmes were not meant to be rigid and inflexible. On the contrary,
they had been derived by observing each child's responses when first
trying out activities together, as well as being strongly suggested by
the anthroposophical understanding of autism. Their actual implementation called for some give and take by both of us, as joint participants in a therapeutic process. At times, for example, I could be more
firm in my expectations towards James and, depending on his state of
health and openness, flexible and amenable to his wishes at other
times. Much depended therefore on feeling my way through each session, and learning together.

Child protection and accountability

The school, in common with other Camphill communities, has clear
policies in place in order to safeguard the welfare of all its pupils. Individual curative educators and therapists are therefore held formally
accountable to the school and to the pupils' parent(s) or guardian(s),
as well as to the local Social Services Department, and the funding
authority for each pupil.

Parents are asked to give their written permission for their child to
receive medical and therapeutic treatments and interventions which

are provided at the school. All measures are prescribed on a purely individual basis, in consultation with the school's qualified medical adviser(s).

My own therapeutic exercises with both boys involved a good deal of very physical, hands on contact — mainly initiated by me — in our one-to-one sessions. Regular progress reports, and descriptions of the actual exercises employed, were shared in the internal school review meetings (see below).

Analysis and evaluations of progress

Each session involved a continuous process of observation and assessment of how we were responding and reacting with each other. I considered my own inner attitudes, thoughts and feelings to be an integral part of the therapeutic situation and process, as well as the children's behaviours and actions.

Written notes were taken by me during the actual sessions, between exercises, and also immediately following each session. This helped to ensure that my observations, experiences, and memories were fresh and accurate.

Changes in the degree of autism could, and often did, occur, in some of the sessions. At one point, contact and communication between us, might be *good*, for example, establishing eye contact, and at another time in the same session, might be *poor*.

The recordings made for each of the sessions therefore described both what was done and, more importantly, *how* we had responded to these activities and interventions.

By comparing the responses recorded with particular intervention exercises, evaluations were made of the progress seen with each child. It could of course be argued that such evaluations carry a strong subjective bias as I was looking for, and indeed hoping to see, progress in terms of alleviating the degree of autism. However as has already been clearly acknowledged, curative educators' attitudes and expectations are to be seen as an essential part of the relationship building process in which they are active participants.

However, if my evaluations of the sessions had indeed led me to a judgment of progress, was this also confirmed by other educators in

the wider school community, and also in the child's own home setting? This issue was addressed through the regular, internal school
reviews attended by educators working and living directly with the
child, together with the school's anthroposophical medical adviser, as
well as through regular written observations and impressions provided
by each child's parents for the school holiday periods.

As the children did not receive any other therapeutic measures
during my intervention period, it was considered likely that any significant changes (for better or worse), could be attributed to the sessions I was implementing, over and above any natural developmental
factors.

It could of course be argued that all those who contributed to the
evaluations, for example the child's own parents, were themselves
actively looking for, and hoping to see, progress, and that this constituted a subjective bias. However, anthroposophically, this should be
accepted as an integral and real factor towards the child's positive personal development. It is difficult to speak of *detached objectivity* when
considering the sphere where autism actually manifests itself — in
human relationships!

Results and discussions

The full descriptions of all the individual sessions cannot possibly be
given here, however fascinating they are. Nevertheless, some sessions
are described in detail in order to try to give the reader a real feel for the
dynamic and subtle therapeutic process involved, and in order to make
clearer the practical exercises and activities which we engaged in.

My overall results from the sessions — that is, any observed
changes — arrived at by my comparison, analysis and evaluation of
the raw data, will be given, and these in turn supported (or perhaps
contradicted), by the perceptions of other educators and the children's
parents.

6. The Sessions with James

Developing a relationship

I had already worked with James, exactly one year before starting these more frequent sessions in September 1998.

In September 1997, he had only just been admitted to the school, and was eight years and three months old when I took him for twice weekly individual sessions over a period of nine to ten weeks in the Autumn term, giving nineteen sessions in total. At that time, we worked in the playroom and I tried to engage his interest in a variety of activities which particularly called upon his lower senses of touch, balance and movement.

During that earlier intervention period I felt that we had gradually developed a therapeutic relationship, built on mutual trust and confidence. James became more actively co-operative in the particular exercises we did, also responding well to hands-on physical contact, such as tickling, but he made very little eye contact and appeared to deliberately avoid it. I worked with him and adapted my expectations and hopes in the light of *his* reactions and responses (part of my fundamental therapeutic attitude), rather than forcing the issue.

James had no speech, and often made rather anxious sounding noises. He also showed obsessive, apparently meaningless, behaviours such as manipulating toy building bricks in his fingers.

Progress was made over these original nineteen sessions in the sense of building our relationship, getting to know each other, and by encouraging James to engage in various joint activities. At times he became more open, and interpersonal contact then increased, for example, when tickling or teasing him, or when imitating his noises.

There were also moments when he looked towards me and smiled, occasionally making brief eye contact, and becoming quiet and peaceful; for example, when touching different surfaces.

While it is not the intention to describe these earlier sessions in detail here, they do give one telling example of the progress James made in engaging himself in a meaningful, co-ordinated activity, with attention and dexterity. In the first session, James had not shown the slightest interest in building a tower with bricks. After working patiently on this together, and as a turn-taking exercise, by the eighteenth session I recorded:

> Today he built a tower more or less by himself! In this activity he is attentive, and shows good dexterity.

He thereafter continued to demonstrate his tower building skills also back in his classroom! Halfway through December 1997, our sessions stopped, as planned, at that time.

Deepening our interrelationship

By September 1998, when I resumed my active relationship with James he was nine years old, and had settled down well during his first year at the school. He was still not toilet-trained and therefore wore disposable nappies.

The three distinct time periods for the interventions provide the obvious structure for what follows.

The first half of the Autumn term, 1998

SESSION 1: 3 SEPTEMBER, 1998

Having spent a short time in the school playground, and also after a much needed change of nappy, we went for the first time into the movement hall.

We went into the movement hall. James was not very happy about that to begin with.

I tried to have some interaction with him using a beanbag and a ball. He screwed up the beanbag in his hands. Didn't hand it back to me. I took it and put it on his head a number of times, in a rather playful way. I also ran up and down the movement hall with James a number of times. He went along with this. I also held his hands and swung him around (but not off the floor). He seemed to enjoy this.

Then I got out the big gym mattress. He showed a real interest in this, for bouncing on. Also he lay down on it, or rather I laid him down on it, and rolled him over — which he obviously enjoyed.

He participated in, and generally enjoyed, these gross movement activities — running, swinging round, bouncing, rolling.

James did make eye contact at various times. He also came and took me by the arm or hand when he wanted me to go with him (e.g. to the mattress). When he didn't want to go with me he would grip or pinch.

He hyperventilates quite a bit. Makes noises; no words or clear sounds. His hands were firm, lean, bony, dry (not particularly warm or cold I think). He is a thin, lean-looking boy, with a largish-looking broad head and a wide mouth.

So today I experienced that:
— he can pull strongly when he wants to go somewhere;
— he can whine and protest when he wants his way;
— he also appears to enjoy various gross movements, and to clearly indicate that he wants more of this (this was particularly so with bouncing on the mattress).

On the basis of these initial experiences with James, the subsequent sessions consisted largely of gross movement and balancing activities, which included:
— walking along, and stepping over benches;
— stepping on to a chair, and jumping down from it;
— carrying weighted shopping bags, containing large stones;
— climbing up and down wall bars;
— walking with James, as he stood on my feet and I held his upper body.

In all these exercises, which called upon James' lower senses, I carefully observed his responses and was open to inspiration as to what to do next. This led to the introduction of touch activities in the fifth session and to *body geography* work — going from his head, down his body, ending at his toes — beginning in the seventh session. An intervention programme was then constructed, as shown below, and this served as the guide for all the activities and exercises which we engaged in through much of the Autumn term, from September until December. However, I felt quite free to select which exercises to do, or not to do, in any particular session, taking my cue from James himself. For example, one session might be given over mainly to touch exercises, and another to the use of the trampette. A certain creativity and freedom was thus available, rather than either of us being tied to a fixed programme. This in no way detracted from the clear aims and intentions of the interventional process which were, above all else, to develop an interrelationship with James which would help to alleviate his strongly autistic, asocial characteristics.

Exercise	Aim
1. Hands on body geography, starting from his head and working downwards — via neck, shoulders, arms, hands, fingers, upper body, waist, legs, feet, toes — accompanied by the naming of respective body parts. Vigorous clapping with his hands, and sometimes his feet also.	To foster James' own body awareness and body image. To also strengthen his inner soul experiences of security, trust and confidence.
2. Tactile stimulation by brushing him (literally) on exposed skin areas, and also touching him with contrasting surfaces and objects, eg. rough or smooth stones, prickly conker case, feather, smooth cold spoon, etc. Also encouraging him to touch/feel these contrasting surfaces.	To help awaken his perceptions for differentiated touch stimuli, and thus exercise his own sense of touch. Also to make him aware, through touch, of his own body boundaries.

3. Walking on my feet, performed by James standing on my feet either with his back towards me or facing me, and with me holding/supporting him with my arms around him.	To enable him to *creep* into my lower senses and, in this way, gain support for his own body senses.
4. Carrying heavy shopping bags as a resistance exercise. Usually with him using two hands to lift one bag, and bringing this to me at the far end of the movement hall. This was sometimes done as a turn-taking exercise.	To come into a stronger experience of gravity and weight, and therefore of his own body.
5. Holding his arms to perform large movements. This could be done whilst I stood behind James or facing him. Such movements could be circular, in the vertical plane or in/out contraction-expansion gestures in the horizontal plane.	To encourage him to relax into making co-ordinated, flowing and/or expansive and contracting, arm movements. I felt this had special importance also in freeing up his middle or rhythmical system, connected to breathing and speaking. Also, to exercise his sense of movement for his own upper limbs.
6. Gross motor activities included: balancing on benches, jumping down from a chair, bouncing on the trampette, walking, running, etc	To exercise his lower senses of balance, movement, and touch, as the basis for increasing his own body experience and self-awareness.
7. Turn-taking activities, such as receiving and giving a copper rod, or a heavy medicine ball, or catching/throwing a lighter ball.	To enter into a social give and take situation. Fostering contact and communication via the objects used.

Table 3. Intervention exercises with James, first half of Autumn term, 1998.

A selection of my original notes is given below.

SESSION 5: 14 SEPTEMBER, 1998

James came in quietly and I sat him down to put on his eurythmy shoes, similar to plimsolls. He had in fact started to take off his trainers and was perfectly co-operative in letting me put his eurythmy shoes on.

As James was quiet and peaceful I decided to begin with touch activities. I touched him with contrasting objects and surfaces — on his hands (back of hand and palms), cheeks, also his bare feet and lower legs (his shoes/socks were removed for this). He allowed this to be done. Items used included: brushes, plastic/nylon abrasive pad, stones rough/smooth and of different shapes, sandpaper, prickly conker case.

Other activities were:

1. *James walking on my feet, with him wearing eurythmy shoes and me normal shoes. His back was towards me, with me holding him with my arms. He appears to recall doing this from last Autumn 1997, as he readily puts himself in position for this exercise.*

2. *Walking along wide benches. He fiddles with his fingers and clothing whilst doing this — I encourage him not to fiddle like this. He does this exercise well, maintains his balance, doesn't look unsteady or fall off. In fact he did this exercise after I had been turning around with him, which made me feel slightly dizzy, but he then went to step up on to the bench!*

3. *Carrying shopping bags. He did this willingly, picking up either of the two bags (one is lighter than the other) with two hands. He was able to manage the heavier bag, which shows he has quite some strength.*

4. *He held the copper rod with me standing behind him and holding his hands to raise arms up (all the way) and down. He doesn't put his arms right up in a relaxed way.*

5. *Also passed the medicine ball between us whilst sitting opposite, with me saying 'you and me.' Also did this with the copper rod. James was reciprocating with this. (Not speaking though.)*

I did not run around with James in this session. I took my cues from his rather peaceful state (not hyperventilating heavily — he only really begins to do this when he fiddles rapidly with his clothing).

I was very pleased with this session with James. He was not at all whingy or whiny, but surprisingly calm and peaceful. There was no protesting at all. He did make some eye contact with me.

SESSION 10: 22 SEPTEMBER, 1998

Did body geography and hand-clapping together.

Did tactile brushing, also using a cold spoon, and then handling contrasting surfaces.

James was attentive in all of this — peaceful — just a little quick breathing and a little twisting/fiddling with clothes. Now sitting very peacefully.

Walking on my feet. He came to do this, first with his back to me, then facing me (he looked up at me).

Carrying the heavy shopping bag — quite willing — hyperventilating more now.

Arm exercises, up/down, out/in. I believe he's less stiff than he used to be.

Passing medicine ball at end. Sometimes big smile, twinkling eyes, even laughing.

SESSION 15: 5 OCTOBER, 1998

I observed James in the playground — he was hopping up and down as he typically does. (It's a sort of skipping he does, up on his toes.) I waited until the bell went and watched him going towards the school house. I called his name, he turned, saw me and came.

I went with him to the movement hall. James sat on the chair (where he is now) waiting patiently. He took the initiative to take his shoes off.

Body geography and hand-clapping. He obviously enjoyed this; smiling, twinkling eyes. Now also making contact — putting his face up to me. Did the exercise again. When I physically exert more pressure he finds it amusing, laughs and enjoys it.

Brushing him. By his attentiveness he seems to be registering impressions. Sometimes smiles. Cold spoon on forehead and neck. He came and sat on me.

Walking on my feet. He comes readily for this, his back to me first, then facing me. Stays on my feet very well.

Moving arms up/down, out/in.

In this session James was co-operative, attentive, mainly peaceful.

SESSION 20: 13 OCTOBER, 1998

James was in his usual playtime position today — up on the climbing platform.

When it was 11am I went across and called his name. He responded by looking in my direction. He sat on the slide (which was wet!) and came down that way. Then as we walked away, he turned to me and put his arms around me. Now he sits waiting as usual ready to start.

Body geography, clapping, rubbing hands and feet. James is not very animated today. Not even the clapping brought a smile. According to his teacher, he has quite a cold. But he's co-operative. I started to do the exercise again, combing his hair with my fingers. But he took my hands down and came and sat on me. I gave him some hugs which he didn't object to.

I tried the exercise again — down his body, starting at the head. But he didn't want this. Sat on me again.

I worked on his feet, rubbing them with rough/smooth surfaces. (He does have quite a runny nose.)

Walked benches, also a narrow one with me supporting him.

Walked a little on my feet.

Then I got the trampette out. He bounced on this a lot, became more animated and was obviously enjoying it. Makes eye contact. I gave him also some hugs in between bouncing.

Today, as James was possibly not feeling too bright with his cold, I was flexible in what we did.

SESSION 24: 22 OCTOBER, 1998 (LAST SESSION BEFORE HALF-TERM)

A dark, rainy day. James was given to me by his teacher. He didn't look too happy when he looked at me. (His usual dour/sour expression.) Now sat on the chair and waiting.

He put his feet up. I rubbed/massaged his cold feet and lower legs. He passively accepted this, not making much eye contact. He indicated he wanted his socks back on.

Then did walking on my feet. He co-operated.

Next, the trampette which brought smiles and direct eye contact. He obviously enjoyed it, smiles, eye contact, looked much more alive!

Also hugs and squeezes from me of his whole upper body. He liked it, smiling, direct eye contact.

In this session the use of the trampette, squeezing and hugging, were the highlights (also some tickling).

In these whole body movement and touch/contact activities, James warmed up, looked cheerful, and was making direct, clear eye contact with me.

However his hands were cool today, not warm as they often are (sometimes very warm). I think his cold, which he still has, is cooling him through.

Initial results of the intervention process

Looking back, what changes/results could be clearly identified by me over this six to seven week period?

A careful comparison of the written notes which had been made during and at the end of each session with James revealed the following.

Observed changes

— large decrease in hyperventilating
— more calm and peaceful
— reduction in obsessive activity, *i.e.* twisting/fiddling with his
    clothing
— increased eye contact
— increased smiling at me
— increased co-operation and attentiveness
— increased expression of enjoyment and pleasure, *e.g.* through
    laughter and liveliness
— sometimes taking initiative, *e.g.* taking his shoes off, coming to sit
    on me, putting himself into position for walking on my feet
— generally less evasive
— responding when I call his name, *e.g.* by looking at me, or coming

Since a therapeutic process is a two-way involvement, had I noticed any changes in myself over this period? To begin with, I had taken a firm and clear attitude with James, and had wanted him to follow my instructions. I had experienced that this attitude seemed to work well, in that James responded positively to this and became more settled and secure, as I had provided him with a clear level of expectation.

However as the sessions continued I felt I could be more flexible, sensitive and open towards James and his wishes; partly depending also on his state of physical health. A warm and light, humorous or playful approach, with some teasing from me, worked well.

Discussion and evaluation

All the intervention exercises done with James called upon his four lower senses of touch, balance, movement and life. With regard to the experiences afforded by the inner sense of life, such as a feeling of well-being, these were stimulated by the regular rhythmic occurrence of the periods of intervention, four times a week, at the same time.

The exercises were aimed especially at strengthening James' own body experience through helping his ego to engage, via the lower senses. However, this would in turn help to stimulate his higher (social) senses of word, thought and ego.

For example, it was observed that during touch exercises, James would often become very attentive and peaceful and engage in eye contact with me. As we know, the sense of touch has a particular developmental relationship with the sense of ego (for the recognition of the *other* person).

It was clear that James responded well to direct physical forms of contact, such as hugs and squeezes, and that he then *warmed up* in terms of his interaction with me — non-verbal communication, eye contact, smiling and expressions of his own enjoyment and pleasure.

The marked decrease in his characteristic hyperventilation during the sessions, his becoming calm and peaceful while sitting on a chair facing me to experience touching, and the decrease in obsessional activities (*e.g.* fiddling/twisting his clothing), were particularly impressive signs of progress towards better ego-integration.

I therefore had good reason to feel pleased with the way the therapeutic process was going so far.

The perceptions of others

Had other educators, such as James' class teacher or his house-mother at the school, noticed any changes with James over this first period of interventions?

James' house-mother wrote:

> James' obsession with tractors/cars has been very strong as
> well as a new interest in the toilet. He will now go into the
> toilet by himself but, as yet, will not perform.
>
> He has been more reactive if he is thwarted from play, and
> makes a fuss when getting ready for bed or if he cannot eat
> the second he hears the dinner gong.

Physically, James had apparently never been so well as in this first half
of the term!

James' class teacher wrote:

> James' way of walking changed. Rather than bouncing along
> he now drags his feet, hardly lifting them at all.
>
> He is extremely stubborn, and cries easily if he doesn't get
> his way.
>
> On the other hand he is much quieter in the classroom sit-
> uation and very patient with activities that require sitting
> behind a desk and sitting still.

After the two-week Autumn half-term, James' mother wrote:

> James has changed considerably since he has been at your
> school. He is generally more calm and does not make so
> many noises (that's good!) He is definitely more aware of his
> body and I actually feel as if he realizes that his legs and feet
> are attached to his body.
>
> He is also (when at home) continually changing his
> clothes — this is good in one sense as I feel he is more
> aware of his body and himself — but he is obsessed with
> stripy tops.
>
> He has become very stubborn about things and tries to
> dictate what he wants to wear each day, but with this comes
> James' ability to choose for himself. He seems less obsessive
> about his Dad's van and not so keen to leg it all the time!

His mother also noticed a clear increase in James' interaction with her in terms of communicating his wishes, and a marked increase in showing interest in his surroundings. James' sister (seventeen months older than James) noticed a clear increase in his communication with other children.

His father had seen some small increases in James' contact and communication with him, but nothing very substantial.

Conclusion

A number of important observations which provide confirmation of my own work in trying to strengthen James' own body experience and ego-integration, are clearly seen in the above accounts. Namely, that he appeared to be more aware of his body as a connected whole, and also that his way of walking had changed so that he seemed to be more 'grounded.'

On the other hand he seemed to be more wilful, stubborn, and reactive, if he could not get his own way. Positively, this could be viewed as a stronger self-assertiveness, in keeping with his actual age (nine years old). The work on his lower senses was intended to increase his bodily awareness as a necessary basis for a stronger inner experience of self.

Both at school and at home James displayed marked obsessional behaviours, and yet, he had also become calmer and quieter, more patient and able to wait in some situations.

Overall, I had the impression that the changes with James were indicative of progress in his own self-awareness, as well as his surroundings, including, at least at home, some communication with other children.

Second half of Autumn term 1998

From November into December, fifteen further therapeutic sessions took place. While some of the exercises given before half-term were continued (see Table 3), others, such as the body geography exercise and tactile stimulation with brushing and objects, were stopped. Some new activities, accompanied by speaking or singing, were introduced in the last sessions of this term, following the internal review meeting of 7 December 1998.

Exercise	Aim
1. Foot rubbing/stroking. Taking each of his bare feet in turn and stimulating them by direct hands-on contact from me.	To help him become more aware of his own feet, and fostering his sense of touch in this area.
2. Bouncing on the trampette, which had sufficient area for only James to stand on, whilst I supported him by standing nearby.	To increase his own body awareness, through this gross motor activity. Also to encourage his expression of enjoyment and pleasure.
3. Upper body bear hugs and squeezes, and whole body spins (with his feet off the floor).	To provide him with considerable tactile stimulation, together with appropriate physical contact in a playful situation.
4. *Walking on my feet* exercise.	To enable him to *creep* into my lower senses, and thereby stimulate his own body senses.
5. Carrying heavy shopping bag as a gravity resistance exercise.	To enable him to arrive at a stronger experience of gravity and weight.

6. Large arm movements per- formed by me holding and directing his hands or arms.	To help him enter into new, sequential, movement experiences, through his sense of movement. To help *free* up his middle, rhythmical system, connected with breathing and speech.

7. Rhythmical clapping with his
hands, and stamping with his
feet, accompanied by me
speaking a verse.
	To stimulate his middle, rhythmi-
	cal system, connected with breath-
	ing and speech.
	   To foster the process of his ego-
	integration through the medium of
	speech (mine).
	   To increase his body awareness.

8. Rhythmical *rowing* exercise, performed by us holding a sin- gle copper rod horizontally, whilst seated, and each of us moving back and forth in rhythm. I accompanied this by singing.	To stimulate his middle, rhythmi- cal system. To encourage him to join in a shared, joint activity.

Table 4. Intervention exercises with James, second half of Autumn term, 1998.

Examples taken from the detailed notes of the sessions are given below.

SESSION 29: 17 NOVEMBER, 1998

I started to rub his feet as usual, but James got up and went to the trampette (which was standing on its side). So I obliged him and put the trampette down.

James used it vigorously, obviously enjoying it — laughing. In between his using the trampette, I gave him big squeezes and hugs which he also enjoyed.

Now he sits quietly again, and I catch his eye! Worked at his feet, and sometimes he looks towards me briefly. Then back to the trampette; he really enjoys it. More hugs and squeezes.

Now sitting quietly again — entirely peaceful. Then the trampette again. Plenty of exercise helps contact, emotional responsiveness and interaction. Now sitting again ready to have his socks and shoes put on.

Then carrying the shopping bag. He did it — I praised him — he responded, looked pleased, smiled.

Then arm movements with me standing behind him. He's still too tense; I want to work on this.

I would say a good, responsive session with James — a lot of interaction. He gives back, through his enjoyment in movement, smiles, laughter, and eye contact.

SESSION 33: 1 DECEMBER, 1998

I was in the playground and James came to me, and so I went to the movement hall with him. He took off his hat, scarf, and coat (I unzipped it).

Went into the Hall — took his shoes and socks off.

James wanted the trampette, so we did this first. He enjoys it very much — really laughs.

Now sitting down for a rest; feet up (to be rubbed). Hyperventilating again; he hasn't done this for a long time.

Used the trampette, then hugs and spins, all of which he enjoys.

He's wilful when he wants his way. His cold is a bit better, no longer has a runny nose. Now he is sitting peacefully.

I let James have his way a good deal, but not always — it's a two-way affair.

A good deal of eye contact and smiling, during gross movement activities.

He carried the heavy shopping bag, twice.

Finally I tried to move his arms in small upward curves (similar to the movements for the 'L' sound in eurythmy). This is not easy as he readily stiffens and resists. However I plan to improve on this.

SESSION 38: 15 DECEMBER 1998

I saw James in the playground as I passed through. He looked at me and would have come then, but it wasn't quite time.

Now in the movement hall. First foot rubbing. He wanted the trampette straight away, but I made it clear he'd have to wait, which he did.

Then trampette, hugs, spins. Now sitting on chair waiting. Did the anapest rhythm (short, short, long) to the verse Brave and true I will be, etc. Clapping it with me holding his hands, and then stamping it by me holding his lower legs/ankles. I sat James on the low bench, (rather than the chair), so that I could really stamp his feet on the floor. We did this rhythm several times.

Then, Row, row, row your boat gently down the stream etc., while sitting down and holding the copper rod between us. James held the rod and went with the movement.

Then ball passing while sitting down, and while standing. He has no clear notion, or skill, how to catch and throw a ball. I feel this should be learnt.

Then moving his arms, with me taking his wrists/hands and making the movements — in and out, up and round. He went with it; very well actually, didn't stiffen up or resist.

Results of the intervention process

Once again the notes of the sessions were compared to see if there were any further observed changes with James. In referring back to the items already identified for the first half of the Autumn term, it would be true to say that the behaviours and responses listed then were maintained in the second half of term, but without any very obvious further changes in their actual levels of attainment. The one exception was an increased expression of enjoyment and pleasure by James, due to changed intervention exercises — more extensive use of the trampette, and frequent physical hands-on contact. With the latter, the rougher the better as far as he was concerned! As I noted after Session 25:

> *James actually shows a good deal of emotional and contact/communication responsiveness when in a situation that he enjoys. I find this to be a real emotional (affective) feedback, such as one would not expect to find in a deeply autistic child. He also responds to teasing and playfulness.*

Considering that James had a cold for much of the second half of the term (he is prone to colds and catarrh) he still maintained a rather impressive level of participation and responsiveness. In Session 31, for example, he continued to thoroughly enjoy using the trampette and receiving bear hugs, despite having both a cold and cough, but the following day he was not in school owing to his ill health.

My notes contained only occasional mention of any obsessional behaviours during the sessions, and this was similar with his hyperventilating.

Discussion and evaluation

As far as I was concerned — and I believe James felt likewise — the sessions had gone well, with a good deal of interaction happening between us.

The exercises had again strongly called upon the functioning of his lower (body) senses, and the overall aim of increasing his own body awareness and self-experience, and thereby of fostering his personal and social awareness, continued to be implemented. However it was interesting to note how James tended to alternate between looking rather dead-pan, often while sitting on a chair, and becoming very animated, lively, and cheerful during very physical activities.

Unfortunately there were no signs at all of any speech development, with no clear syllables or sounds being heard by me.

The perceptions of others

An internal review meeting took place at the school on 7 December, when I had had a total of thirty-four sessions with James (with only five remaining for that term). What follows is derived, firstly, from the record of this review, and then his parents' observations during the three-week Christmas holiday.

His house-mother reported that there had definitely been changes with James, since the Autumn half-term. These are summarized below.

> James' obsessive behaviours became more intense, and there were also more of them. For example, obsessed with getting the cutlery containers, he will get out of bed in the morning

to find these. Obsession with stripy jumpers, which he wants on and off. In these behaviours he hyperventilates and has a manic impression.

When the first gong goes in the house (to signal ten minutes to lunch-time), James immediately wants food. Sometimes he laughs, occasionally tears. You often don't know why he reacts as he does.

Since half-term there have been five occasions of soiling and poking himself (though not masturbation). The fifth incident was a major event, with faeces around the dormitory. Previously James has never liked to be dirty, but this has now changed to an oblivion of being dirty!

James has become more aware of sensory matters relating to his own body — he is into his lower senses. A couple of days ago, and for the first time, James wanted grown ups to tickle his knees!

In the review meeting the medical adviser (who has had considerable experience with autistic children in a Camphill school community in southern Germany working with Dr Hans Müller-Wiedemann), asked if there had been any changes in James' environment at the school since half-term. The house-mother said that a new pupil came then, who now shares a room with James. He first came as a day pupil, and then as a weekly boarder. However, she did not feel that this new situation had influenced James particularly.

The question was then asked whether any improvements had been seen with James since half-term, and the house-mother's answer was a clear *no*.

James' class teacher reported that:

He had shown strong obsessive behaviour in the class since half-term, expressed by him going for music stands at the slightest opportunity.

How then did James appear, to his parents' during the holidays? *His mother wrote that:*

> James is really getting to know what he does/does not want
> to do, but because he is unable to express himself verbally he
> gets very frustrated. He appears to have a greater understand-
> ing of himself. He is more aware of his body and his feel-
> ings. This however means he is not so easy to persuade, and
> if he has made his mind up about something, that's it! I think
> that in the long term this is all good. It's just a question of
> enabling him to communicate without shrieking and being so
> stubborn.

His mother had also observed a marked increase in James engaging
in two-way communication with her but, interestingly, a decrease in
communicating his own wishes.

His father had noticed slight decreases in James' contact and communication with him.

Conclusion

Whereas I continued to have very positive experiences with James in
our sessions together, others were reporting new changes of a difficult
and problematic nature for them — if not for James himself!

The medical adviser was able to throw a very helpful light on all
this, from the anthroposophical perspective.

Bearing in mind that the clear aim of the interventions was to facilitate James' ego-integration — the penetration of his soul spiritual
nature into his physical life body — we could interpret the problematic
changes and developments as a part of this deeper incarnation process.

The stronger obsessive behaviours, the greed for food, the increased
self-will, were expressive of James' astrality (the astral body carries
soul wishes and desires). It appeared therefore that he was now
becoming more involved with his soul-astral nature. Together with
this was a growing awareness of, and penetration into, his actual physical body. This was evident from James walking more on the ground
and less on tiptoe, an awareness of his limbs, and perhaps even his
interest in poking himself and soiling, which had never been known
before.

What was then required to aid this incarnation process further,
beyond just the astral nature? It would need therapeutic exercises to

engage James' ego (the Spirit), so that the ego could help to bring order, peace and direction into the rather wild astral nature (from which the obsessions arose).

The medical adviser recommended exercises in which speech would be combined with rhythm and movement. Interestingly, in all the work which I had done with James before the review meeting, I had not consciously incorporated speech. After the review I immediately took up this recommendation. Furthermore, the doctor said that he could understand (and would even have expected), that by stimulating an incarnation process in James his behaviour could 'get worse before it became better!' Both resistance and aggravation (from the child) can become evident as soon as you encourage 'a more incarnated situation.'

It was agreed that I should continue with my sessions during the Spring term, in the New Year, after the three-week Christmas holiday, but three times a week rather than four.

As James was often unwell with colds, medicines were prescribed to treat the colds, but which wouldn't interfere with the interventions.

Another review meeting was planned for the Spring term.

Spring term 1999

During the Spring term there were twenty sessions from mid-January until the end of March. There were some changes to the intervention exercises, as well as continuity from the end of the previous term.

In particular, I decided to stop using the trampette, because I did not want this to be the main focus of James' attention at the expense of other helpful activities.

Exercise	Aim
1. Foot rubbing/stroking taking one of his bare feet at a time in my hands, as we sat facing each other.	To make him more aware of his feet through his sense of touch. I was also aware that, according to reflexology, foot massage can work helpfully on the whole body.
2. Rhythmical clapping with his hands, and then stamping with his feet, accompanied by me speaking a verse.	To foster the process of ego-integration, through speech and rhythm.
3. Rhythmical *rowing* exercise performed when sitting facing each other and holding a copper rod, horizontally, between us. Accompanied by me singing.	To foster ego-integration through a rhythmical, and joint turn-taking movement exercise.
4. Upper body bear hugs, squeezes and whole body spins.	To provide considerable tactile stimulation, of the lower senses, combined with physical contact.
5. Playful chasing/catching game situation, by running away from or towards James in the movement hall.	To provide a new form of playful and enjoyable interaction between us.
6. Giving or throwing, receiving or catching, a copper rod or ball, using his right hand.	To bring his upper limbs into purposeful actions, in a give and take interactive situation. To foster right-handed dominance as it is well-known that dominance development is closely associated with language development.
7. Symmetrical and harmonious arm movements, performed by me holding his hands or arms.	To mainly help free up the middle rhythmical system, connected with breathing and speech.

Table 5. Intervention exercises with James, Spring term, 1999.

As before, a few illustrative examples have been selected from notes made during the actual sessions.

SESSION 3: 20 JANUARY, 1999

James came willingly with me into the movement hall. We sat down and he put his feet up for his socks to be taken off. I worked on his feet. (His hands were warm today, his feet coldish.) He did some hyperventilating.

Then we did the anapest rhythm (short short long) accompanied by speech, Brave and true I will be; first clapping then stamping. He seems to enjoy it; smiling and looking at me. The more vigorously done, the better.

Now he's gone off bench walking again. (James had taken the initiative to walk along the benches, at the sides of the movement hall, since the first session this term.)

Hugs and spins. Obviously enjoyed it. Very direct eye contact.

Then did the other rhythmic exercise, Row, row, row your boat. He was smiling throughout.

(Hyperventilating stopped — very calm as I rubbed his feet.)

Big arm movements — he went with this — up and round, in and out. Stiffened once. But then when I had to put his boots on to take him back to his class, big protest. Definitely didn't want this (the boots I think).

However had to be!

SESSION 7: 2 FEBRUARY, 1999

At break time James was making a big fuss. Apparently he wanted to get into the classroom to the music stand.

I've rubbed his feet — he sat peacefully for that — apart from breathing a bit noisily.

Now he's walking along the benches. We've had eye contact and smiling. (He's still got a cold, but not coughing.) Hands warm, feet cool.

Now he's touching/fingering the wall — fingers in the gaps between the blocks — interested in the wall?

Hugs, spins. He liked this, smiled and laughed.

Game — 'You can't catch me' — really interrelating.

Sat down again — peaceful.

Did the Brave and true rhythm. He often gives the impression of enjoying this. Then Row, row, row your boat. He holds the copper rod, looked at me directly, smiling. (I do feel I have good, positive, contact with James.)

Now bench walking again in between. I still want to do arm movements — ball/rod throwing/passing to get his arms and hands in use.

I experienced this as a good session, with interaction, contact and communication. James co-operated. No protests.

SESSION 14: 10 MARCH, 1999

I fetched James. He came willingly as I led him by the hand. He hung up his scarf, hat, and coat, with a little help.

Bit of hyperventilating (has a cold). Was a cold day; his hands are cold. I rubbed his feet, then teased him a bit. He liked it.

He's running round now quite happily. Running and chasing in the Hall. Hugs and spins. The spins make me dizzy, but don't appear to do much to him!

Did the rhythm and the rowing exercise. Well, I felt it was a positive session. James actually did well, considering he's got a cold.

A good deal of contact in the session. We do a lot of physical, bodily contact. He doesn't speak — not a word-like utterance. He also doesn't breathe rhythmically.

SESSION 20: 30 MARCH, 1999 (THE LAST ONE THIS TERM)

James came with me before the bell went. I do find him more with it in the impression he gives, and the way he looks at me also.

Foot rubbing first.

Did the rhythm with speech — he resisted going with me at times.

Then hugs/spins/chasing.

Then rowing with singing, Row, row, row — peaceful — eye contact is good when it takes place. I do feel I can meet James in this eye contact.

Now he's taken off his jumper and is standing on a bench. Breathing through his mouth. He still has quite a cold.

At times James was protesting a bit today. Co-operated mainly, but at times screeching/whining a bit. He does this, I presume, to say that he doesn't want any more — that it's enough!

Did some large arm movements with him — up and round, in and out.

Could do some of these with him, but he stiffens up when he doesn't want to do them.

At the end he went quite happily with me back to the classroom.

Results of the intervention process

Usually, the sessions went well, with a good deal of contact and communication taking place.

Observed changes

— more direct eye contact in which I felt we really met
— the impression that James was often more with it; more there and open; less distant and aloof
— he was more interactive, *e.g.* in playing a chasing game, or in responding to teasing
— sometimes resisted in an exercise, so that what was done had to be achieved with his willing co-operation
— generally he warmed up during a session, and there was more contact, interaction and involvement as we proceeded
— he took the initiative to go bench walking and touching/fingering the walls of the hall, rather like marking out the boundaries
— interestingly, while I felt thoroughly dizzy after spinning, he showed little, if any, signs of dizziness
— although he continued to have colds and often a runny nose, mostly this did not appear to hamper him from becoming active, and enjoying himself
— sometimes he would be more relaxed in making arm movements with me, but often he would stiffen up. This was an activity he couldn't readily enter into
— on the other hand he generally participated well in the rhythmic exercises which also involved arm movements, such as clapping and rowing
— he was not yet able to catch or throw a ball or a rod
— I was not aware of any obsessional behaviours in the sessions.

Discussion and evaluation

The warming up phenomenon of James becoming more animated and alive, and participating as we got into a session is, I think, very important. Even in physical terms I could see the difference in James' responsiveness if he was warmly dressed. On the soul level a warm, light-hearted, friendly approach from me, met with a positive response from him, which showed James' ability to reciprocate appropriately.

From anthroposophy we know that warmth is the element that provides the link between the physical and the spiritual levels. The human ego (spirit) lives in the warmth and, within the body, it is the warm blood which is the vehicle or bearer of the ego.

Therefore warmth on the physical, soul and spiritual levels was very important to help James' process of ego-integration, and his human, social interaction. He could also then respond to me in a warm, friendly way.

It was important also to ask the question, When is James more there and present, or more distant and away? It was also important to be sensitive in order to perceive and feel these situations. Clearly in physical contact activities he was there, making eye contact, smiling, and looking, but this state could also be experienced when he was peaceful and calm. The Row your boat exercise had a calming effect, and could be accompanied by good eye contact and smiling.

However, the lack of any obvious dizziness on his part (not mine!) after whole body spins performed by me holding him from behind, under his arms and around his chest, did perhaps suggest a lack of being centred in himself.

The bench walking of his own initiative, and touching/fingering the wall might be seen as exploring the boundaries of the room, as he was also becoming more aware of the boundaries of his own physical body.

His difficulty to relax sufficiently when making large arm movements with me in the vertical and horizontal planes, as well as an inability to catch and throw a ball, seemed to reflect a tightness or lack of freedom in his middle, rhythmical system. There was also no indication of any development, however slight, towards speech. I also noticed no clear imitative ability with James, in the realm of movements.

However, overall, I felt that progress had been made in engaging James, and making more direct, interpersonal contact with him.

The perceptions of others

The internal review meeting, provisionally scheduled for February, actually took place on 29 March 1999, just the day before my last intervention session with James, and the fifty-ninth in the series. Therefore the review was well timed to hear how things had been going, from the perspective of home and school, in relation to my therapeutic efforts with James.

His house-mother reported that:

> Leading up to Christmas, James had presented the picture of a rather unhappy and disturbed boy. However, when he returned to school for the start of the Spring term, James was in a far better state.
>
> He was much calmer and more in control, and less obsessive, than before the second half of the Autumn term.
>
> He was more responsive now to challenges, but also showed greater resistance and self-assertiveness. More self-willed.
>
> In the realm of communication he seemed to be at a standstill, and the important question was raised as to how to help James make further steps in the area of language and communication. Seemingly, in the daily pattern of life, James understood basics.
>
> A totally new development with James was that he would now willingly take medicines, whereas previously this had been a constant battle!

The class teacher confirmed that:

> James was much calmer now, more balanced, without the mood swings he had shown last term.
>
> His strong obsession with music stands had completely fallen away, and he now showed no interest in them.
>
> He was more open to do things now, and it was much easier for him to sit and wait. He was more relaxed in class.

There was an issue of him wanting to be in charge.

James liked games and activities, which also involved turn-taking.

Importantly, in both house and class, there were small signs that James was taking more interest in other children.

A letter was received from James' mother towards the end of April, to share his parents' perceptions during the Easter holidays. This is given below.

Dear Bob

Re: James

Thank you very much for your letter. Before we received the letter we had noticed how much more openly and spontaneously affectionate he has been. This has also been noticed by other people who are close to James. He cuddles without asking, comes into bed in the morning and just generally seems to want attention and to be around people. Although, on occasion, James had done these things in the past it has usually taken a great deal of effort on his part and indeed ours!

The improvement in James since you have been working with him is incredible. I think I fed back to you in the beginning how he now realises his feet are attached to his body and he actually owns them! It gave me great pleasure the other day when we were out walking that he kept lifting up his foot for me to tie his shoe laces.

James still has his obsessions and at the moment it is jumpers with zips (and his Dad's van) but what is great about that is that he can actually do up zips.

We would like to thank you again for all the time you spend working with and helping James, it really is appreciated and quite obviously paying dividends.

Conclusion

It seemed clear that the crisis of the second half of the Autumn term had been surmounted, and that James had progressed to a new level of balance within himself, and in relation to his surroundings. He was both calmer and more self-assertive, and importantly, more in control of himself.

This suggested that steps were being achieved in the process of ego-integration, which included overcoming James' obsessions, arising from his undirected astrality. He appeared to be more in charge of his life, and to be able to express his affections for others.

As our medical adviser had said in the December review meeting, things 'may get worse before they get better.' This appeared to have been very clearly borne out by the latest reports and observations.

It seems reasonable to conclude that the intensive, one-to-one, interventional process had made a significant impact on James' positive overall progress — that is, in alleviating his former degree of autistic withdrawal and aloofness, and in fostering a greater participation, interest and involvement with others. No other special therapies or treatments had taken place during the intervention period.

Therefore, the evidence which has been presented does, I believe, strongly support the value and effectiveness of the interventional process with James.

It is, however, important to note that in the course of such a planned process, a child may go through a period of greater difficulties, such as more intense obsessional behaviour. This occurred in James in the second half of the Autumn Term 1998, and was interpreted as a result of the deeper processes of incarnation and ego-integration which were taking place (see Chapters 8 and 9).

Confirmations of progress

The interventions stopped on 30 March 1999. In the statutory annual review meeting which took place in June, and in the annual school and house reports, written in July, the following significant remarks were recorded.

James' mother:

> ... is very pleased with James' growing involvement to be in
> a group. She and James' family have noticed that James is
> more mature, calmer and observant. During a conversation
> James looks from one person to the other. ... His obsessions
> are still strong at home. She has been encouraging James to
> be more upright when walking and to lift his head up and
> make more eye contact.

She has observed a lot more involvement with other children.

James' house-mother at the school:

> James has progressed well with self-help skills and begins to
> take a little initiative. He has gained more confidence and
> one can demand more from him to do things with a greater
> independence. Recently there has been direct contact with
> other children, and James has shown an interest and warmth
> towards them which so far had not occurred.

James' class teacher:

> James is in a class with seven other children. He is well liked
> by the others and even though he is still more adult-orien-
> tated he does show more and more interest in his peers. He
> does not seem to be so much of a loner anymore but is
> always right in the centre with all the other children.

Postcript

When James returned to school in September 1999 after the long
summer holidays, an important new change had occurred. He was toilet-trained and now took himself to the toilet whenever he needed it!
This breakthrough, age ten, was further clear evidence of a new bodily awareness and inner self-experience that had developed in James
following our intervention sessions.

7. The Sessions with Roger

I had not worked previously with Roger, who was already fifteen years old when I began one-to-one intervention sessions with him. The frequency of these sessions was the same as with James, and Roger was fetched by me after I had returned James to his class. As shown in Table 2 (p.77), the actual distribution of the sessions was very similar to James, and the total number of sessions was exactly the same for both boys.

The first half of the Autumn term, 1998

A pre-conceived intervention programme had not been constructed to begin with, as it was a matter of getting to know Roger initially, and to start to build a trusting interrelationship together.

As the notes are extremely interesting, it has not been easy to choose which ones to include here. However, my intention has been to give as comprehensive a picture of the exercises and Roger's responses as possible.

SESSION 1: 3 SEPTEMBER, 1998

I went to fetch Roger from basketry. This was a new subject for him. He was sitting at a table with a basket (base and uprights) in front of him. I watched him being helped for a while (not that I saw him doing anything much), and then said we could go. Roger got up to come with me, he understood what was required.

He is a very good-looking boy. We went outside. With a helping hand he walked on the balance logs. He also went up the log steps to the platform where the slide is (after I had done this first), and he went down the slide after having sat at the top for a while.

It took Roger some time to do things, e.g. to cross from the grass on to the wood chippings. There wasn't a free continuous, smooth, flow of actions. (An indication of threshold problems?)

He didn't want, apparently, to repeat the slide, so we went to the movement hall. I tried to engage him by using a ball — first a blue ball, then an orange/black one, then a tennis ball. He held and smelt the balls. Ball throwing/catching was not for him.

The big gym mattress was still out from James' session and Roger lay down on this, and was in no hurry to get up again! I tried to interest him in throwing the ball through the netball hoop. He had the ball a couple of times in his hand, whilst lying down, and only threw it a small distance.

As he didn't appear interested in doing anything else (apart from lying down), I told him we should leave the movement hall. We went to the playroom.

Here we used the coloured discs on vertical sticks. He took these off, as a block, not just one at a time, and then later replaced them on the sticks — used his right hand consistently and skilfully. However he (how shall I describe it?), also picked up and manipulated the discs — first he had wiped/rubbed a disc against the wallpaper.

After this he used simple shape-fitting boards. He replaced the shapes correctly and easily.

Then I cut a piece of paper with scissors. He could also cut skilfully, though he didn't do it in a straight line. When I drew a triangle for him to cut out, Roger cut through the shape. Did he not understand what was meant?

Finally, I let him draw freely on a sheet of paper. He did a line drawing of nothing recognisable (to me) and then proceeded to shade over the lines. He might have continued with this but it was time to finish.

Roger was more interested in fine motor (desk top) activities, than in gross motor ones (whereas James liked the big movements).

Roger was co-operative overall, and placid. Not protesting, as James had done.

Roger screws up his eyes sometimes. Sometimes smiles. Makes some noises — no words or clear sounds. Right-handed dominance. Makes some eye contact. He also makes finger movements, extending and closing.

My feeling is that it would be good to get him moving more freely (less hesitation), in gross movement activities of various sorts.

In a sense the first sessions were of an exploratory nature, with both of us seeing how each responded in this special one-to-one, non-class-room situation. There was time for trying things out.

SESSION 4: 9 SEPTEMBER, 1998

I went to fetch Roger from his classroom. Met his helper coming out with A. to go swimming, and then Roger came. Looked quite happy.

We went across to the entrance of the movement hall. I took off my coat and asked him to hang his up. Hesitation. Then he did it — find-ing the loop — and put it over the wooden peg. Came in and went straight to lie on the gym mattress. Lying there now — looks very happy — broad smile on his face, looks towards me. (Has taken his red jumper off.) Puts his vest near his mouth/nose. Masturbating? (Looks like it.) Lying on his side, looking up at ceiling.

I fetched him off the mattress, by physically helping him (he didn't come off just by asking him to).

Walking, then running with him, the length of the hall. Joins with me. So far, much more willing to be active than yesterday.

Balancing on benches. He did it with my encouragement and some physical support.

He gets stuck — can stay in one place for quite a time as if rooted to the spot. Now sitting on mattress (put his red jumper on, then he took it off again). Makes some noises (not much).

Parallel benches, to walk over. Did it today with me — happy about it and did it quickly (not much hesitation). What a surprise! Today things are a lot different from yesterday; much more active and willing.

Wall bars to climb up. Roger lay on the mattress. I went up the wall bars to show him what I wanted. I helped him off the mattress. He came across and climbed up and down — skilfully!

Shuttlecocks and rackets. I showed him how to hit the shuttlecock with the racket. I put one on his racket and he flipped it off. He didn't actually hit a shuttlecock with the racket, as I had done, but went across and picked it up. Smelt it, and put the end in his mouth!! He seemed more interested in eating it than hitting it!

After this Roger indicated that he wanted to go out, and he went to the door. I reminded him to put his jumper on first, then we went out. He took his coat and put it on.

Today was very positive. Yesterday I was rather concerned as he wasn't keen to do things. Today was the opposite. Couldn't have been better for the fourth session.

He does make eye contact, and he can smile reciprocally.

SESSION 5: 14 SEPTEMBER, 1998 (FIVE DAYS LATER, AFTER THE WEEKEND BREAK)

The majority of time in this session was used in activities where we sat facing each other.

Touch activities. I touched Roger with various objects/surfaces. He accepted my doing this. Touching him on his hands (back and palms), forearms, lower legs, and feet. In this exercise Roger made better, and more, eye contact, than I have observed before.

We also used a copper rod, which I balanced on his head and then on mine. Roger kept his head still and the rod was in balance. Then he tilted his head forward to let it roll off. I also balanced the rod on my head, then let it roll off. He looked at this. This was altogether an amusing activity to do, and I laughed at this, and he also laughed.

While sitting facing each other we also passed the medicine ball back and forth. He did not do this very actively — I had to initiate the gesture of passing it to me — though at least once he did send it back to me.

Walking hand in hand — we did this a number of times — up and down the length of the movement hall. I also then tried running with him. However, he was sluggish and heavy in this and, I think, rather on his heels.

Also did walking along wide benches. He did this well and, today, more or less jumped off at the end.

Stepping on and over six parallel benches. At times Roger hesitated (as if rooted to the spot), however he could also go quite quickly at times. It's like an exercise of overcoming, or crossing, thresholds.

Carrying weighted shopping bags. He did this several times. A bag in each hand.

Roger was less open and more tense when doing these big movement exercises. (I mean, closing his eyes, shutting out), than when we had been sitting face to face.

However there was more clear and direct contact in this session than previously. He co-operated well, there were no protests.

By this stage an intervention programme had been constructed as shown below.

Exercise	Aim

1. Tactile stimulation on exposed skin areas, through, brushing, touching with various surfaces (rough/smooth, flat/pointed, etc.)
 	
   Also rubbing/stroking his feet and lower legs.
	To exercise his sense of touch through differentiated stimuli. Also to increase awareness of his own body boundaries, and foster a feeling of security and trust.
	
	   To help make him aware that he has feet!

2. Turn-taking and joint activities, such as balancing a copper rod on his head, then tipping it off, and being caught by the other person (me), and vice versa.
 	
   Rolling/passing a medicine ball back and forth.
 	
   Rowing while holding a copper rod between us.
	To enter into an interpersonal (I-You) relationship through activities.
	
	   Encouraging eye contact, and communication.

3. Weight/resistance exercises, such as carrying heavy shopping bags, walking with ankle weights on.	To stimulate his mastery of gravity and thereby *lightening* him up. Also to exercise 'sense of balance.'
4. Gross movement activities, such as balancing on benches, stepping on and over benches, walking, jogging, running, trampette, etc.	To increase his skill, confidence, motivation in these activities, and to reduce hesitancy, possible anxiety and threshold difficulties. Exercising his senses of movement and balance.
5. Positional arm movements, both facilitated and by imitation. Also flowing and expressive arm movements.	To increase his awareness of his arms in space, and bring about greater freedom of movement and expression.

6. Throwing/catching of a medicine ball with two hands, and a copper rod with one hand, using right and left.	To actively engage him in a give and take interaction, and, thereby, to increase his sense of self.

Table 6. Intervention exercises with Roger, first half of Autumn term, 1998.

A wide variety of observations and impressions were made, and recorded by me, over the course of the twenty-two sessions during the first half of the Autumn term. Some of these are summarized below.

> Roger gave a stiff, cramped, heavy impression; sometimes he showed lots of involuntary, twitching movements of his body; and sometimes looked very uncomfortable. I had the impression that he was mainly unpenetrated by his ego, and especially his arms. It was difficult for him to relax.

> Usually he did not use speech, although I had the feeling he could have spoken. On rare occasions a word did emerge. In Session 7 he distinctly said 'happy;' also in Session 21. In Session 15, he said 'Roger.' Often he made tight, jerky sounds, and often appeared to hold his breath. He did not breathe freely. Occasionally he laughed.

> It was impossible to predict how Roger would respond from one session to the next. One day he could be open, another day closed off and uptight. He surprised me constantly. He was ambivalent, alternating between showing himself, and then withdrawing and covering up or hiding again. Appearing happy/unhappy. He gave a rather over-sensitive, vulnerable impression.

> Sometimes he smelt me as well as objects. Sometimes he flicked his fingers, or twiddled with his sock. Often he would rearrange his shoes (which had been taken off for touch exercises), or my pens, and put them in parallel order. Surprisingly he didn't appear at all ticklish on the soles of his feet!

Initially he seemed much more withdrawn than James, and less willing.

In the beginning he did not imitate arm movements, nor could or would he stretch his arms.

Initially he showed a lot of restless, involuntary, movements of his eyes.

Initial results of the intervention process

It was certainly possible, in carefully comparing the notes, to see that quite a lot had happened, even if sometimes inconsistently and sporadically.

Observed changes

— Although he varied from being open, towards making contact with me, and closed off and withdrawn; good eye contact and smiling did occur again and again
— His eyes became more steady, whereas previously there had been a lot of restless movements
— He demonstrated an ability to imitate at least approximately, with arm movements and positions
— His occasional speech utterance confirmed that he could speak
— He was able to perform gross motor activities, sometimes much more freely, with less hesitancy or without getting stuck. He had, for example, bounced on the trampette, and looked as if he was enjoying it
— He demonstrated that he could catch and throw back a ball (the large, quite heavy medicine ball), with two hands, and also the copper rod using either hand. He could even do this with some strength and force. He actually progressed well in such turn-taking activities
— He could participate well in a joint exercise, such as rowing together whilst holding a copper rod between us. He could put himself into this, and was not limp
— He demonstrated that, sometimes, he could see the funny side of things, *e.g.* in the sixteenth session, he laughed when the copper rod fell off his head backwards to his neck

— Whereas to begin with he had shown no response at all when I
had touched the soles of his feet, observable reactions were
seen as the sessions progressed. This clearly indicated that he
was (now), visibly registering sensations
— He was very willing to receive physical contact through touch
— Occasionally he took the initiative, such as in the seventh session,
when he suddenly got up and sat on me!

Repeatedly, I had to ask myself whether I was being too demanding
with Roger, and to what extent I was giving him the opportunity to
join in an activity when he felt ready, and able, to do so. At the end of
Session 18, for example, I noted:

I felt he was more with me today; much happier than yester-
day — and making much more contact — through eyes, and
physically.
   (Interesting; I was trying to leave him more freedom and
let him show me what he wanted.)

Discussion and evaluation

A main aim with Roger, as with James, was to strengthen his own
body awareness and self-experience via the lower senses. In normal
child development this provides the basis for social, interpersonal
relationships, to form and grow. I had the impression that Roger had
perhaps only really penetrated, or incarnated, as far as his head, with
his soul-spiritual being. It was striking that he first showed no reaction
on the soles of his feet, suggesting a hyposensitivity in his extremities
which might, conceivably, be due to a deliberate holding back on his
part.

It was striking also, how in one session he appeared to be very open
to making contact and communicating with me and seemed happy,
and, in the next session, was the opposite. All this pointed to a lack of
balance and harmony, particularly in the middle rhythmic system. This
middle realm needed strengthening and warming through.

His breathing was not relaxed and free and although he had some
speech he was not using it. I had the strong impression he was
restricted or blocked in the area of his larynx and chest. When he stood

up he lacked a certain free uprightness, and tended to be hunched up. I felt his neck, shoulders and arms all needed to become freer and loosened up.

I felt that Roger was an aware and sensitive person, and in my own consciousness I recognized his real being behind the autistic symptoms. My own inner attitude was an essential part of the therapeutic, interventional process.

I was confident we had established a good relationship and it was, of course, a delight when Roger engaged himself in activities, and looked happy. On the other hand it was rather painful to see him when he looked tense, uncomfortable or agitated.

The perceptions of others

Roger's house-mother reported that:

> Since 18 September he has had some cold/flu symptoms which have lasted, on and off, for one month. During this time he fluctuated between a tense, withdrawn and agitated state, to one of calm. As in past experiences with Roger, when he is in an agitated phase, sleep and appetite are affected. Of late Roger is engaged in periods of masturbation and will remove clothing if not supervised at any time of the day, as well as at night time.

Both Roger's house-mother and upper school teacher, noted slight decreases in his eye contact with them, and in accepting physical contact from them.

Interestingly, his own mother, reporting on the two-week half-term holiday, also noticed similar slight decreases in eye contact and accepting physical contact from her. However she saw small increases in his reciprocal smiling, joining in turn-taking activities, both with her, and with other children.

Roger's mother also wrote that:

> Roger did surprise me on a number of occasions this half-term. Sometimes he used his own initiative to do things. He

was beginning to be more co-operative when asked to do things. More strong-willed when he decided on a course of action.

Roger's father had not really seen any changes, in their interaction together, over this first intervention period in the Autumn term.

Conclusion

While Roger surprised me again and again through his responses in our sessions, I felt we had achieved a good amount of interaction, contact, and communication. Therefore I was pleased, and hopeful of making further positive steps.

In contrast, others had mostly not noticed any definite positive changes in their observation of, and relationship with, Roger, except for the very important remarks of his mother. She had referred to his taking initiative, beginning to be more cooperative and showing a stronger self-will.

In an internal review meeting held at the school on 10 September 1998, the biggest problem with Roger was said to be his almost complete lack of motivation. He required guidance and prompting to get involved in anything, including basic self-care skills and toileting. Therefore any signs, however small, of him taking the initiative and showing a stronger self will, were very significant.

I expected that any changes with Roger were likely to be subtle, rather than dramatic. The intervention period had only been going for six weeks and, furthermore, it appeared that his health had not been very good for about a month of that time. I looked forward to working with him again after the half-term break.

Second half of Autumn term 1998

From November into December, Roger and I had another fifteen sessions. An internal review meeting was planned for 10 December which would provide a forum for sharing experiences and impressions amongst those educators who were most involved with Roger. He was now sixteen years old, and yet despite his age, I felt that a good deal of tactile stimulation was both needed, and justified, in this half of the term. The intervention programme was as shown below. Not all the exercises needed to be done in any one session, and although the sequence of doing them was fairly consistent, there was also freedom to manoeuvre.

Exercise	Aim
1. Foot rubbing/stroking, with me working on each of his bare feet in turn, as we sat facing each other.	To help him incarnate into his body, right down to his feet.
2. Therapeutic touch. I stood behind Roger and first put my two hands on his head. Then, put one hand resting on his neck and the other near the base of the spine. Then I sat at his side, one hand over his chest and the other on his mid-spine.	To help him feel better in his body, more comfortable and relaxed, and to strengthen a trusting relationship. This can also stimulate the warmth organism.
3. Resistance/interaction, via his feet and my hands, as we sat facing each other. I held both his feet and pressed against the soles and toes, encouraging him to resist and respond to this.	To stimulate his incarnation into his feet, and to engage in a two-way interaction with me.
4. Standing behind him, or sitting facing him and massaging his shoulders. Guiding him into large, flowing, arm movements, and stretching.	To help loosen up and relieve tension from the shoulder girdle. To bring some freeing up to his middle, rhythmic system.

5. Greek wrestling, in which we stood facing each other and made contact through the palms of our hands, exerting a give and take pressure, and entering into movements of arms and upper body, whilst maintaining balance.	To enter into a dynamic balance/ movement interaction by engaging in giving and taking pressure and resistance.
6. Clapping and stamping, in rhythm, to a spoken verse. I gave him hands on guidance, but also encouraged his independent, imitative, movements.	To stimulate ego-integration through rhythm and speech, and his motivation in own movement.
7. Rhythmic rowing exercise, accompanied by singing, as we held a copper rod horizontally and sat facing each other.	To help free up the middle, rhythmic system, through a give and take joint interaction.

Table 7. Intervention exercises with Roger, second half of Autumn term, 1998.

SESSION 24: 10 NOVEMBER, 1998

Today Roger was, on the whole, open. He did have his eyes closed at various times (closing off), but overall I experienced this as a positive session with interaction and contact being made.

The session was almost entirely given up to tactile touch stimulation, initiated by me.

Such things as massaging/rubbing his feet. Today his toes on both feet were being moved by him, i.e. to exert pressure against my hand. This I see as helping him to get down into his toes. His feet strike me as being less insensitive and unanimated than they used to be. He's moving his toes and, in a sense, taking control of them.

I also worked on his shoulder area, trying to loosen it up by moving his shoulders alternately. At one point he was moving with this quite freely — rolling/moving his head at his neck. (I think that's good since usually he's sunk into his shoulders.)

I also tried to encourage warmth to go down from his head, through therapeutic touch.

Roger made a good amount of eye contact in this session.

Towards the end we used the copper rod to balance on each others' heads — a turn-taking exercise — like a game. He's quick to catch the falling rod (also with one hand), he's there in that moment. He smiles, and I think he enjoys this.

Finally some Greek wrestling. Standing up, his and my palms against each others, and dynamic give and take. I feel this is a good exercise to free and loosen up his arms, shoulders and chest. Also moving his arms up and then out in a wide circular movement, our palms still in contact. I then asked Roger to do this himself — showing him what I wanted him to do — but he's quite incapable of getting his arms straight, either upwards or to the sides. Therefore I did this with him.

I have a very clear impression how insufficiently Roger has penetrated his body, and this is what I'm trying to encourage. He was not relaxed all the time today. At times a tense look on his face, at other times smiles and, in some things we did, almost laughing, but he didn't quite get there!

SESSION 29: 23 NOVEMBER, 1998

I fetched Roger from the classroom where he was sitting at a table with others doing a shopping game.

He came, but was stilted and slow in his movements. Now sits with eyes closed and making tense, uncomfortable, noises.

So can I help him to relax?

Worked on his feet, he was quite willing. He looks a lot happier. Eyes open, looking at me sometimes, smiling. Now seems sensitive/ticklish on soles of feet, even laughed. He's now holding his right foot with his right hand, feeling his toes, perhaps discovering his foot?

I worked on his feet again — wrestled with his toes in my hands — he responds to this, uses pressure. (At one point it was almost as if he was speaking in sentences — not clear — but moving his lips and sounding.)

After this, I did therapeutic touching of his head, spine and chest. With this he leant over and made physical contact with me when I was sitting at his side.

Then working on his feet again; again verbalization. My two hands on his two feet, pressing/responding. He seems mainly happy, pleased with all this.

There were new experiences with Roger today.

At one point, after I had done touching of head, spine, chest area, he started to stamp his right foot. I encouraged him to stamp the left also, which he did, with his bare feet on the floor.

Towards the end of the session I stood behind him (seated) and moved his arms up in a loop. He was much lighter today. I felt he was going more with the movement.

Did some Greek wrestling — standing — he co-operated, went with me, but not much pressure from him.

Finally, standing with me moving his arms in a curved loop. Definitely lighter, and larger movements. I asked him to move my arms, and I felt that he did! There was no doubt he was much more in his arms today.

SESSION 37: 16 DECEMBER, 1998

Fetched Roger. He came with a smile (his usual smile on his face). Now on the toilet.

He's very happy today. I worked on his feet. No grimace, no tension, no constricted noises, but rather sort of cooing sounds of pleasure I would say. Eyes open, looking at me directly at times.

Now he's whirling his sock around.

Did rubbing of feet; then touch on head/spine/chest. He leans over to me when I sit side on to him. Relaxes and makes himself comfortable.

After this, I rubbed feet again.

Then, to finish, Greek wrestling and moving his arms up and round, in and out. Today he really managed to stretch fully, I would say.

This was a good session to end with. Roger seemed in a particularly happy and relaxed state. Smiling a lot, and a good deal of eye contact. No constricted sounds, but rather pleasurable sounds.

A happy, enjoyable, satisfying session for me and, I hope, for him.

Results of the intervention process

Reviewing and comparing the recordings over the fifteen sessions, yielded the following results.

Observed changes

— A greater reactivity and responsiveness in his feet
— A good deal of eye contact, smiling, and communication between
   us in the sessions, facilitated through touch contact
— Greater relaxation
— Taking the initiative. For example, to stamp his feet, lean over
   towards me, make physical contact
— At times, much more in his arms, not so heavy ... lighter. Man-
   aged to stretch fully in last session
— In several sessions, speech-like vocalizations
— His eyes were steady, not showing all the restless movements
   they used to
— No strong obsessional behaviours, just some finger flicking/click-
   ing at times
— Often showing his pleasure, or enjoyment and openness

Discussion and evaluation

The emphasis given to tactile, hands on stimulation in these sessions
was intended to do a number of things. Namely, to increase Roger's
own body awareness, to strengthen his self-experience, to provide
security, trust, and confidence, and to foster openness, communication, and contact.

   We know, from anthroposophy, that the lower sense of touch has a
developmental relationship to the higher sense of ego (for the recognition of the other person). Therefore, as well as supporting Roger's
process of ego-integration, the exercises were also helping to open up
his higher, social senses.

   The results, observed over the sessions, gave clear indications that the
therapeutic process was being effective, at least to my perception.

   However, it was true that Roger still had a strong tendency to hold
himself back, and be uptight. Was this deliberate and, if so, why? What
was blocking or restricting his incarnation into his body? I did not
profess to fully know the answers to such questions. His parents were
convinced, so I understood, that Roger knew a great deal and was intelligent. However his possibilities for free self-expression, and especially

motivation, even in very practical, everyday matters, was extremely limited and curtailed. I had observed, for example, that he was not able to wash and dry his hands properly after going to the toilet.

However Roger, now sixteen years old, had been autistic from an early age and therefore, he had a lot of catching up to do developmentally.

The perception of others

An internal review meeting was held at the school on 10 December, 1998, which enabled educators to share their observations and impressions of Roger since his previous review on 10 September that year. Verbal reports were given from house and school, and these were minuted.

Roger's house-mother reported that:

> He had recently shown clear motivation on three occasions in connection with food and drink.
>
> Stripping of himself and his bed (both of which had been problems for others, in the first half of the Autumn term), had stopped since half-term.
>
> Three to four days ago he had clearly hummed the tune of a song, well known in the school.
>
> He still needed prompting all the way with self-help skills so that, for example, although he would put his shirt on, if left alone, he would get stuck and do nothing further.

Roger's upper school teacher reported that:

> Some changes had been seen in terms of initiative and motivation. Namely, instead of Roger being propelled to school, having his coat taken off and being led to the classroom, as had been the case previously, he would now do these things himself at the start of each school day. He will hang his coat up, come to the classroom, and, if his chair is upside down on his desk, he will put it on the floor.
>
> In teaching situations such as crafts, or in reading, writing and arithmetic, Roger required one-to-one support from an adult.

Roger's bodily awareness was described as being very
poor indeed and, for example, he would not deal (or perhaps
be aware), of his runny nose. His physical posture is hunched
up, and he still often holds his breath.

He made less noises in school which, previously, had been
a disturbance in the class.

Interestingly, the basketwork teacher had remarked to me on 9
December, 1998. that when she saw Roger outside, a day or two
before and had said hello to him, he had looked at her and said hello
back. This had taken her by surprise!

It was agreed in the review meeting that I would continue to have
individual sessions with Roger in the Spring term, on a frequency of
three times a week (as with James).

What about the perceptions of Roger's parents during the three
week Christmas holidays? Had they noticed any changes?

Roger's father had noticed some small increases in Roger both
accepting physical contact and in initiating such contact, and also in
co-operating with him. An increase was also seen in Roger's interest
in his surroundings.

His father wrote that:

Roger's level of interaction is very dependent on his mood.
He seems to get depressed by his disabilities. Boosting his
confidence raises his spirits, which in turn improves his level
of interaction.

Roger's mother wrote:

We did have a good Christmas holiday with Roger and, on
many occasions, we remarked on how he was much better
than last year. This was especially surprising as we had just
moved into a new house and it was quite chaotic. He was
more keen than usual to go to any social occasion offered.
Although it is obviously difficult for him and for others as he
doesn't talk, he enjoyed any attention shown him and coped
with noise, people he didn't know, and late nights.

Conclusion

While changes with Roger were often subtle, requiring careful observation over weeks, the verbal and written reports from others were supportive of my own positive perceptions. Especially in that there were small, but definite, signs of some increased self-motivation and initiative. This, in turn, was indicative of an improved process of ego-integration.

Interestingly there was no mention of any obsessive behaviours, whereas in the first half of the Autumn term at school, stripping his bed, moving the bed, opening curtains and windows, and removing his own clothing during the day, had been marked problem behaviours, and he had been said to have:

An obsession with moving furniture around.

In comparison, he now seemed more settled and peaceful.

Spring term 1999

Intervention exercises were drawn from those used in the second half of the Autumn term, 1998 (see Table 7). However, for a few of these new sessions I also tried again with active gross motor activities such as jogging around the movement hall, walking on benches, ball and rod throwing and catching.

His reactions in the sessions varied; one day open and expressive, but the next day he could be closed and holding back. The first two sessions of the term illustrated this puzzling variance.

SESSION 1: 18 JANUARY, 1999

Roger had been in the toilet and, meanwhile, I was talking with J. in the painting room. When I went to check on Roger he had already gone into the movement hall.

He was standing by the piano where I had left his folder open, ready for my notes. He had taken the pen and repeatedly made clear crosses on a page!

Roger was in good humour. I worked on his feet, first the right, then the left. When I had finished with his right foot he touched it himself. An awareness that the foot is his? I was in no rush with his feet — they were cold, and needed warming up.

Afterwards I moved my chair round and put my hand over his heart/chest area, and my other hand against his spine. He liked this it seems, and turned towards me.

Afterwards, when rowing with the rod, he was rather stiff in his arms.

Then Greek wrestling, standing facing each other, palms together. I asked him to go with me but then, after a while, to push more against me — this he did — daring to show more of himself, and then he was ready to finish! It was time anyway.

I experienced that Roger made a good deal of contact in this session — he was open, not withdrawn with closed eyes. In fact he looked towards me quite a lot. Sometimes, he had a slightly perplexed look on his face, as if not quite understanding. At other times smiling, almost laughing.

I feel there is a rapport, and I also feel it's best just to proceed slowly, gently, with an inner connection. I'll try to get him to stretch his arms tomorrow, and become freer in his chest/speech area.

SESSION 2: 19 JANUARY, 1999

Roger came willingly. Now in the toilet. He doesn't look so happy or relaxed today, I don't know why. Eyes closed much more than yesterday.

Worked on his feet — separately — then both feet up and wrestling against my two hands. He pressed quite hard with his feet.

Very closed off today, but I've no idea why. Holding his breath in.

Now putting his own socks on — but again in fits and starts — gets stuck.

Did rowing with the copper rod, but his arms were stiff and straight, not relaxed and going with the movement ... He really didn't seem to want today.

I tried putting my hands on his chest and back, and kept them there for a time. But there was no usual leaning towards me, and in fact Roger took my hand from his chest. Greek wrestling also no go today. So could he have a headache, or something else wrong? Seemed off-colour and not happy, as if it was too much.

The next day however he was again much more open and happy, and participated well in the exercises!

SESSION 16: 16 MARCH, 1999

Roger came from the classroom — seemed relaxed, was smiling. Now in the toilet.

Now sitting on the chair, facing me. His breathing is not free. I did the therapeutic touching in the usual fashion, starting at his head, then top and bottom of the spine, and then chest and back areas. There was certainly plenty of reaction from Roger, and he started clapping spontaneously.

We then did the rhythm with speech to the verse Brave and true I will be etc. clapping, then stamping it. He stamped very firmly.

In the rowing exercise his arms were not straight and tense, but much more relaxed.

Then at the end of the session after some further therapeutic touching he was clearly singing. He also made steady eye contact at various times.

I felt it was a very positive session with Roger expressing himself through clapping, stamping and singing.

However the next day he was more closed off again, and I felt he was holding back and not allowing himself to show so much. The holding back gesture was clearly reflected in his breathing and I felt, again and again, that just his middle, rhythmic system, needed freeing up.

Results of the intervention process

The results which had been seen in the second half of the Autumn term were again evident from these further twenty-two sessions, despite the unpredictable variance in his responses from one session to the next. However, it was not easy to identify any clear further progressive developments over this period of time.

Certainly there were many examples of good contact, communication, and interaction between us, to be found in the recordings.

There were also intimations that he was continuing to become more aware of his own body. For example, in several sessions Roger took the initiative to touch/explore his foot, after I had rubbed it. Or when I clapped alternately on his right and left legs he appeared to like this.

Visiting the toilet before beginning a session in the movement hall, had become part of Roger's pattern this term. Often he did perform there, but he also played with himself if he had the opportunity. I discouraged this by asking him to get ready quickly.

Although Roger had sometimes responded well even when I took a more challenging and demanding attitude towards him (for example in a few sessions with gross motor exercises), I mainly felt that a gentle, sensitive and encouraging approach was best for him, and also I felt happier with this! I wanted him to feel reassured and secure, able to relax and express himself when he wanted to, and not to impose my will on him.

However there were no occasional speech like utterances, such as I had observed in the previous intervention period.

The next internal review at the school was in June, but the advantage having it two months after stopping the interventions meant that it might then be possible to gain a clearer picture of any progress that others had seen, or experienced, with Roger.

The perceptions of others

A letter from *Roger's mother,* written towards the end of April 1999, gave some observations from home of the Easter holidays. She wrote:

> No dramatic changes but he was very happy and calm. He still needs constant attention otherwise he resorts to twisting his sock — but he will stop if requested.
>
> He is always keen to go places, do things, etc. but sometimes looks anxious if actually spoken to directly. It must be difficult for him when asked questions as he cannot reply in the conventional way.
>
> He prefers to have someone sleeping in his bedroom at night, but is adaptable about where he sleeps.

In the review meeting on 10 June, *Roger's house-mother reported* the following (as recorded in the minutes):

> Roger is very settled into our life, and he seems happy and well. His parents describe that he smiles when approaching school again.

Initial problems in the Autumn term, such as moving furniture around, and undressing himself, stopped.

Roger goes through phases when he is more vocal and
more responsive, but there is no clear pattern for this. Around
Christmas there was incredible contact, and he was very
lucid and open, and he clearly hummed a (Michaelmas)
song.

He can say *please*. There is definitely speech, under the
surface. There has been an increase in his motivation to a
very small degree. He will go into the larder to get a biscuit.
He has more purpose in his movements (used to get stuck
like a statue). He has quite considerable strength, and can
push wheelbarrows.

It is laborious to try to involve him in practical tasks in the
house. However, he will do the fishing out at washing up time.

With self-help skills, such as washing and dressing, he
needs a lot of prompting, but how much depends on his general mood. His moods can change during the course of a day.
Toileting needs supervision — he can block the toilet with
paper.

However he is more open and relaxed than he ever was.
Holding his breath has changed, and is now much better.
Breathing is more even. He doesn't smell people as he used
to. He's been healthier.

There have been two or three tempers from February to
April, in the mornings, and lasting for some minutes.

Motivation has increased. He will go and get a book or
photo album.

Twiddling of socks has stopped and he is less obsessive.
More on an even keel, and a bit more communicative. His
parents are happy with how he is getting on.

From the school side, *Roger's main class assistant* who had also
worked with him on a one-to-one basis throughout the year, reported
the following:

There has been a great improvement this term. He will do
more by himself. For example, colouring in on paper, bringing

his chair to the computer, going to get a book; using the computer.

I found him much more co-operative. In basketry he will hum a tune with me, and sometimes says 'bye to C. (the basketwork teacher). In the weavery he needs prompting, but will then do the correct movements, up and down. He knows what to do.

After listening to these reports, and also to my own contributions in regard to the intervention sessions up to the end of March, the medical adviser commented that he found what had happened with Roger:

Rather impressive, particularly as he is already sixteen years old.

Conclusion

I had also found the perceptions of others impressive! Of particular interest to me was the observation that Roger's breathing had become more even and balanced. In working together with him in the sessions I had repeatedly hoped to loosen up and free his middle, rhythmical realm. Normally, in breathing, we enter into a continuous give and take relationship with the surrounding air, but it is also true to say that there is a definite breathing quality in our social relationships with others. If the inhalation is too strong we become caught up in our organism and socially withdrawn. If there is too much exhalation we can lose ourselves into the surroundings and weaken our inner experience of being centred. (Interestingly, both Roger and James showed imbalanced breathing rhythms, but in opposite directions! James tended to hyperventilate, whereas Roger held his breath in.)

The reports clearly indicated that Roger had come to a better, more balanced relationship with himself, and his social surroundings. He was less tense in himself and more open to make contact and communication with others. Very importantly there were small, but significant signs of increased self-motivation, in spite of the fact that he still depended on much prompting from others in order to implement basic daily skills. Also, there were important instances of vocalisation, in speech (single words), or song.

All these small signs, taken together, can be interpreted as symptomatic of an increased ego-integration, and a better incarnation both into his own body and into earthly life. Often he seemed happy with life. Obsessive behaviours had decreased.

The few tempers, seen from February to April, could be seen positively as self-assertiveness; making his feelings known to others, instead of being simply placid and unmoved.

It seems reasonable to conclude, as previously with James, that the rather intensive one-to-one interventional process had had a significant positive influence on Roger's progress. That is, in helping to alleviate Roger's autistic symptoms and in increasing his sphere of contact and communication, interest and participation with others.

No other special therapies or treatments had been given him during the intervention period.

Confirmations of progress

Both the annual house and school reports written in July 1999 provided clear confirmation of the new steps Roger had made over this school year. As the reports were comprehensive and detailed only a few selections from them are now cited below.

From the house report:

> ... after the half-term (in the Autumn), there was quite a change in Roger where he was obviously more relaxed and open, and the breakthrough with bedding occurred. Since this time there have been no occasions of bed or clothes stripping at all. During the October-December time an increased eye contact and vocalisation was also experienced ... Christmas was a very good period in which we have not experienced him so open, happy and motivated (even if it was towards the chocolate!) ... and there were also the first signs of initiative.
>
> Roger now moves around more freely, less stuck and staccato, with more motivation to get from A to B. He also walks more firmly ... There has been a decrease in breath holding and his breathing is more even.

The report ended, importantly, with reference to his relationship with others in the house community:

> Roger has continued to be very popular with children and adults alike and has shown this year that he is undoubtedly very settled and secure in our environment, thus enabling him to make these small, but progressive, developments.

The school report was written not only by Roger's main upper school teacher but also included the perceptions of other specialist teachers, *e.g.* for the subjects of woodwork, basketwork, swimming, gardening and weaving.

The remarks below have been drawn from some of these contributors.

> This year Roger has continued to be well settled in the school routine and to gradually increase his level of involvement in most areas of the curriculum. He comes to school more purposefully than before. He enters the building by himself without having to be told, hangs up his coat and goes straight into the classroom to find his place and sit down.
>
> When he goes to the toilet he will now come out again by himself without needing a search party to be sent ... In certain lessons, such as craft lessons, he seems very happy and will spontaneously begin vocalizing words and break into song ...
>
> A very important factor, not to be underestimated, is the fact that Roger is very well liked by the other pupils and his presence brings out the best in them. *(his main upper school teacher)*

In this last comment recognition is made of the strong social interrelationships within the mixed ability peer group. Certainly, an important factor for an autistic youngster.

> When he first arrived in the woodwork shop Roger spent many lessons completely disengaged and directing his attention outside the window. He did not respond to any attempts to communicate with him, such as greetings or goodbyes.

Little by little he became more involved, though the process was slow, and he now acknowledges that people are speaking to him by looking at them. *(woodwork teacher)*

Now he is able to work through the whole lesson with a little assistance. With encouragement he counts the canes and weaves the basket. He is willing, patient and precise in his work. In the short breaks Roger laughs, talks and sings. *(basketwork teacher)*

With some encouragement and a little help Roger has been able to engage in the activity quite happily. Although his interest in the work and his degree of attention varied considerably, he has generally been co-operative and has shown a positive attitude towards his tasks. *(weaving teacher)*

Roger enjoys activities which enable him to build up his own momentum and rhythm. One of these is to push a moderately heavy wheelbarrow over a longer distance, which he does with good control and perseverance. He also enjoys sawing logs for firewood ... Roger visibly thrives on encouragement and praise. *(gardening teacher)*

Roger has become more interested in others. Sometimes he will take A's hand or just want a handshake or a game of Give me five. He will initiate this by giving you his hand ... Roger has been a delightful pupil, quite well motivated and very determined in his own ways. *(main class assistant)*

It is clear from all these accounts that clear progress in alleviating Roger's autistic symptoms had been achieved over the year. He still is a young man with autism, but his interest and participation in the world, with others, is slowly increasing.

A final word

In Chapters 6 and 7 we have seen how the anthroposophical model of autism has been practically implemented within the broad context of curative education. This holistic model generates specific therapeutic attitudes and intervention exercises, which can help to alleviate the degree of autism shown by individual children. The educator's awareness and recognition of the child's unique spiritual being is a crucial factor in the attempt to build empathetic and supportive interrelationships with each child, and clearly encourages increased mutual contact and communication.

As is the case with most of us, we respond positively and become more open and relaxed, when we sense and feel that we are both understood and recognized, in our uniqueness by others!

III

An Anthroposophical
Approach to Autism

8. Anthroposophy's Holistic Image of Man

Rudolf Steiner and anthroposophy

Rudolf Steiner (1861–1925) explained anthroposophy's Image of Man in his thirty-five written books (Seddon 1988) and some six thousand lectures. At the outset it is important to stress that Steiner did not formulate theories, or even hypotheses. Instead, he claimed that what he described in his books and lectures was the content of rigorous scientific research which had employed spiritual faculties of perception. Such spiritual faculties could, according to Steiner, be developed by anyone who was willing to undergo a strict and systematic inner soul training and self-education (see Appendix 1).

> In every human being there slumber faculties by means of
> which he can acquire for himself a knowledge of higher
> worlds. ... It can only be a matter of how to set to work to
> develop such faculties. (Steiner 1993, 19)

Steiner did not expect or want his readers or listeners to simply accept unthinkingly what he had discovered through his own methodical spiritual research. He did, however, expect a certain open-mindedness and freedom from prejudice from those who considered his work. He maintained that the results of spiritual-scientific research were accessible to lively thinking, and could be verified in the experiences of life itself.

The usual scientific way of obtaining proof or validation, via the independent replication of research findings and the power of predictions, was well-known to Steiner, and he encouraged his pupils to undertake their own research on the basis of his indications.

It is clear that Steiner's spiritual-scientific findings are immensely practical and innovative from their applicability in many diverse fields (Davy 1975). Of these, education provides a striking example. Since the founding of the first Waldorf or Steiner school in Stuttgart, Germany, in 1919, Waldorf Education has become a worldwide movement with nearly nine hundred schools in fifty-six countries.

Steiner's Image of Man

What then are some of the broad essentials of anthroposophy's holistic Image of Man, which underpins Steiner's concepts for new approaches in education, curative education, medicine, and also for a new understanding of autism?

1. The human being is threefold in nature and consists of Body,
     Soul, and Spirit.

Each one of these principles is also clearly differentiated by Steiner in a threefold manner (Steiner 1973, Chapter 1). As Lievegoed (1993) explains, Steiner's tripartite image of man clearly contrasts all other models that have been influential in the twentieth century. This is mainly because other models have failed to recognize the essential spiritual being of man in its relationship to the psyche and the body. Needless to say, a purely biochemical or computer-like model of the human being completely rejects any independent reality for both the spiritual and soul principles. However, the soul which functions in the three psychic forces of thinking, feeling, and willing, is the mediator during earthly life, between body (matter) and spirit. The human soul therefore receives influences from both the material world and the spiritual world as shown in Table 8. The soul is the stage where upon our manifold experiences are enacted.

One of the most far-reaching of Steiner's discoveries was the precise relationship and connection between the three psychic, or soul forces, of thinking, feeling, and willing, and the bodily organism. After more than thirty years of spiritual-scientific research, he found that each soul force corresponds to a particular organic system (Harwood in Davy 1975). See Table 9.

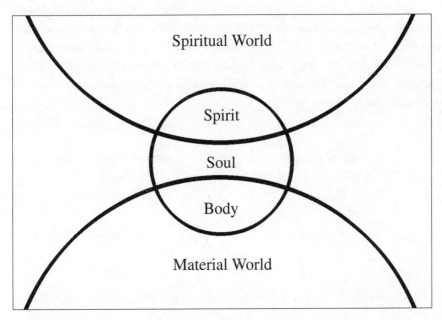

Table 8. *The soul as mediator between body and spirit.*

Soul Force	Organic System
Thinking	The Nerve-Sense System, with the brain and sensory organs. Principally centred in the head.
Feeling	The Rhythmical-System, with the organs of heart and lungs. Principally centred in the chest.
Willing	The Metabolic-Limb System, with all the organs below the diaphragm. Principally centred in the lower body.

Table 9. *Relationship of the soul forces to the bodily organism.*

Steiner was also aware that in the human body the functions of these three organic systems interconnect with each other.

Moreover, the three soul forces are active on three different levels of consciousness (Zeylmans van Emmichoven 1982), so that the conscious awakeness of thinking stands in contrast to the unconscious sleep state of the will. The feeling life however occupies a middle realm, between thinking and willing, and the consciousness there is dream-like.

Soul Force	State of Consciousness
Thinking	Awakeness
Feeling	Dreaming
Willing	Sleeping

Table 10. Relationship of the soul forces to different states of consciousness.

2. Each human being is, in reality, a spiritual being. This being is often referred to by Steiner as the ego, and it is important that this term is not confused with its usage in any totally different Images of Man (see Lievegoed 1993, Chapter 6 for a comparative survey of such images). For each of us, our true being or ego, existed before birth, and will continue to exist after death. However, our ordinary day to day self-awareness, or ego-consciousness, is narrow and restricted in comparison to the transcendent nature of our true, or higher, ego.

3. Our being is partially subject to periodic re-embodiments, or reincarnation (Steiner 1973). The conscious impulse for this arises strongly during life in the spiritual world between our last death and the new, pre-planned, birth (Wachsmuth 1937; Steiner 1975). It is only by entering into earthly life once again that we can further evolve and mature.

4. However when effecting a new incarnation on Earth, the human
   being does not arrive as a tabula rasa. Instead he brings with
   him certain consequences from the actions and circumstances
   of his previous earth-lives, together with definite goals for the
   current life. Collectively this constitutes his or her personal
   karma. Karma, seen anthroposophically, is not however fatalis-
   tic, but can be realized in more than one way, and therefore
   allows for individual initiatives and for freedom.

   ... life can only be understood in its details if we can find
   how the various karmic influences are interwoven. (Steiner
   1969c, 30)

5. The human being is engaged in a continuum of purposeful spiritual evolution and development, which involves complex
   processes of metamorphosis and transformation. Chapter IV in
   Steiner (1989) describes in great detail the successive evolutionary stages of Man and World. When seen in this broad
   context, our modern, individualized and personal self-
   consciousness and reasoning ability are relatively recent
   acquisitions, and can lead us towards ever greater independence, freedom, and a strong sense of moral responsibility.

6. The unique Christ Event, (the life, death and resurrection of
   Christ), and the healing redemptive impulse that flows from it,
   was seen by Steiner as absolutely pivotal to the whole course of
   world evolution. He claimed that:

   All that was conferred upon human evolution through the
   coming of Christ, has been working in it like a seed. ... We are
   but at the beginning of Christian evolution. (Steiner 1989, 218)

   Steiner (1976b) perceived this Christian evolution as being
inwardly linked to the development of individual ego-consciousness
within human beings in modern times, and it therefore transcends any
particular religious dogmas or beliefs.
   It is important to emphasize, for our later understanding of autism, that
the unique biography of each person develops karmically in relationship

with others, and that the core of each individual is a spiritual being in the becoming *(i.e.* involved in a continuous process of evolution and further development), thoroughly imbued with meaning and purpose. Indeed, as an individual becomes more spiritually aware and awake, his sense of purposefulness increases because he can more clearly perceive his own standing in the stream of human evolution *per se.* On the basis of this broad anthroposophical background we will now turn to child development.

Child development

Certain essentials which are needed for our deepened, spiritual-scientific understanding of autism, are given below.

The child as a being in the becoming has consciously set his own goals and aims for this particular life, long before he is physically born on earth (see Appendix). According to anthroposophy, child development is a differentiated process whereby the child's spiritual being, or ego, strives to incarnate into earthly existence in order to fulfil its personal karma in social relationships with others. We can call this process ego-integration. As Meadows observes:

> If it were possible for a child to grow up without any social relationships at all, and it probably is not, that child would not be recognizably 'human' — would not have spoken language, would not have the intellectual skills we revere, would not, probably, have self-awareness or empathy. Social interaction is necessary for all this ... (Meadows 1986, 173)

Therefore it is clear that the process of ego-integration must take place within, and is indeed dependent on, the child's social context with others. Fortunately, the child is not normally conscious or awake, to the enormity of the leap he must make when crossing over from the spiritual to the physical modes of existence. As a neonate, infant, and young child, he literally sleeps and dreams his way into the surroundings of his new life, which includes his inherited body. The following quotation from Steiner vividly captures the importance, for the child's well-being, of sleeping into his new, earthly situation.

... if the child were still living in this pre-earthly consciousness
his (new) life would be a terrible tragedy, a really terrible
tragedy. ... He had prepared himself according to his karma,
according to the result of previous lives. He was fully contained within his own spiritual garment, as it were. Now he
has to descend to earth, [where] ... he clothes himself in a
body that has been prepared by a number of generations.
(Steiner 1982, 25)

This physical-material, hereditary body, then serves as a model
(Steiner 1972), on the basis of which the child's ego endeavours to
form and fashion its very own individualized body, according to
karmic laws. This organic building process takes approximately seven
years to complete, and is achieved through the use of certain formative
life forces which Steiner often called etheric forces. In three succeed-
ing phases (see Steiner 1986, 111), these etheric forces are gradually
withdrawn, or freed, from their exclusively biological functions, and
then become available, on a different level, as soul faculties within the
child; for example, as memory and mental image capacities.

Normally, around the seventh year, the child's own body has been
built, and some of the etheric forces are metamorphosed into living,
imaginative powers of thought, which are in no sense abstract
thoughts. Steiner summed up this new step in a child's development as
the birth of his own etheric body.

At around fourteen years of age, other new soul capacities emerge,
leading to the formation of independent judgments, abstract thoughts,
and a much more personal feeling life. These capacities are due, in
anthroposophical terms, to the birth of the child's astral body, and are
accompanied by the physical changes of puberty.

Therefore, the process of incarnation, involves not just one, but
three distinct bodily births. Namely, the birth of the child's physical,
etheric, and astral bodies. (Here, the term body is used to mean an
organized and contained system of forces, not only a material-physical organism.) The full impact of these different bodily births and
metamorphoses need to be clearly understood by educators who are
active in Waldorf Education (Steiner 1975a; Harwood 1982; Aeppli
1986; Lievegoed 1987; Childs 1991), and also by anthroposophical
doctors (Bott 1982; Glöckler & Goebel 1990).

It is precisely through incarnation into these three bodies that the child's ego enters into earthly existence. Therefore, anthroposophy often refers to the fourfold constitution; namely, the ego with three bodies. It is important for us to note the following:

1. The physical-material body provides earthly building blocks (minerals also have physical-material bodies).

2. The etheric (or life) body, not only underpins growth and reproduction, but is the bearer of memory and imagination in Man. Organically, it functions through the glandular system (plants also have etheric bodies).

3. The astral (or soul) body enables sensations, inner consciousness and ensouled movements to come about (that is, movements that are expressions of the soul through the physical organism, rather than mechanical movements). Organically, it functions through the nervous system (animals also have astral bodies).

4. The ego, as the essential being of Man, alone enables the process of individualization of the three bodies in each person through ego-integration, self-consciousness and individual biography (Hansmann 1992). Organically, the ego functions through the warm blood system. (Only human beings have egos, in earth existence).

In our attempts to understand autism in a new way, we realise that the ego of the autistic child is unable to sufficiently penetrate into and individualize its three bodies. This shows itself in the child's lack of imagination, in connection with the etheric body, and in repetitive and compulsive movement patterns, when we consider the astral body, while in respect of the ego itself, the autistic child invariably fails to establish a secure and reliable self-consciousness.

With reference to human fourfoldness, Steiner (1990b) often pointed out that when we are awake the ego and astral body are united with the physical and etheric bodies. However, when we sleep, the ego and astral body are withdrawn from them and enter into a spiritual existence. We can illustrate these two situations, in a simple schematic way. See Table 11.

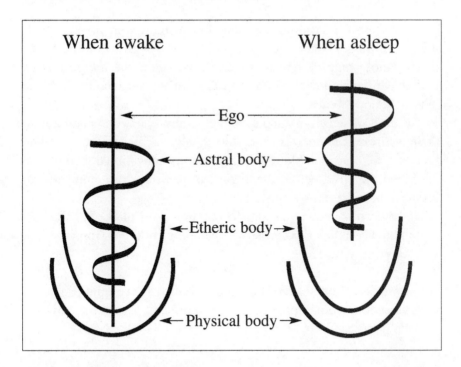

Table 11. Man's fourfold constitution.

Normally, when we awake in the morning, the process of ego-integration takes place and we regain our self-consciousness, personal identity and conscious memory. However, when the ego and astral body are withdrawn during sleep, we lose our self-consciousness, personal identity and autobiographical memory. We shall see later that autistic children do not wake up properly to self-consciousness, nor do they easily go to sleep. This can be explained as a disturbed ego-integration in relationship to the three bodies.

Environmental factors

Great emphasis was placed by Steiner on the social and moral, as well as physical, environment which surrounds and influences a child throughout their early years. He said that we should think of the very young child as a single, highly sensitive and perceptive sense-organ

(Steiner 1988). Everything that the child perceives in his surroundings, even thoughts and feelings within people with whom he establishes a close rapport, has a profound effect upon the reorganization and active development of the child's own physical body from the inherited model body.

The marked sensitivity and acute vulnerability of young children to their environment derives from the faculty of imitation, to which Steiner gave considerable importance. In his educational lectures, he described the child before the change of teeth as, 'pre-eminently an imitative being' (see Appendix 1).

However, it is known that autistic children show marked difficulties in imitation compared to normally developing children (Hobson 1993, 72). As Wing states:

> Imitation is one of the skills that is basic to developing social behaviour, so its impairment is a significant part of the autistic picture. (Wing 1996, 50)

The first three years of life

While the acclaimed Swiss child psychologist, Jean Piaget (1982), was particularly concerned with the evolution of cognition in the young child, recent years have seen a growing interest in the emotional and social development of infants (Harris 1991; Dunn 1988). The sequential developmental behaviour of young children from birth has been observed and mapped since the 1960s (Sheridan 1988).

However, the nature of a young child's inner experiences, and the quality of their varied perceptions, still remains a field for continued exploration and discovery (see Appendix 1). According to Karmiloff-Smith:

> For a long time it was thought that the newborn perceives and interprets objects in a kind of chaotic, surreal way, famously described by the early twentieth-century psychologist, William James, as the infant's 'buzzing, blooming confusion.' But recent research suggests that the infant's world, although blurred, isn't that different from the adult's. (Karmiloff-Smith 1994, 47)

However, in contrast to this recent research, the inner process of early child development can be seen, as Weihs (1984) suggests, as effecting a withdrawal from an initially global and vague perceptual field, towards increasing discrimination and objectifying of the world. In other words, a contraction from a wide peripheric awareness towards a centred, and sharper consciousness, in which self and world are increasingly separated. We shall see later that the autistic child retains something of this sensitive early peripheric consciousness, instead of achieving a clear self-awareness and developing interpersonal relationships with others.

In order to understand autism better we should take particular note of the lower and the higher senses as characterized below (see Appendix 1 for fuller explanation).

The four lower senses

König (1971) provides us with a detailed study of the lower senses from which the following brief accounts have been drawn.

Touch — gives us a first dim awareness of the boundaries of our bodily existence, and results in a sense of inner security and trust. Moreover, it is through touch that we can have a sense for the divine in the world; if a person had no sense of touch they would have no feeling of God.

Life — gives us a feeling of bodily well-being (or otherwise). Moreover, the initial feeling of self comes through the sense of life, with the experience of wholeness in our corporeality.

Movement — gives us an awareness of the co-ordinated movements and relative positions of our own body parts, and therefore of our integrated bodily existence.

Balance — gives us orientation in the three dimensions of space, and provides us with an enduring inner certainty.

It is specifically through the combined perceptions of the four lower senses that we can arrive at a sense of certainty of our own body, and a complete body image. Together, these body senses give an existential, and largely unconscious self-experience, which is distinct from an awake, sharp self-consciousness. However, if any one of the four lower senses does not function adequately, the very basis of our earthly existence can become uncertain and insecure, and we shall see later how this situation applies to autistic children.

The four higher senses

Steiner (1990b) gives very clear descriptions of these distinct cognitive senses.

Hearing — makes us aware of sounds and tones. It also conveys the musical element of spoken language. As such it already appears to function in the embryo (Verny & Kelly 1982).

Word — makes us aware that a language is being spoken. This awareness, according to Steiner, is distinct from what is conveyed through hearing alone.

Thought (or Concept) — makes us aware of the thoughts of another person which may be conveyed to us via spoken or written language, or gestures. The perception of thoughts or concepts, and therefore also of sense and meaning, is in reality a sensory, not a cognitive thinking process.

Ego — makes us aware of the ego-nature of another person. Through this sense, which is the most spiritual of the twelve senses, another's essential humanness is recognized. Steiner (1990b) precisely described the functioning of this highest sense within our interpersonal relationships.

It is through the co-ordinated functioning of the four higher senses that we are able to become truly social beings (König, 1990), who can communicate and learn to empathize with others.

Additionally, it is important to note that there are specific developmental relationships and correspondences between the four lower and the four higher senses, which are shown below in Table 12 (see Aeppli 1993).

The exact reasons for these specific relationships cannot be dealt with here but in brief, it means that a healthy development of the higher senses depends on the proper functioning and maturation of the lower senses. This dependency is very important when we come to interpret childhood autism, precisely because such children appear to have some higher sense impairments or dysfunctions, resulting in a profound lack of social sense and awareness. This therefore, also has implications for their lower senses.

Self-consciousness

It is commonly known that when small children learn to speak they do not yet use pronouns in reference to themselves. They still refer to themselves by name in such a way that Johnny or Jane wants this or that. However, as Sheridan (1988) observes, by the age of two and a half years children are typically able to use the pronouns I, Me and You correctly. By three years, they use both personal pronouns and plurals correctly and also most prepositions. They also ask many questions beginning What, Where and Who? How then does the child come to the

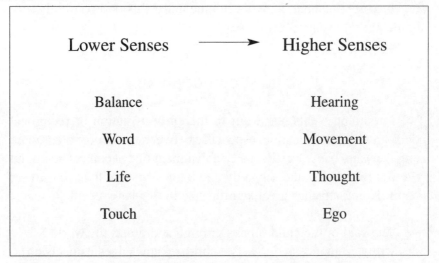

Lower Senses	⟶	Higher Senses
Balance		Hearing
Word		Movement
Life		Thought
Touch		Ego

Table 12. Correspondences between the lower and higher senses.

realization that, in language function, he is not only Johnny Brown, but also I? Is this knowledge arrived at by some intellectual inference or deduction, as is often assumed to be the case (Flavell 1985, 259). Is there a totally different explanation for this phenomenon? Steiner asserted that the emergence of this pronoun was an outer expression of inwardly experienced self-consciousness in the child.

> In the course of his development as a child, there comes the moment in the life of a man in which, for the first time, he feels himself to be an independent being distinct from the whole of the rest of the world. (Steiner 1973, 35)

Steiner (1973) emphasized a simple fact which, in its uniqueness, is mostly overlooked. Namely, that while all of us can apply every other name that exists to its corresponding object, I can only be applied and used by an individual speaking of his or herself. Therefore, when children in their third year begin to use I properly and consistently, from this time onwards they begin to experience the continuity of personal, autobiographical memory which forms the thread of their entire earthly life (see also Appendix 1).

It may also be possible that a child who, for some reason, does not speak, still arrives at consciousness of self. However, it seems that speaking autistic children do not refer to themselves as I in a normal and consistent manner, and, developmentally, this observation is very significant (Hobson 1993, 95-101).

The social context

Two important events stand out in the early evolution of reciprocal contact and communication, especially between mother (or other main caregiver) and baby. Firstly, the establishment of eye contact at around two to three weeks, and secondly, the baby's first smile at four to six weeks. König attaches great significance to this latter event.

> The soul of the child breaks through and greets the world with acceptance and joy. The child acknowledges its decision to become a citizen of the earth. (König 1994, 67)

However we know from the literature that the absence of eye contact and social smiling can be early indicators of the presence, or onset, of autism. (See Appendix 1 for further explanation of the anthroposphical social context).

Play

The developmental importance of the stages of play, for the child's active integration into the world, are now well recognized (Garvey 1991).

It would not be going too far to say that play is one of the most important activities in a child's life. König once pointed out that a child's spiritual being, the ego, leads them into earthly life through play.

Fantasy and imagination, pretend and social play, play with adults, siblings and peers; all of these constitute a creative and increasingly socially-shared world of transformations and metamorphoses. What could better accompany the parallel, inner transformation of the body during the first seven years? For a child play is as natural and vital as eating and sleeping. In the deepest sense, play during the first seven years, is 'the preparation for life,' and for later realizing personal karma (Britz-Crecelius, 1979). As Steiner remarked:

> The way in which such a young child plays is a clear indication of its potential gifts and faculties in later life. (Steiner 1986, 118)

Unfortunately, the lack of creative play and fantasy is a characteristic feature of infantile autism.

Summary

From the preceding sections on early child development, and according to anthroposophy's holistic Image of Man, we can now state that:

— Children undergo a process of incarnation, from a pre-birth spiritual existence to a post-natal earthly life.

— The child's spiritual being is active, via etheric forces, in the complete organic reconstruction of its own individualized body from the inherited model body. The brain is worked upon and refined in the first two and a half years.

— The child is, above all, an extremely sensitive sensory and imitative being; the more so the younger he is.

— In the course of the first year, the child's lower or body senses develop, accompanied by existential feelings of trust and security. These are linked to the subsequent functioning of his higher or social senses.

— In the course of the third year, the child first achieves individual self-consciousness and thereafter starts to refer to himself as I. This is the result of an existential recognition of his own uniqueness, and is a crucial moment in his biography.

— There then follows the age of defiance, of self-assertiveness, and the continuity of autobiographical memory.

— The child's development is integrated into, and dependent on, the social context. Early awareness is peripheric and at one with the soul surroundings.

— Creative play is an expression of the ego's incarnation process, and is instrumental for the later realization of karmic intentions.

Two key concepts

Finally, underpinning all that has been discussed above, are two fundamental anthroposophical concepts. The first of these is expressed by the term ego-integration, which is defined by Hansmann (1992) as:

> The process of the spiritual individual entering through conception and birth into his body and the environment of family and nature, of folk and historic time. (Hansmann 1992, 165)

It is precisely through ego-integration that developmental processes of metamorphosis and individuation are able to take place effectively in the growing child.

The second key concept centres on the very *raison d'être* for ego-integration. Only through incarnation into earthly existence can individuals achieve new steps in their own spiritual evolution (Steiner 1959). This means that man is still a *being in the becoming*. (See Appendix 1).

If we keep these two far-reaching concepts in our minds, together with the understanding of child development presented in this chapter, we are now ready to propose an anthroposophical interpretation of early infantile autism.

9. Autism seen Anthroposophically

A typical three year old displays a vivacious interest in life. He has long since mastered to stand straight on his own two feet, and to walk where he wants in his active exploration and conquest of the new world. He can speak well and clearly communicate his basic needs, wishes and questions. He refers to himself as I, and can be extremely self-assertive in word and action, especially determined to have his own way. He still sometimes imitates what he has seen his father or mother or other adults doing, irrespective of whether they approve of it or not. His whole nature dictates that he follows the examples which he has observed. At play, he is the master magician, whose power of fantasy can create and transform anything in his surroundings, whether he is alone or with other children. He shows obvious affection and trust with familiar others, which can include younger siblings, and is generally emotionally responsive and alert to his social surroundings. The three-year-old child is, therefore, a thoroughly active little person, expressing his full participation in that world, which he shares with others, in his own increasingly individual way. However, behind him, giving intention to all this visible outer involvement and expression, is the strong inner drive for successful incarnation, for ego-integration, into this new earth life. There are indeed important and pressing things which can only be done, learnt and achieved in this particular down-to-earth existence.

Hypothesis

What would happen if the invisible, yet normally empowering, drive for ego-integration were to break down and fail early in life? What would this mean for those hidden and complex processes of transformation and metamorphosis which underpin typical child development? What would this mean if outwardly, the child appeared to be physically perfect, even beautiful in appearance, and was apparently also organically undamaged?

Anthroposophically, from what we have already described of early childhood, and assuming it to be true, we could expect and in fact predict, certain serious developmental consequences of such a failed, or at least a disturbed, ego-integration. However, in doing so we must be quite clear that these specific consequences are not due to any of the variety of afflictions or dysfunctions which can also disrupt the course of normal development, such as an early encephalitis. We must be sure that they have their root on the deeper soul-spiritual level of the basic existential drive, the will impulse, to enter into physical incarnation. Usually this drive is strong enough to withstand, and surmount, any early illnesses, accidents or traumas, experienced by the incarnating soul-spirit of the child in the first years of life or later, without autism occurring.

Implications of an unsuccessful early ego-integration

1. The inherited model body is not sufficiently taken hold of and transformed by the ego. This results in the insufficient development of one, or more, of the lower senses. This leads to an underlying lack of bodily self-experience, inner security and trust, and an incomplete body image. Thus the very ground of existence is missing, as is likely to be the case for the autistic child.

2. Because of the lack of development of one or more of the lower senses, there would be impairment or even non-functioning, of certain higher social senses, resulting in an autistic inability to make sense of the world, especially other people.

3. The general sensory organ and the power of imitation, which are essential in the building up of the new individualized body and in early communication and contact with the

human social environment, are either weakened, or else break down altogether. This inevitably results in early isolation and aloneness.

4. The release and particularly the metamorphosis of certain etheric forces are impeded. It is just these forces which normally lead to the development of vivid fantasy and imagination and find expression in the child's natural urge to play. Therefore, these most child-like attributes are markedly absent in autistic children.

5. The motor achievements of talking and thinking, which are intimately linked with the senses of word, thought, and ego, are seriously disturbed, or perhaps altogether fail to take place. This results in further isolation from, and incomprehension of, the human environment.

6. During the third year, the contraction of the initially wide peripheric consciousness of the infant towards a more centred self-consciousness does not fully take place. If spoken language has been attained, the use of personal pronouns, especially I, will either be missing or confused. This results in an inability to separate self from the surroundings, and to establish a personal identity.

7. The failure to effect typical ego-integration (even allowing for normal individual differences in development), shows in disturbed or deficient sensory functioning, as well as in an inability to establish secure self-consciousness through the continuity of personal, autobiographical memory.

8. Therefore, the most singular and dramatic effect of the above, is seen in the almost total inability of the child to integrate himself actively into the stream of social life, and to establish reciprocal human relationships. To a large extent, the child appears alienated from his closest human surroundings. He is already, or will soon become, autistic.

These specific implications of the consequences of a disturbed ego-integration, are supported in theory, when we historically survey the complex evolution of the anthroposophical interpretation and understanding of autism. We shall include the work of König (1960), Weihs (1984), and Müller-Wiedemann (1988); all were informed by decades of direct practical experience and observations, through living and working with autistic children in Camphill schools.

The evolving interpretation of autism

Dr Karl König

In 1960, Dr König gave two lectures on the theme of The Autistic Child. After a review and consideration of the typical symptoms of autism, he came to the following initial conclusions:

> The inability of a child to integrate into the sense, the meaning, of the environment and social surroundings is not primarily due to a dysfunction of walking, speaking, and thinking but to a dysfunction in the development of the three higher senses of word, thought, and ego.

> The general organ of sensitivity whereby the child especially perceives the persons in their surroundings is, for one or another reason, not functioning.

> The ability to imitate is absent in these children.

In seeking the deeper reasons for these dysfunctions, König came to further important, yet still initial, conclusions:

> The active power of imitation depends on the child's general sensory organ. (This seems reasonable, since the child must first perceive something before it can imitate it.)

> Imitation and the sensory organ are both intimately concerned with the as yet-unborn, etheric body of the child. This etheric body only comes to full birth around the seventh year, and meantime is normally protected by what Steiner (1975) described as the mother's etheric envelope (or sheath or shell). König's view gains clear support when Aeppli points out that: 'Steiner often speaks of how the small child,

approximately up to the fourth year, still possesses a kind of "general organ of perception," in his etheric body ... The child still possesses the liveliness of perception caused by the enlivening etheric forces in the sense processes.' (Aeppli 1993, 46–48)

If before, or soon after physical birth, this maternal etheric sheath is ruptured, this will directly affect the child's own unborn etheric body, and consequently their general sensory organ and power of imitation. König thought that such a rupture could be caused by a traumatic event, and an examination of the case histories of autistic children led him to conclude that: '... you never find an autistic child where you cannot elucidate very clearly a shock, an accident, an illness — something which disturbs this time of becoming and birth.' (König 1960)

The overall effect for the unborn child or infant would mean that they then prematurely wake up in their consciousness, when they ought to remain healthily unconscious and asleep. The profound, formative power of imitation is only possible because children, in their expanded consciousness, sleep into their surroundings (see Steiner 1990b, 150). Therefore, it follows that if this sleeping into life is prematurely disturbed, so is the capacity for imitation.

Furthermore, König pointed out,

If you study what is thought today about child autism you will find one school which sees the whole thing purely organically — for the one the brain is damaged, for the other (school) certain psychological things are the cause and reason for the disturbance.

But where does psychology start in a baby without being at once organic. Where in a baby does an organic lesion start without at once having mental consequences. It is all one. 'If such a child wakes up too early, at once the whole body suffers.' (König 1960)

Here, we are immediately reminded of Bettelheim's views on the intimacy of soma and psyche in earliest development (see Chapter 1).

Finally, and most importantly, Dr König saw autism as the reaction of the soul or being of the child, towards difficult existential circumstances. König therefore considered the acknowledgment of the child's spiritual being to be absolutely essential for any real understanding of autism and its symptomatology.

Dr Thomas Weihs

In 1970, Weihs put forward a developmentally based interpretation of autism. He was not concerned primarily with the identification of possible underlying aetiologies which, he believed, could be heterogeneous — organic, psychogenic or environmental — and which needed to be diagnosed for each child individually. Rather his aim was to understand autism in the light of the first three years of normal child development, as illuminated by anthroposophy.

Weih's observations strongly emphasized the unique inner awakening to self-consciousness, from an earlier, peripheric awareness. In essence, he proposed that the phenomenon of autism could be understood as a reaction of the young child to the incipient, and potentially over-powering and threatening, emergence of its own self-hood.

> To sum up, the attempt has been made to interpret childhood autism as a panic-reaction to the moment when the ego first makes itself known to a child between his second and third years. ... In consequence of the panic-reaction, there can develop avoidance of the realisation of the self. (Weihs 1984, 91)

With reference to autistic children who speak, Weihs stressed the significance of the well-known phenomenon of pronominal reversal (see also Wing 1996, 39):

> This transposition of the personal pronouns is perhaps the most unique and classical demonstration of the panic-reaction against the dawn of one's ego-experience. The failure to lodge the ego-experience at centre is probably the core of childhood autism. (Weihs 1984, 91)

Interestingly, Weihs remarked that among hundreds of histories of autistic children, he had only found a small number showing signs of autism in very early infancy. Whether or not early signs are observable (Muller-Weidemann (1988) believed that this was frequently the case), recent literature certainly agrees that the characteristic symptoms of autism are typically seen by the third year. As we saw in Chapter 1, the ICD-10 definition of childhood autism clearly specifies the full manifestation of the Triad of Impairments before three years of age. This is, therefore, in keeping with Weihs' particular interpretation of the unique significance of the child's third year.

Additionally, Weihs considered that first-born or only children were more likely to be at risk of showing an autistic reaction, because of their position of special responsibility in the family. His views were partly based on the evidence from a survey of children with special needs in Camphill during the 1960s, which revealed:

> ... a strikingly higher percentage of first-born children among the psychotics. (Pietzner 1966, 213)

At that time, the term *psychotic* was often used to describe children who might now be placed within the autistic spectrum. There is, however, no recent published evidence I am aware of to confirm these early observations.

Similarly, Weihs suggested that the numbers of autistic children who appear '... with large beautiful heads, and are potentially intelligent and gifted,'(Weihs 1984, 90) were also more vulnerable, through their constitution, to the over-powering force of ego-awakening. As he had described in an earlier chapter in his book when speaking of large-headedness:

> Large-headedness is an expression of these children's own reluctance to be born. (Weihs 1984, 42)

It is interesting to note here that Kanner observed that of the eleven autistic children he originally saw, 'Five had relatively large heads.' (1943, 248).

This 'reluctance to be born' as a longing to remain in a spiritual pre-birth existence can, in the case of some autistic children, be shown as an early lack of motivation with a weakened drive towards achieving ego-integration and the acceptance of personal karma.

Dr Hans Müller-Wiedemann

In the 1970s and early 1980s, Hans Müller-Wiedemann published his own attempts to try to come closer to a still more comprehensive and detailed anthroposophical understanding of autism. These were based on thirty years of practical experience living with autistic children. He also indicated some new perspectives in the areas of differentiated sensory developments.

Like König, he acknowledged the inability of autistic children to integrate themselves into the specifically human environment via the power of imitation.

He also emphasized their fundamental inability to achieve an experience of their own body, and consequently to gain the inner security afforded by an existential, bodily-based self-experience.

He maintained that there was both an insufficient maturation and functioning of the lower senses and that in fact:

> The extent of the 'autistic disorder' depends, according to our experience, on the time-appropriate degrees of the development of the maturing of the Lower-Senses. (Müller-Wiedemann et al 1988, 69)

In particular, the sense of life which normally develops during the infant's first year, is often severely disturbed. This had also been pointed out by König:

> We must only call to mind quite concretely what it means when the sense of Life cannot develop as a contained uniform sense experience.
>
> If that happens then the child will not have a correct relationship to his own body. What is otherwise an immediate experience, starting in early childhood, by which we feel ourselves as being 'a complete within-ness' and thereby as a matter of course sense ourselves as a 'bodily self filling space,' this is not present.

The identification between bodily corporeality and spirit-soul does not come about and thus severe contact disorders ensue. The child's soul experiences the body as not belonging to him, but rather as a part of the world. To a large extent the certainty of earth existence is thereby lost, and features and symptoms of severe autistic disorders appear. (König 1971; free translation by J.Holbek)

What König and Müller-Wiedemann both assert, is vividly confirmed in the autobiography of a recovering autistic person:

My perception of a whole body was in bits. I was an arm or a leg or a nose. Sometimes one part would be very much there but the bit it was joined to felt as wooden as a table leg and just as dead. The only difference was the texture and the appearance. (Williams 1994, 228)

Furthermore, impairment of the sense of life would satisfactorily explain the often unusual and perplexing reactions of autistic children towards conditions that, in a normal child, would be the cause of severe pain or illness. For example, the self-injurious behaviours to which Wing refers (1996, 113).

The failure in the maturation of the lower senses does not allow a normal differentiation to develop sufficiently between the body and the shared inter-human world of natural objects and other people.

Consequently, as the process of individualization of the body (towards the seventh year) is only partially achieved, facial expressions and movement patterns often remain almost unchanged up to the seventh year.

In terms of consciousness, it even appears that the autistic child may become unhealthily awake in the perceptual realm of the lower senses, where they really ought to remain unconscious. This unusual awakeness is, for example, evidenced in the child being strongly drawn in a compulsive way into the area of spatial-geometrical and mathematical relationships.

This appears in some autistic children in the ritualistic ordering of objects. Elly Park (see Chapter 1), would, for example, arrange a hundred building blocks in perfectly parallel rows. A marked tendency to reduce the outer world to number and measure is seen, which is due to the pathological descent of consciousness into the lower sense realm:

> Everything, which can be determined in our surroundings by
> number, measure and weight, belongs to the experience
> realm of the four lower senses. (Aeppli 1993, 24)

This important realization at once helps to explain the outstanding savant type activities of some autistic people in the area of numbers and drawing. (Wiltshire 1991). This led Müller-Wiedemann to write that:

> The child is 'imprisoned' in the world of the lower senses
> which then also 'invades' the field of the middle soul senses.
> (Müller-Wiedemann et al 1988, 75)

The autistic child does not however become awake where he naturally should, namely in his head-centred thought life and self-consciousness. Therefore we can speak of a certain reversal of normal consciousness which comes about in autistic children. This significant insight was expressed by one anthroposophical researcher in the following way:

> ... the autistic child as a whole assumes the character of a head,
> [but] the actual head itself is as though almost eliminated. The
> brain and the sense organs connected with it are restricted in
> their functions and altered. (Holtzapfel 1995, 42)

We can better understand Holtzapfel's remarks when we consider how the head nature normally enables a certain detached antipathy to come about specifically in the cognitive thought pole. Typically, the autistic child seems detached and antipathetic to their entire human social surroundings.

Moreover, the far-reaching seriousness of just this reversal of consciousness for biography is highlighted when, from anthroposophy, we further learn that our karmic intentions are actually embedded in the normally unconscious, lower sense will realm. Therefore, through the child waking up pathologically into this realm, his personal

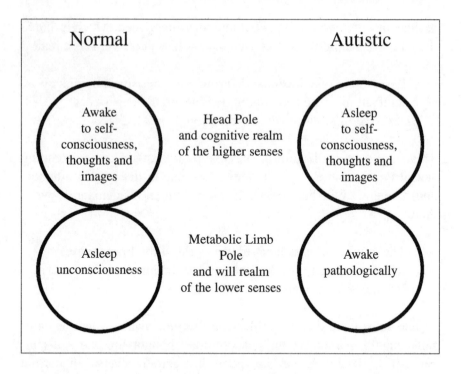

Table 13. The reversal of consciousness in autism.

intentionality and motivation for life are greatly impaired. To a degree, they actually become conscious of their karmic intentions, and this awareness is then experienced as a very real burden, which can cause them pain and even acute despair (Müller-Wiedemann 1982). In Table 13 the form of a lemniscate represents the two opposite poles of consciousness in the human being.

Furthermore, this reversed consciousness also prevents the autistic child from attaining an inner world of living images and imagination. These images normally arise as the result of metamorphosis from early sensory-motor activities, since perceptual consciousness precedes the formation of such inner images and representations. However the head remains empty because the normal mirroring faculty of the head and brain has been undermined.

The sense of thought, which is dependent on the healthy functioning of the sense of life, is also developmentally impaired or is rendered non-functional. Since concepts cannot then be perceived, other sensory percepts, including those arising through language and gesture, lack both sense and meaning. It becomes clear that without enlightening concepts, the plethora of everyday percepts must present a confusing, painful, frightening and unpredictable world to the autistic child. (In his *Philosophy of Spiritual Activity* (1992), Steiner explains how reality is confirmed for us only when percept and concept unite together.)

Faced with this situation, and probably in desperation, the autistic child tries to create a controlled and predictable *pseudo world* for himself, in which he can somehow exist. Often the child strives to maintain sameness at all costs, precisely in order to reduce his existential fear.

> When we meet an autistic child it has to be clear to us that his world is not just deficient to ours, but that he creates for himself a world in which he can live. (Müller-Wiedemann *et al* 1988, 66)

Only in a restricted, closed space, without change and development, can he perhaps manage to gain some measure of inner security. However, if this space is breached, the child is quickly filled with anxiety, fear and panic, as he immediately loses control over his environment. As Tustin (1992) expressed it, autistic children are often 'traumatized and terror-stricken.' These powerful emotions are certainly confirmed in the autobiographical accounts of Grandin (1986) and Williams (1992).

The senses and autism

The great importance which Müller-Wiedemann attaches to the under or over-functioning of certain senses in autism, is partially recognized by mainstream literature (Delacato 1974; Ayres 1995). Delacato, for example, was convinced that for neurological reasons the autistic child had an 'unreliable sensory system.' The disturbing experiences in autism due to abnormal sensory functioning and inadequate perceptual integration, are clearly confirmed in the autobiographical accounts of Grandin (1986) and Williams (1992 and 1994). However, through anthroposophy's description of the twelve senses, and especially their specific relationships, the various possible sensory dysfunctions can now begin to be more fully understood. In particular, we have pointed earlier to the clear developmental relationships between the lower and the higher senses, such as the correspondence between the senses of touch and ego, and the senses of life and thought.

A classic example of the correspondence between *tactile* perceptions and an inner awareness of other people is vividly described by Temple Grandin (1986). By constructing a *squeeze machine* for herself in order to experience whole-body pressure in a controlled way, it seems that she was able to first develop some empathy for others.

> At College I was making great strides in communicating
> with people. I attributed this 'break-through' in getting along
> better with people to my maligned squeeze machine. It
> enabled me to learn to be gentle, to have empathy... (Grandin
> 1986, 104)

We have suggested, and clearly predicted, the failure of certain higher senses, particularly those of thought and ego in the autistic child. This prediction, if verified, would go a long way to explaining the so-called *mind blindness,* which Theory of Mind protagonists refer to, in just these children (Frith 1989; Astington 1994). *Theory of Mind* refers to a person's natural ability to understand the connections between others' external behaviour and their inferred internal state of mind. This ability, which Frith (1989) calls *mentalizing,* is essential for us to function as socially aware human beings. In autistic children, the lack of mentalizing then leads to a blindness regarding the minds of others.

We know that impairment in the functioning of the higher senses will undoubtedly have serious consequences for social communication, understanding and empathy. Their proper functioning, however, should come about precisely through the being, the ego of the child, incarnating into the circle of the twelve senses, and actively using them to perceive, contact and communicate with the three different perceptual fields of: own body; the natural environment; and the social-human surroundings.

As Müller-Wiedemann (1966) described, it is precisely by the ego working in the child's social relationships, that the whole realm of sensory perceptions can be properly assimilated and metamorphosed, into meaningful and coherent personal experiences. However this assimilation does not seem to happen with autistic children, so that their perceptions lack coherent integration and meaningfulness. Therefore, Müller-Wiedemann seems convinced, as I am also, that we find *a fundamental problem of active ego-integration* in these children. If the ego, the being of the child, is unable to properly take hold of its physical, etheric and astral, bodies, and gradually penetrate and individualize them, then this situation will have consequences, sooner or later, on both the organic and psychological levels, as current research into autism strongly suggests.

We could perhaps compare the complex process of typical ego-integration in a very simplified and schematic way, with the atypical autistic state, as shown in Table 14.

In a sense, the autistic child remains more closely connected to its pre-birth spiritual existence than the normal child but, because of this, does not develop sufficiently into the social-moral sphere.

Müller-Wiedemann believes that this ego-integration difficulty has often arisen even before physical birth.

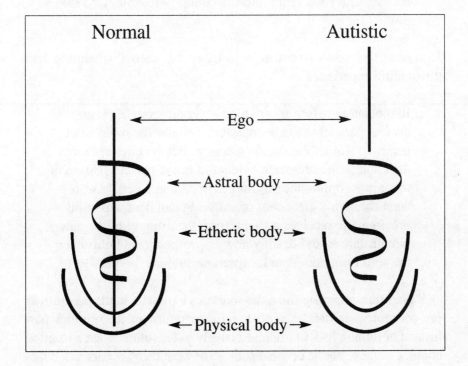

Table 14. Typical ego-integration and autism.

Primary causation

If the unborn child's soul-spiritual being (soul and spirit are united in pre-birth existence and also in the young child) receives a shock, then the initial impulse and motivation towards the new incarnation may be seriously thwarted. Consequently, the crossing of the threshold between spiritual and earthly forms of existence, will not be achieved successfully. Steiner gave indications that such an existential shock can indeed occur, and thus prevent personal karma from being fulfilled. He described that, on the path of re-entry into physical life, the soul-spirit being experiences a pre-vision of its coming earthly life, and that:

> What he thus sees becomes the source of active forces which he must carry with him into the coming life. (Steiner 1989, 89)

However, this pre-vision can sometimes be an overwhelming and threatening experience.

> Immediately before incarnation a very important event occurs, parallel to the event which follows the moment of death. ... Not all the details are seen, but the circumstances of the coming life are made evident in broad outline. This is of the utmost importance. It may happen that a person who went through a great deal of suffering and hardship in his previous life receives a shock from the glimpse of the new circumstances and destiny now in prospect, and holds back the soul from complete incarnation. (Steiner 1970b, 49)

Rather than incarnate fully, the soul tries to remain in the pre-birth or pre-conceptual existence, and thereby to return to its spiritual past instead of turning its will impulse actively to the future. Such a reaction could, I suggest, be the original source for what then appears as a deep-seated and primary, early autistic condition, with a withdrawing from the sphere of human, social life. This sphere is, however, precisely the scenario where past karma must be encountered and new, future karma created. In the light of this let us again recall to mind some typical characteristics of classical autism, shown by a child of about three years old.

The child with pure autism

He is a beautiful, perfectly formed boy, who has an almost unearthly air about him. He is skilful, with good body co-ordination, balance and dexterity, yet he walks on his toes. Sometimes, and for no obvious reason, he suddenly flaps his hands quickly in front of his face, or puts his fingers into his ears, or rocks his body backwards and forwards. In the presence of other people, including his peers, he always appears strikingly aloof and distant. He seems to deliberately avoid eye contact, even with his own caring family, and often simply looks through other people as if they do not exist. He does not explore his surroundings, with the usual childish curiosity and intent. However, each and every day, he spends hours arranging his large collection of toy cars in straight lines, always in precisely the same order and patterns. He is usually good at doing jigsaw puzzles, even when the picture side is turned face down, but has no imaginative or pretend play either alone, or with his peers. He does not imitate the gestures or actions of others.

He shows no signs of outward affection or love, but will sometimes smile to himself, or even giggle. He seldom speaks and, though he is not deaf, does not respond when others call him by name. At times, however, he hums a tune in near perfect pitch, and sometimes echoes words he has just heard with almost identical intonation. Nevertheless, he walks alone in a busy world of people , only taking the initiative to reach out by sometimes taking a passing hand or arm as a useful tool, to fetch some needed item, or perhaps to reach a high door handle. This three year old, outwardly so perfect in appearance, remains a stranger, even to those who most long to make contact with him.

He seems to have no intention, enthusiasm or time to enjoy his life with others, but at best seems to eke out some pseudo existence.

Primary and secondary autisms

We recognize that there are different degrees of autism — a spectrum — from severe to mild. In terms of differential diagnosis it is very important to discover if the autism appears to be of a deep-seated primary or pure nature, or rather of a secondary form. If secondary, then the autism could be due to a reaction to some other primary difficulty; for example, an early encephalitis, the birth of a sibling, or a developmental aphasia. In the latter instance, Sahlmann (1969) clearly described, with examples of specific children, how when the aphasia is identified and treated, the secondary autism can then recede; sometimes quite quickly. However as Wing (1993) emphasized, accurate differential diagnosis can only be made by taking a detailed developmental history from infancy, and obtaining an equally detailed description of behaviour in different settings.

When pure autism is present it is likely that these children will suffer some degree of autism as a life-long disorder unless, perhaps, we can already begin to build trusting human relationships with them through early empathetic interventions which are based on a deepened understanding of their special existential predicament.

Asperger's Syndrome

The anthroposophical view of autism specifically relates to Early Infantile Autism, as described and identified by Leo Kanner in 1943, and which is usually referred to as Kanner's syndrome.

However, in 1944, Hans Asperger published a paper entitled 'Autistic psychopathy in childhood.' (See Frith 1991, Chapter 2).

In recent years a great deal of interest has focused on gaining a better understanding of the nature of Asperger's syndrome and its chief characteristics, as well as on distinguishing its similarities to, and differences from, Kanner's syndrome (Attwood, 1998).

Thus, to emphasize the differences, the young classic Kanner's child has good manual dexterity when engaged in his or her preferred activities but has delayed and deviant language development, as well as social impairment of the aloof kind. Those with typical Asperger's syndrome have good grammatical speech from early in life, passive, odd or subtly inappropriate social interaction, and poor gross motor coordination shown in gait and posture. They also tend to be in the mildly retarded, normal or superior range of intelligence, while Kanner's group covers a wider range of the IQ scale ... However, the more able among Kanner's group can, over the years, develop the characteristics, including the types of social interaction, of people with Asperger's syndrome, and become indistinguishable from them in adult life. (Frith 1991, 115)

What is however very clear is that children and young people with either of these syndromes show characteristic, often severe, difficulties and limitations with respect to their social interaction and integration. This can unfortunately lead increasingly to aloneness and isolation, and perhaps also acute frustration and despair in the comparatively more able person with Asperger's syndrome.

The question as to whether autism and Asperger's syndrome should be seen as distinct, and mutually exclusive diagnostic categories is not yet clear (Frith 1991, 2). However, there does seem to be a strong argument for including both of these syndromes on the spectrum of autistic disorders, and considering them as valid sub-groups on this continuum (Wing 1996).

The anthroposophical interpretation of Kanner's autism, as a fundamental problem of active ego-integration, with an insufficient individualization of the child's three bodies (physical, etheric and astral) may need to be modified in order to explain Asperger's syndrome. With the classically autistic child we can quite easily imagine a certain withdrawal, and a consequent failure to achieve a typical incarnation process of soul and spirit into the body. However, it may be necessary with Asperger's syndrome to speak of a too deep, or exaggerated, incarnation process; perhaps a plunging down too strongly into earthly physicality. This would then give rise to the characteristic clumsiness of these subjects, with a singular inflexibility of thought and complete lack of ordinary social understanding and empathy, in spite of their often impressive language and intellectual abilities and specialized talents.

However, a detailed anthroposophical explanation of Asperger's syndrome, and also any specific therapeutic and curative educational exercises to alleviate it, would require further research work.

Self-consciousness and social life

We have come to understand that autism, whether primary or second-ary, follows as the result of a reaction of the child towards existential difficulties of incarnation. When this reaction occurs, before or soon after birth, or in the third year, will be crucial for the child's on-going biographical development. The very word autism, from the Greek word autos meaning 'self,' strongly suggests that the child fails to achieve a normal process of earthly self-development, and therefore of success-ful ego-integration. Historically, with the fall from favour of psycho-dynamic approaches, and the increasing emphasis on behaviourism and organic causes of autism, the real significance of the meaning of the word autism, for the child's inner self-experience, has been eclipsed. As autistic children are unable, or perhaps sometimes unwilling, to come to the developmental experience of a secure and permanent self-consciousness, an active social life with truly interpersonal I – You rela-tionships, is inevitably either absent or, at best, very confused.

There are some other (non-anthroposophical) authors who have also recognized the central significance of the failure of these children to achieve inner self-consciousness. For example, Hobson writes:

> The clinical vignettes of earlier chapters provide a rich
> source of insight into the children's relative lack of self-con-
> sciousness as well as their seeming obliviousness towards
> other people as 'selves' with their own interests, inclinations,
> motives, sensibilities, and so on. In addition, I have already
> linked autistic children's dearth of imitation with their less-
> ened propensity to identify with the attitudes of other people.
> (Hobson 1993, 76)

Jordan and Powell also stress that 'There is, in autism, a failure to develop satisfactorily an *experiencing self.*' (Jordan & Powell 1996, x)

As Leo Kanner originally described, this failure results in the typical outer appearance of 'extreme self-isolation, or aloneness.'

The challenge

These children are, however, not alone. It is, therefore, very much our responsibility to discover ways to bridge the isolation which an autistic reaction has created, and to build interpersonal relationships with these children. Autism is not merely an in-child problem, which perhaps has its roots in some form of brain damage or dysfunction. Anthroposophy views it as a special challenge to develop deepened, empathetic relationships with people who have encountered major difficulties on their particular path towards incarnation. To form such evolving relationships is indeed the foremost task of Curative Education based on anthroposophy. It is of the greatest curative and therapeutic importance to recognize that each child, whatever their behaviour, has a real transcendent spiritual being, and this stands firmly at the heart of curative education (Hansmann 1992, 17). This clear and objective recognition of the child's true being can then help to give the child's soul new forces of strength and courage with which to cross the threshold from the spiritual pre-natal state to the human social world. This is where ethical and moral capacities have to be newly acquired in each incarnation (Steiner 1972). We could, therefore, say that each earthly life enables the individual to realize some part of their full human potential, precisely by facing up to life's challenges and obstacles.

10. New Ways Forward

The New Image of Man

The new way in which we have come to understand childhood autism in this book has evolved over time, based firmly on anthroposophy's Image of Man. This image is multifaceted and differentiated, and yet forms a holistic and consistent totality. Centrally, it takes account of the fundamental human threefoldness of body, soul, and spirit, and of the relationships of these realities to the physical, material world on one hand, and the spiritual, non-material world on the other. The human soul as intermediary, is the dynamic scenario where influences from both spheres of existence mix and mingle, and it is here that experiences unfold, both in the drama of daily existence and in the course of our individual biographical development.

In any comparison of the anthroposophical interpretation of autism with other mainstream explanations, it is always essential to try to identify exactly which image or model of the human being underpins the explanation. Furthermore, within any particular model it may be possible to focus at different levels, such as the biological or psychological (Happe 1994). Clearly, different interpretations of autism are likely to emerge from a predominantly biological or behavioural model of man, as compared to a largely psychodynamic perception in which the importance of inner soul-states and dynamic relationships between people is emphasized.

The anthroposophical model is clearly inclusive, rather than one-sidedly exclusive. It fully recognizes the level of biological processes, (underpinned by the physical and etheric organization), and also the psychological levels of consciousness within the soul (underpinned by the etheric, and especially the astral organization). In addition, it acknowledges the spiritual level, (underpinned by the ego), on which we encounter the unique being of ourselves and others.

We have argued in this book that a holistic, anthroposophical perspective, is able to provide us with a more complete understanding of autism than is to be found at the present time in literature, which emphasizes the biological, organic view of autism. This view is, however, not contradicted by the anthroposophical perpective, provided that the organic is seen as one level of explanation, and is not accepted as the be all and end all.

The same proviso applies if we focus on the child's cognitive faculties at the psychological level, as currently done by Theory of Mind researchers (see Chapter 9), who suggest that the autistic child often appears to be mind-blind with regard to his own mind, and to the minds of others (Astington 1994). The anthroposophical model can throw light on this particular problem, through an understanding of the differentiated functioning of the four higher senses. However, through anthroposophy we do not only encompass a variety of different levels within the totality of the human being, but also, and more importantly, we are led to a recognition of the child's essential being. The child's individual spiritual being, (the ego), is not sufficiently, if at all, acknowledged by mainstream models of man, not even on the psychodynamic level (Lievegoed 1993). It is precisely the awareness of the real being of the child, which underpins curative education, and the wide choice of interventions which this generates. Therefore, the Image of Man gives us the necessary spiritual-scientific foundation for new ways of both understanding and alleviating autism.

New research

There is no known cure for autism, and indeed a search for a cure may well be misguided because it is not a sickness in any simple sense, but our knowledge of its causes and how to intervene to help the child and family is growing rapidly in a period of unprecedented research activity and public interest. (Trevarthen *et al* 1996, 3)

The anthroposophical interpretation of autism, and the attitudes and interventions which curative education makes available, deserve to be fully included in this current and on-going research work. There is an urgent need to critically examine the uniqueness of the anthroposophical contribution. However, it requires further study and research in order to describe, and investigate in detail, the physiology, functioning, genesis and development of the total sense organism. The developmental correspondences between the four higher and the four lower senses, which are clearly an essential component in the anthroposophical interpretation of autism, could constitute an extensive and exciting, new research area. As König (1984) indicated, we have hardly begun to explore thoroughly, or to differentiate between the three higher senses of word, thought and ego which Steiner originally described (1981 & 1990b).

Another area which begs investigation, and which is central to the anthroposophical model, is the development of typical self-cognition in the young child. Only when this is more thoroughly understood shall we be better able to confirm the importance of that inner awakening to the self, and to self-referencing through language.

> It is not yet possible to provide an adequate account of early 'self'-development in autistic children ... (Hobson 1993, 76)

Although Hobson may be correct, it has to be admitted that such an account would be of central importance to the understanding of the asocial behaviours of these children. Linked to this theme of self-cognition is the autistic child's sensitive peripheric awareness which, in terms of curative interventions, generally calls for a correspondingly indirect and gentle approach. More generally, the nature of cognition and thinking in relation to the development of self, should certainly be examined further.

> Just as the colour-blind see only differences of brightness without colour qualities, so someone who lacks intuition sees only unconnected perceptible fragments. (Steiner 1992, 64)

Steiner's remark is indicative of the precise situation in which autistic children so often find themselves in. This appears to be clearly corroborated by autobiographical accounts of recovering autistic individuals who have struggled to make coherent sense of their sensory perceptions (Grandin 1986; Williams 1992).

Yet another essential research theme which autism highlights is an investigation into the deeper nature and important developmental role of imitation, as it has been referred to in this volume.

> The first thing to note is the general agreement that autistic children demonstrate abnormal delay and limitation in their imitation of others. (Hobson 1993, 73)

As we showed in Chapter 9, this delay and limitation is evidence of the lack of early ego-integration and individualization in these children.

Finally, an area that urgently warrants special attention is that of how to arrive at exact differential-diagnoses, with correspondingly appropriate curative educational measures, for primary and secondary forms of autism. Sahlmann's (1969) initial observations and researches into the identification and treatment of children who have a secondary autism due to an underlying primary aphasia, should be developed further. In this respect it is not sufficient, either diagnostically or in terms of effective individual interventions, to simply place a child on the broad autistic spectrum, without also making specific reference to any other accompanying disabilities or impairments (Wing 1993).

From the previous chapters, it is clear that the anthroposophical model of autism does generate important avenues for valuable research, including practical implementations in the variety of curative education interventions. Although curative centres aim to provide an integrated holistic environment, this does not mean that the effects of specific types of intervention cannot be investigated and monitored. Clearly, it is important to develop this kind of evaluative research so that clearer differentiations of progress, in relation to specific measures, can be seen. One obvious difficulty in ascertaining the effectiveness of a specific intervention when conducted over six months or even longer, is to know to what degree natural processes of maturation have contributed to any progress which has been observed. Therefore when specific interventions, such as curative eurythmy, art therapy or

lower sense exercises, can be implemented intensively, over comparatively short periods of time, with the child's responses clearly monitored, it should be much easier to evaluate their actual effectiveness.
However, the specific relationship between child and educator in curative education is a central and inclusive factor in whatever therapy or
intervention is employed.

New moral issues

The whole subject of interventions, whether anthroposophical or otherwise, is based on a fundamental assumption that it is justifiable, and
indeed morally right, to try to alleviate and, if at all possible, cure
autism. This assumption is implicitly underpinned by the notion that
the differences which autistic children exhibit in their behaviour, are
deviant from the normal child, and socially unacceptable. It follows,
therefore, that we should do everything possible to socialize and nor-
malize these children, and this necessitates some form of intervention.
Exactly what type of intervention may be applied to a particular
autistic child depends upon a number of factors: the latest fashion
(Facilitated Communication; Auditory Integration Training; or Bio-
chemistry); parents' perceptions and understanding of their child; the
resources on offer etc. We could however question this whole line of
thinking and, from an ethical and anthroposophical perspective, ask if
there are deeper reasons than the goal of *normalization*, for wanting to
change autistic children?

Rudolf Steiner questioned the whole notion of *normality*, when speaking of the child's observable life of soul expressed in its various behaviours.

> This life of soul, which can show itself in varied expressions
> and manifestations, may be normal or it may be abnormal.
> But now the only possible grounds we can have for speaking
> of the normality or abnormality of the child's life of soul, or
> indeed of the life of soul of any human being, is that we have
> in mind something that is normal in the sense of being aver-
> age. There is no other criterion than the one that is custom-
> ary among people who abide by ordinary conventions...
> (Steiner 1972, 17)

Steiner then pointed out that when people apply this criterion, based entirely on what is average or typical, they may readily *intervene* with children who have been judged as *abnormal*.

> When they have in this way ascertained the existence of
> 'abnormality,' they begin to do — heaven knows what! —
> believing they are thereby helping to get rid of the abnormality,
> while all the time they are driving out a fragment of genius!

Steiner goes on:

> We shall get nowhere at all by applying this kind of criterion,
> and the first thing the doctor and teacher have to do is to
> reject it and get beyond the stage of making pronouncements
> as to what is clever or reasonable, in accordance with the
> habits of thought that prevail today. (Steiner 1972, 17)

I have quoted Steiner at length to show that he did not accept the concept of superficial normalization, seen in terms of individuals conforming to expected, average standards of behaviour.

Steiner claimed that any interventions must be thoroughly grounded on a deepened understanding of child development that went far beyond superficial observations and judgments. Therefore, he described the nature of the child's real spiritual being; the processes of incarnation into the threefold bodily organization; the individualization of the child's model, inherited, body; and even spoke of karmic necessities and reincarnation.

Steiner repeatedly emphasized the moral tenor which should underlie any interventional methods, and educators were called upon to have reverence and respect for the child's real being above all else. In a sense, the child's own being could tell them what needed to be done, in each individual case, but this required educators to consciously develop their powers of empathy.

As our understanding and appreciation of the autistic person's experience grows and deepens, for example, helped by biographical accounts (Williams 1992 and 1994; Grandin 1986; Barron 1993; Sellin 1995), so our own judgments and expectations can change considerably and positively.

New relationships

A purely organic explanation of autism, which puts the source of the problem firmly in the child, is unlikely to do justice to the role of relationships in contributing to the degree of autism seen in different situations, with a particular child. The case studies with James and Roger, clearly indicate that increased contact and communication was achieved through the implementation of curative educational attitudes and exercises which recognized the inner dynamics between educator and child — thus achieving a reduction in autism.

One of the most difficult aspects of living with these children is their seeming indifference and disaffection. This is particularly poignant for those who have a close family connection with them, as is apparent in published parental accounts (Hocking 1990; Kaufman 1976; Lovell 1978). The educator must search for deeper reasons for the child's behaviour, while maintaining a definite warmth of soul and respect for the child.

Steiner gave specific indications and guidelines for the self-education of the educator, to enable them to develop relationships of the right ethical and moral quality.

> So long as the teacher meets the situation with any kind of
> bias, so long as it can arouse in him irritation or excitement
> — so long will he remain incapable of making any real
> progress with the child.(Steiner 1972, 41)

Instead of inner irritation towards the child's difficulties or responses, the educator has to develop a conscious calmness and composure so that the phenomenon he encounters becomes an objective picture.

> Once this has come about, the teacher is there by the side of
> the child in a true relationship and will do all else that is
> needful more or less rightly. (Steiner 1972, 41)

The despair, frustration and disappointment which an autistic child can arouse within someone who very much wants to help, underlines the considerable challenge posed by the type of rigorous self-education which Steiner expected curative educators to earnestly pursue.

The development of new relationships is furthered by the holistic context in which curative education is practised, especially in those centres that have residential provisions. The relationships between children with different social abilities, is often of great therapeutic value and benefit. While this might perhaps also be seen in schools which only cater for autistic children, the exacerbation of the autistic environment that is inevitably formed by such specialized provision, may not be able to generate the diversity and social enrichment which is available in a more holistic setting. This is not a criticism of the special relationships which educators can form with their pupils in schools specifically for autistic children, but simply contrasts the differing environmental resources on offer.

New knowledge

Anthroposophy, as presented by Rudolf Steiner in his books and lectures, is described as a path of knowledge. It calls upon those who meet it to begin to actively exercise their own faculties of knowledge. Although a critical and questioning mind is certainly required in studying anthroposophical literature, careful self-observation is also needed to guard against the limitations and narrowness of perception resulting from preconceived notions and prejudices. An openness for something new, and perhaps unusual at first sight, is required even of the seasoned scholar.

Anthroposophy is neither a religion nor a new faith. It is a spiritual-scientific way of coming to a new and detailed understanding of evolving human beings, and their relationship with the evolving universe. Spiritually, both mankind and our planet are viewed as intimately and inextricably linked in their past and future developments (Steiner 1989). Central to this new evolutionary understanding and perception, is the knowledge of the profound and transformative intervention of the Christ-Impulse in earthly existence. This impulse has a direct relationship with the development of human ego-consciousness and the process of individualization, seen both historically and in each individual biography (Steiner 1976b). Steiner's spiritual research revealed this relationship as an objective evolutionary reality, quite irrespective of peoples' preferred beliefs or opinions.

In the fourfold constitution of the human being, it is the spiritual ego which enables the complex processes of transformation, metamorphosis and individualization to come about during incarnation into the physical body. However underlying this is the working of the Christ Impulse, and this is very especially the case during the child's first three years of life when the faculties of walking, speaking and thinking are typically achieved (Steiner 1976a). However, this is the same period of childhood in which the symptoms of autism first manifest themselves in children who, for one or the other reason, fail to achieve centred ego-consciousness and active ego-integration.

The new knowledge which anthroposophy provides, enables us to properly acknowledge the real and intact being of each autistic child and this, in itself, is the most far-reaching curative intervention. Through it the child receives both support and encouragement to face the challenges of his earthly existence, painful and difficult as they often are.

Autistic behaviour and state of mind are distinct from the person's real, spiritual being. Anthroposophy, therefore, gives a new cognitive and holistic perspective which, when implemented in curative education, may eventually enable many more autistic children or adults to discover what Donna Williams (1994) felt to be the most important thing she had learned – AUTISM IS NOT ME!

IV

Source Material
from Hans Müller-Wiedemann

11. Early Diagnosis and Aspects of Early Consultation with Parents

The following text is taken from a lecture given to paediatricians in Brixen, Italy, on 5 September 1980. First published in the journal Kinderpsychotherapie, *Volume 4, Biermann, Munich, 1981.*

Part 1

Early diagnosis of autistic children, and the resulting therapeutic attitudes and curative educational efforts, depend essentially on the initial assumptions under which the diagnostic conclusions of the case history and the observations are made. Kanner and Eisenberg viewed early childhood autism as a developmental disturbance of the emotions, emphasizing aspects of communication. Other investigations and theories have been undertaken in the medical-psychological realm, which infer that autism is caused by cognitive disturbances, which can ultimately be traced back to insufficient brain function. As a result, behavioural therapy is directed at the modification of symptoms. However, the biography of the child and their parents is not taken into account.

Another, psychotherapeutical approach, presented primarily by Bettelheim (1967), Ekstein (1973) and Mahler (1968), investigated the manner in which an autistic child first of all communicates with their human environment, or rather, how their communication is disturbed in this respect.

In anthroposophical curative education, autistic children are regarded as possessing a serious handicap in their relationships with the earthly world, which occurs immediately after birth. According to Rudolf Steiner's *Science of the Senses* our perception of the world, which continues to develop after birth, differentiates itself into the experiences of one's own body, surroundings and specifically human environment. In these three areas the autistic child suffers from a disturbed development, and the symptoms that appear early on can express themselves in severe symbiotic disturbances, as well as in fixations with respect to conditions of time and space. There is always a marked disturbance in the use of language, which is independent of the levels of semantic or syntactic abilities.

In the normal development of the child, every perception is directed towards the child, through the knowledge gained through perception, being able to communicate with other people, mainly through the use of language, including non-verbal language. This facility, however, appears largely unavailable to the autistic child.

Interviews with parents regarding their own experiences around the time of the child's conception, show that disturbed communication with the child is central to a diagnosis of early childhood autism. Often we hear the mother saying that before the birth, she had the curious feeling that her relationship with the child was disturbed, and that this feeling developed only after she had felt the child move in the womb. Other mothers report that throughout the pregnancy they had looked forward to the birth, but that afterwards a marked and unexpected lack of relationship followed, often accompanied by an inexplicable fear regarding the future of the child.

These comments reveal the fact that, even before birth, a child has a soul-spiritual relationship with the mother, and that this relationship, after birth, adapts for new, earthly life conditions.

It is crucial to picture the important and dramatic character of this extraordinary change in the incarnation process of the child after birth, in order to understand and assess the symptoms of autistic children.

We shall never understand the autistic child if we start from the viewpoint that the child is born as 'a blank page' and that after birth their human-cultural behaviour is merely imprinted on to them.

Where the adaptation towards an earthly sensory world does not sufficiently occur, mothers often report, as one of their earliest observations, that the child *looked through* her, did not see her at all, so that the mother experienced herself as not perceived by her child. On the other hand, the child, in the course of his development, made use of the mother in an external sense, as if encountering a useful object. These experiences of interrupted symbiosis are early indications of an autistic syndrome.

I should like to leave the question of the cause of autism open, and to proceed with the description of some of the aspects of early symptoms. We should remember that the symptoms described are not the illness itself, but point to a communication disturbance. The child develops symptoms in order to *survive* his earthly environment, and at the same time calls on us to further his maturing of the senses therapeutically. The analysis of sense perceptions, as described by Rudolf Steiner, directs us to begin with the development of the perception of our own body. In the first year of life, the normal child acquires an experience of self, through the upright position, by orienting himself in the forces of gravity, and through his own movement. This existential experience of his own life enables the child to constitute a world of objects, and a shared world of the *you*. For an autistic child already in the first sensory motor phase, the individual relationship with a key person, usually the mother, fails to appear, and the child's attention is directed mainly towards the spatial world.

Active eye contact is disturbed in the first months, or breaks off intermittently later in life, when the child is approached and when he is addressed.

Autistic children are often strikingly quiet, do not cry and do not convey their needs, or they demonstrate fear when touched, looked at, or when moved quickly. This can sometimes be seen when the child's nappies need changing, when early gestures which typically accompany daily communication between mother and child, may not appear.

There is also an absence of curiosity of gaze, of movements of the head and hands. Invitations to imitate do not flow into the movement-organism of the child, and autistic children show anomalies very early on, revealing that reflex behaviour is not developing sufficiently.

By contrast, there is an extreme sensitivity to impressions of movement close by, and to acoustic, visual and tactile stimuli.

The change to earthly nourishment already shows signs of early disturbances, even if the child first accepts the mother's breast: resistance to chewing solid food; phases of constipation; avoiding eye contact when being nursed and when taking nourishment; and, compulsive staring at objects instead of the person concerned. From early on only special foodstuffs are accepted and others are rejected.

The adaption to culturally-provided rhythms of taking nourishment, turning to another person and seeking care, is usually delayed early on, and for a long time. The autistic child has difficulty entering into circadian rhythms, which result in disturbances of the sleeping/waking rhythm.

Furthermore, it is striking, in the first year, that the child does not explore objects and usually does not seek contact by mouth. Later, the exploratory and constructive attitude to play does not occur. Activities of touching and grasping do not develop progressively, the child becomes a *spectator*, lets others act for him and alternates these states with chaotic phases of excitement, especially when too much is demanded from him.

Between the second and third year new symptoms occur which are mostly related to the fact that the autistic child does not succeed, or only partly, in making the world objective; that is, one of objects. Instead, the world of objects remains only a part of the insufficiently structured bodily experiences of the child.

This shows, above all, in the area of language where the child's efforts at speech do not develop into a language of meaning (Ekstein 1980, 102–19). The insufficient objectivity of the world extinguishes the indicating function of language as a decisive medium of increasing communication. As an expression of this, the child's first use of *echolalia* appears. The child does not establish ego-consciousness *vis-à-vis* the non-ego of the world of objects, and does not experience himself as a speaking individual, even when he does speak. Imitation or the beginnings of play do not develop and, at this stage, the first fear caused by change usually starts to appear. This tends to happen when the child is anxious to set up or keep to the same spatial arrangements. There also arises a lack of orientation with regard to happenings in time, demonstrating a disturbed living experience of time.

No habits of communication are formed with reference to common rhythms of life, and this in particular leads to the first serious burdens on the family.

Phases of *being absent,* alternating with restlessness or compulsive fixation on certain objects, appear increasingly around the age of three. The lack of further development in movement by not imitating, now causes stereotypical movements to appear, that are not related to the environment. Paths of successful communication such as pointing, gesturing, and miming fail to appear.

With more damaged children speech does not appear, and the children try to communicate through the *language of their organs.* In normal sensory development, a child increasingly learns to teach the body through a developing *sense of life,* usually resulting in the experience of a sense of self, as well as the release of language and the polarization of self-experience with the perception of another person as another ego.

Thus, the speech disturbances of autistic children and their use of language are closely linked to retarded perception of the other person as an ego. Speech remains only a limited expression of self, occurring as echolalia or, if further developed, as a warding off of demands from the environment. Around the third year, it is especially frustrating for the mother or another person new to the child that they cannot make themselves understood to the child through language.

Early disturbance in making eye contact already indicates later problems in communication through speech with the autistic child. Therefore, monitoring eye contact always plays an important part in the early recognition of autistic children. According to our observation, obtained mostly from mothers, the child either makes no eye contact at all or eye contact decreases the more the child grows into earthly conditions and demands. Looking is an intentional act in which we participate intensely with our ego. The other person must be able to endure this gaze, to place something against it, otherwise eye contact cannot be maintained.

What the normal child learns to place against this is the experience of his own bodily nature, gained through the four lower senses, as a foothold in the world which can be seen by others, *i.e.* from outside. The lower senses are touch, life, movement and balance.

You will have noticed how careful one has to be, when one wishes to make eye contact with a baby in its cradle. You then also see immediately that the therapeutic enforcement of eye contact, as practised for many years by behaviourist therapists, constitutes an inhuman over-powering of the child and his own initiatives. However, the more we assist the child in forming his own body-experiences as experiences of self in the field of the lower senses, the more the child will perceive the gaze of someone else as communication and respond to it.

From this understanding many therapeutical activities have resulted in the early treatment of these children. However, I only wish to point out, that normally, early eye contact between mother and child, usually in the course of the first weeks of life, begins to extend to objects, so that an inter-humanly constituted world of objects develops. In the autistic child, this development is disturbed early on. The establishment of this shared world is, however, the prerequisite for the use of language as a means of reference between people.

Towards the end of the third year problems related to the experience of self in the child, through saying *I,* usually become fully apparent. The autistic child often calls itself *You,* although they are not awake to the ego of the other person as *You.*

Rudolf Steiner showed that the perception of another person as an ego, as well as the perception of their language and thoughts, constitutes a direct sensory experience to which the child, after birth, becomes increasingly awake. Up to the third year, the perception of another's ego as *You* is formative for the child's awakening ego-consciousness, which has consolidated itself through the experience of the non-ego of the world of objects.

Through child development, experiences within the various areas of sense perception are made on different levels of consciousness, and a mere polarization of consciousness and unconsciousness does not suffice for the theory of sense maturation. The connection between fully perceiving the self in the body, the awakening towards the world of objects, and the highest wakefulness in perceiving someone else, must develop in a harmonious relationship which entails a well-developed ability to communicate together with the arising of one's inner ego-consciousness. However, the displacement of perceptive consciousness constitutes a central problem in the diagnosis and therapy of autistic children, and does not exist in this general form in any other handicap (see von Arnim in König 1978).

The autistic child's lack of awakening to the perception of his fellow men, their thoughts, speech and ego-being, represents perhaps the most serious trauma for the relationship between the child and his human environment. When the child only perceives sequences of sound instead of the meaning of words, or only sees the other person as a thing among things, one can understand what this means for the parents of these children, and also perhaps for the therapist. They are not perceived as soul-spiritual beings. The significance of this fact is experienced by the parents, and especially by mothers of autistic children, since the development of communication is a reciprocal relationship, in which the child increasingly perceives the people nearest to him on earth, acknowledges them, and thereby also contributes to *their* development as parents. This is especially clear with the first child of a family. The people nearest to these children become part of the autistic situation, for example, when the child uses the mother as an object for the fulfilment of his wishes and takes her hand in order to do something that he cannot do. As the other person is not being perceived, he or she is manipulated as an object in the environment. This parental experience seems to be representative of early childhood autism. There is no statistically or clinically objective diagnosis, without reference to mutual experiences of communication.

The early symptoms mentioned so far are only indicative of the autistic syndrome if they appear firstly in groups and, secondly, over a prolonged period, and increase according to the dynamics of development, usually towards the third year in cases where early therapy did not take place. Many of the disturbances described, if they occur temporarily or in isolation, can point to critical phases of development in a normal child.

The paediatrician, when first confronted with autistic symptoms, must also consider comparative diagnoses of other developmental disturbances which can occur in the first three years of life, from aetiologies which can cause autistic reactions. Here, one must take into consideration so-called *prenatal* or *perinatal* brain damage, as well as the rather symptomless varieties of encephalitis that can occur in the first three years of life. One should be aware of the barely noticeable changes that may occur after smallpox inoculations, and that show autistic symptoms. Further attention should be paid to early symptoms of deafness, when speech does not develop after the babbling phase. Fundamental disturbances of visual perception, and in hearing and speech, should also be considered. These latter symptoms can only be eliminated over longer periods of observation and with repeated investigations. Moreover, autistic reactions can also appear as a result of prolonged hospitalization, or neglect. These can usually be overcome through a change of environment or therapy, but not always.

Early childhood neuroses, with delayed ego-maturation, which becomes apparent around the third year, can also show symptoms of an autistic reaction.

The *autistic psychopathy* described by Asperger, usually with regard to early symptoms, shows a different course. The primary perceptive ability of a common world-of-action remains, and speech formation is

mostly undisturbed. However, the children shut themselves off in a
world of their own, show intellectual abstract precociousness, and flat
soul-less forms of movement, often with a delayed development of the
total psycho-motor co-ordination. As a rule this pattern only appears
clearly around, or after, the third year, and according to generally available information, relates mostly to boys.

However, isolated symptoms, before three years of age, should not
be seen as a primary declaration of the possible presence of childhood
autism. Therefore, for the purpose of diagnosis and necessary therapy,
several examinations and, whenever possible, prolonged observation
and repeated conversations with parents over a longer period of time
are necessary. Insufficient diagnostic clarification and early advice to
parents, the absence of therapeutic attitudes directed to the development of imitation, and above all, early efforts at conditioning, can
quickly lead to *autistic situations* between child and parents. This then
leads also to the increasing social isolation of the parents and, related
to this, wrong attitudes towards the child. Consequently, the already
problematic inter-human dynamic can be negatively influenced, often
for a long time.

Contrary to Bettelheim's conception, with the children we have
observed and educated curatively over the last thirty years, there seems
to be no direct parental cause of early childhood autism. We must, however, accept that considering the rhythmical relationship that exists from
the start with their child, the parents find themselves in a situation where
the child's disturbed actions and perceptions prevent the creation of a
mutually accepted world. This situation often causes them to despair
with regard to their own role as parents, as they are increasingly forced
to adopt a paedagogical attitude which often demands too much from the
child. The earlier and the more intensively mere behavioural measures
are offered to parents, the more medical doctors and therapists may
themselves become part of the fundamental problem of communication
in the framework of the family. This situation, therefore, requires more
intensive initial work with the parents, which is necessary in the family
situation where, especially if the autistic child is the first child, the relationship between the parents is often difficult. The father can withdraw
after the birth of an autistic child, leaving the mother alone with the child.
In this situation continuing advice and help are therapeutically necessary.

Through his disturbed perception, the autistic child often becomes the mirror of his parents' behaviour and habits of relating. The normal child actively absorbs these impressions, whereas in autistic children there is already a failure of imitation or a weakness of incorporation. The sooner after birth the child's autistic symptoms begin to show, the more fundamentally the decisive developmental steps of the first three years appear to be disturbed. Early diagnosis and courses of therapy are therefore of decisive importance and, above all, support for the people nearest to the child must be provided.

The child's *weakness of incorporation* is certainly not genetically determined and in-born, but nevertheless it is in a certain sense *native* to the family situation. In the mothers of autistic children quite frequently we find a relatively strong verbal-intellectual activity, as part of their lifestyle and relationships. However, the lifestyle of the father, in our experience, is often marked through professional, or extra-professional, special interest in his achievements, which is sometimes fanatically pursued. These parental attitudes are certainly not direct causes but often add to the picture of the family group. In the course of therapy with autistic children it is therefore suggested that the parents' habits of their inner and outer way of life are changed, so that they may become helpful partners in the destiny of their child. With regard to the problems of autistic children, the therapist is also continually called upon to be ready to give up certain habits, which in dealing with a normally developing child remain inconspicuous, since the child can cope actively and in a transforming way with them. However, the inability of transforming the earthly experiences for the autistic child, is in contrast to other handicaps, especially pertinent to autism. Perceptions cannot unfold themselves in the dimension of time; they cannot be incorporated into the child's biography.

So, the need for intensive work with the parents is clear. This is usually prolonged, and takes a positive course when the initially isolated parents discover the curative educator to be actively participating in their situation.

I have tried to give some points of view of the curative educational diagnosis, based on spiritual science, for the early recognition of these children. From this, corresponding therapeutical beginnings can be made, aimed at solving the autistic isolation of child and family, and avoiding continuing damage, through any inappropriate behaviour of the child and his parents.

Part 2

People living with autistic children must realize as soon as possible that the symptoms — such as, contact disturbances with other people, stereotypical behaviour and fixations — are not the illness itself, but desperate efforts of the child to survive in a stressful, chaotic world of sense perceptions and relationships. In this effort, the child's perceptual world, as well as its world of activity, becomes considerably narrower than it is for the normally developing child. Through this situation the original expectations of the parents are also deeply and lastingly disappointed.

A situation arises when the family's rhythms of life are so enduringly disturbed through the child's behaviour, that the child's relationship with the family is reduced to mutual outer dependence and, finally, each only reacting to the other. Increasingly, the parents' ability to gain insight, with regard to their conduct and actions, which might be helpful for their child, is lost. As a result, autistic children are often either challenged too much or too little.

Adopting a number of basic therapeutic attitudes can resolve this kind of situation, while involving a considerable and lasting adaptation of family habits. This appears to us to be the essential first step in therapeutic understanding before any special therapy exercises are implemented, aimed at the specific situation.

Basic Therapeutic Attitudes

1. Autistic children are not just handicapped or badly adjusted — they are injured by a world that is foreign to them. Their symptoms are efforts to find their way in this world within the specific limitations of their ability to relate.

2. Autistic children have a long way to go. Rapid results of adjustment may initially make family life easier. In the long run — and parents must learn to be prepared for this — what matters is the independence which the child achieves in their

relationship with the world, also when this relationship seems different from what we are used to.

3. Nobody can manage the problems of these children alone. Therefore, as parents, look quickly for advice and assistance from other experienced parents, medical doctors and therapists.

4. It is not your personal fault that your child is autistic. As long as you think so you will demand too much from your child because you believe that you have to compensate for something.

5. Rather, create for yourself an attitude which is directed towards the real being of your child, that lies behind the symptoms, and which wants to become healthy. Cultivate this attitude at all times, even when you are not together with the child. It is an injustice to your child if you only direct your attention to the symptoms of his behaviour.

6. As parents discuss your experiences and observations together, so that you can find a common attitude. The child is helped through this, as otherwise one parent is often over-demanded and the other not engaged enough.

7. Autistic children have the inclination to reduce relationships of soul to relationships with objects. Perhaps you are sometimes treated like an object by your child.

8. Try to look for the true soul-spiritual being of your child, behind the symptoms; a being that cannot grasp, or sufficiently penetrate, the physical body as an organ of perception and cognition.

9. Your child has the inclination to replace relationships with the living world of people, with his fascination for gadgets, especially those of a technical kind. Strictly limit the use of tapes, television, computers, technical-didactic toys, etc.

10. What your child needs above all is access to simple human activities in which he can slowly learn to participate. For example, washing-up, laying the table, folding linen, looking after a flower etc.

11. Be critical in the matter of fixed programmes of education and therapy. You should act only after having acquired new therapeutic attitudes towards your child.

12. Above all, you need compassion and loving observation with regard to what you demand from your child, and what you should not demand. As parents you must agree on this, and what happens is ultimately dependent on your mutual understanding of your child. Try therefore, through your observations, to distract the child from an expected act that is socially disturbing or self-destructive, before you say no. Your child is disturbing but he does not want to be so.

13. Plan your day in such a manner that at certain times you can devote yourselves entirely to your child. He needs a rhythm and time when you fully turn to him, and that is reliable. At first do simple things with your child, for example, guide his hand when he puts forks on the table, or when he opens a tap. Go on doing this until he can do some of these things on his own and/or imitates you.

14. Try, in the rhythm of your special times together, to stimulate reciprocal activity. Do not confront your child to begin with, but at first remain behind him, then next to him and then, finally, opposite him. Play reciprocal games, such as, building bricks, saying rhythmically, 'I put a brick down, you put a brick down,' and otherwise, do not talk too much. With such simple games it is not a matter of construction, but of communication. Do not force any eye contact. That will come of its own accord to the extent that the child discovers you as a partner in a joint activity.

15. Do not talk too much or too little with your child. Aim always for an increase in their perception of speaking. Speak simply and with gestures. Avoid intellectual language which has a strong reflective element, as this is at first only a noise to your child.

16. Plan well what you wish to demand from your child as regards language. Do not expect the child to always immediately repeat what you say. In an appropriate situation say

a word to the child and do this repeatedly and regularly, even for days and weeks, without always demanding that they repeat it. Learn to wait without becoming inert.

17. Refer all that is spoken to the ordinary surroundings of the child. Try to increase the child's understanding of simple sentences that express a request, rather than merely the imitation of single words. For example, 'Fetch that ball for me.'

18. Do not correct all the time. At first, allow the child to pass the sausages when they are asked to pass the butter. Initially, relate speech to actions, and later to instructions and objects. Avoid using words and pictures together. Your child may perhaps manage to show the correct card for a word, but they do not know what is depicted. Your child must therefore first learn to live with the words in the actual world before the picture world is opened to him. This transition often occurs suddenly and unexpectedly, at first in only a few isolated situations.

19. Autistic children learn a lot in situations in which they are not confronted. You should take this into account. Autistic children notice more than you might at first assume. Speak softly, and not always from the front but also from behind, for the autistic child is not yet self-assured when confronted by someone. In such situations the child will do or say all kinds of things in order to be left in peace.

20. Do not talk about the child in his presence.

21. Do support every spontaneous meaningful thing the child does, through joining in or through imitating him in confirmation.

22. Try to observe the rhythms of life of your child, the rhythms of sleeping and waking, eating and excretion. These rhythms are always disturbed, and as a result, the child does not appear to be socially adjusted. Try to alter these rhythms slowly to a reliable rhythm, by at first using strictly determined times. In some cases this can take months.

23. Autistic children also need other children, to whom they are often less strange and distressing than adults. Depending on

experience, you must decide between the fourth and seventh year of age whether the child will be educated at home, in a day kindergarten, in another therapeutic setting, or in a residential therapeutic centre outside the family. By this time you have most of the experience necessary for making such a decision. Autistic children do best among other children who are not all autistic. There is no scientifically valid theory of any kind which relieves you of this decision.

24. It is always a matter of your child being seen as an individual, and today there are enough experienced people who can advise you. Of course, these people occasionally have different ideas about what may be right in the situation. In any case what is decided should be specifically related to your child, and not merely follow predetermined theories and models.

Aspects of schooling

1. Because of the autistic disturbance it is not easy to decide on the right kind of schooling for each child. The usual methods of testing do not provide sufficient criteria.

2. Therefore it is necessary to approach the total picture which each autistic child presents with regard to:
   a. ability to meet others,
   b. perceptual areas available to them or in need of development,
   c. their independence relating to impulses of will,
   d. their ability to express themselves in gestures, play, and language,
   e. their ability with regard to visual memory and other essential symbolic activities, such as perception of language.

3. From this it follows that only through prolonged observation in a relevant class situation, can specific ways be found to approach each autistic child.

4. A special factor here is how deeply established are any pathological forms of reaction against the environment, which would prevent the child's openness to learning.

5. Formal programmes of learning must therefore always be tested in relation to the personality of the child.

6. It is necessary, before school age, to establish whether the autistic behaviour of your child has any single determining cause, for instance, hearing damage, specific disturbances of language understanding or speech, or brain damage following an infection or encephalitis.

7. The extent of what can be asked of the child, and the kind of educational method and the therapy, are dependent on such diagnostic clarifications, and you should get advice from an experienced child psychiatrist.

8. The autistic child is, in most cases, a multiply-sensory handicapped child in that he is not able to integrate new sensory impressions in a meaningful way. This is especially apparent when one has the opportunity to live for years with autistic children. Autistic children need small, even very small, classes for their schooling, and, added to this, some single one-to-one lessons, especially at first. These individual sessions cannot be limited to the area of school learning, but must also extend to special curative educational, therapeutic measures. However, the aim must always be that the autistic child becomes more and more able to integrate into the class group.

9. According to our experience the autistic child also needs the presence of differently handicapped children within a class context (Feuser 1980).

10. Autistic children often show special abilities, such as a pronounced local memory, manual-technical skills, and other intellectual semi-talents. This often leads to the one-sided advancement of these talents. In the area of school, however, the aim is to work towards a harmonious, all-round development — above all, the educational-therapeutic cultivation of artistic and manual craft activities.

11. Above all, we should be aware that autistic children, during the course of their school time, and especially at the

beginning of the third seven-year period (around fourteen years of age), go through considerable crises, but that even in these circumstances the ability to learn remains for a long time. However the initial autistic symptoms may change considerably over the course of the school years. Often stereotypical movements and fixations are not so obvious any more, and the child, as he grows older, becomes more open to social relationships with other adults and children. The older the autistic child becomes, the more he wants to grow beyond his initial autistic situation or autistic environment. For this, he also needs other kinds of children and adults than just those in his own family.

12. It is especially important for the autistic child — if it has not been prevented by earlier wrong approaches — that the ability to learn can continue for a long time, and therefore school and therapy should go on until his twenty-first year. Here, it is a matter of fostering the disturbed earth-maturation of the ego. Autistic young people acquire identity especially through the acknowledged contribution they can make in practical activities, their experience of success, and social recognition given to them by others.

13. The autistic child is autistic because he is culturally and socially isolated, through the fact that he cannot initially manage to make the world of his perceptions meaningful.

What is necessary to overcome this isolating situation for the autistic child, is the suport of a therapeutic community of teachers, therapists and parents, and ultimately of society in general.

Therefore in the education of autistic children, the most important aim should be to enable these children to live as people, as freely as possible, albeit handicapped, with other people in community.

12. The Topsy-Turvy World: An Anthroposophical Understanding of Autism in Early Childhood

From a privately published manuscript, Die verstellte Welt – Zum geisteswissenschaftlichen Verständnis des frühkindlichen Autismus, *1970.*

Since autism in early childhood was first described by Leo Kanner and his collaborators in 1943, as a disorder of the affective contact with the environment, a great number of physicians, psychologists, therapists and curative educationalists have tried to come closer to an understanding of this disorder. In 1960, Karl König summed up the findings at that time in two lectures, and he made the first step towards a spiritual-scientific penetration of the phenenomenon. He especially pointed to the disability of these children to imitate. The stages of imitation which unfold and differentiate during the first seven years of life, include the ability of the child to interiorize their human environment and thereby to make it his own.

This phenomenon of human development and learning, which is often not sufficiently acknowledged, signifies nothing other than the early stage of inter-human relationships and recognition. As increasingly demonstrated by a multitude of observations during the last years, autistic children show a profound disorder, which is manifested quite early in life on the level of relationships with the world. The most essential manifestations are summed up as follows:

1. The relationship with another human being is disturbed or lacking altogether. The child does not react to the speech or gesture of the other person, avoids his gaze and sometimes also touch.

2. An autistic child does not experience things within a human space of reference, but in relation to their position in geometric space

(situation, position, relation, form), and strives towards unifor-
mity of spatial object arrangements and sequences in time.

3. If an autistic child can speak, they use words as if they were
   things, in a way which does not include meaning or relationship
   to the environment. The personal pronouns I and you are often
   exchanged. With regard to these linguistic connections G.
   Bosch (1962) published an important study based on phenome-
   nological points of view (see also Rutter 1978; Schopler 1978;
   Kehrer 1978).

Here, then, the basic phenomena are mapped out which, since Kanner's descriptions, have been verified by almost all authors, and which
in all their many variations, show the disturbed relationship of the
autistic child to their surroundings and contemporaries. When we
meet autistic children we have to be clear that their world is not just
deficient to ours, but see that they create a private world in which they
can live, even though this world appears narrowed down to us and, to
begin with, unapproachable.

The spiritual-scientific knowledge of the senses, described by Rudolf
Steiner (1981), differentiates different fields of perceptions, which results
in a realm of higher, middle, and a realm of lower (or body) senses.

These differentiations have proved particularly fruitful for understanding the autistic child, but also for approaching other developmental disorders. I will often refer back to the spiritual-scientific
understanding of the senses in the course of these contemplations
(Steiner 1980; Lauer 1977).

Sensory experience and the development of consciousness

Soon after birth, the autistic child shows behaviour which is often overlooked and which points to their inability to grasp their inter-human
environment. There is no response to maternal care. In the gaze, in
smiling, in the corresponding movement of the arms when the mother
lifts the child from their cradle, every original contact seems to be lacking, which otherwise would make up the richness of the early mother-
child relationship. Mothers who relate instinctively to their child as a
responding soul-being, sense this disorder in pre-verbal relationship.

However, mothers who concentrate chiefly on the bodily needs of the child, often overlook this deficiency, and only notice it later between the second and third year of life when the child does not communicate through gesture or language. These occurrences, which are fundamental to the mother-child relationship, have been the subject of many valuable observations and investigations which all concur in recognizing the significance of early experiences of environment for the entire development of the emotional and recognitional functions.

What happens during the first months of life, belongs to the recurring mystery of archetypal human encounter, by which the ego of the child actively integrates into the surrounding human world and culture and, by way of imitation, makes this world the child's own: part of his body. In this environment, too, belong those things which, for a long time in early childhood, remain objects within the context of inter-human relationships from which they gain their functional significance, and later on, their verbally communicative symbolic content. Among the many phenomena which show the participation of the child with his human environment, it is in the child's smiling that what really matters can best be shown.

Through the child smiling on meeting his mother, a bodily participation with the environment comes to expression, or, through the higher senses the soul-attitude of the mother is experienced. More precisely, the newly born child primarily perceives the given intentions of the mother, still far removed from the ability to objectify the outer bodily form of the mother. This encounter finds a response in the plasticity of the body, which appears in the expression of smiling. As the child experiences itself in the mother, so the mother experiences herself in the responding smile of the child.

We notice here one of the many encounters of early childhood, which we can describe as the formative circle of mutual human acknowledgement which, as we will see, is similar to the instinctive behaviour of animals, and yet is fundamentally different. Child and mother awaken to themselves, and thereby construct a mutual environment in the process of human relationships. Revealed in this process is a stage of imitation first described by Rudolf Steiner, the primary happening of which lies in the sensory activity of the child meeting the empathy of the mother. Basic to this is an active process of seeking and finding in the child, which E.H. Erikson simply and truthfully called hope, which:

...grows out of the unbroken early trust and mutuality and
produces a feeling of fitting into the personal and cultural
environment ... As a consequence this hope is always filled
again through all those rituals and ritualising which are
engaged against the feeling of forsakenness and hopelessness
and, instead of this, promise throughout life a mutual recognition face to face until we recognize that we are recognized.
(Erikson 1968)

Child psychology has only, in the last twenty years, started to recognize and understand the active achievement of the child in integrat-
ing himself, or participating, in the mutual and also personal world,
and has thereby focused on the intentionality of the soul-spiritual centre of the being of the child. In a treatise on the essential aspects of
autism in early childhood, J. Lutz has pointed to ego-activity and its
weakness in autistic behaviour, by clearly showing it as the:

... individual kernel of the human being... Through the
activity of this kernel the human being grasps the world,
becomes conscious of himself in the world, and senses his
connection with spiritual powers. (Lutz 1968)

The forms of early inter-human encounter, from the morning greet-
ing by the mother to the moment she says goodnight, which Erikson
called ritualizing, help integration into the shared environment,
including tuning-in with the child's bodily experiences in this world.
There is an interaction between the experiences of the surrounding
world and the bodily experiences of the child, in thirst, hunger, positions and movements, and also tension within organs. The small child
perceives all of these phenomena with the lower senses more intensively than later on and, every time, these expressions of the child's
perceptions are met with the tuned-in behaviour of the mother as a
response.

In these early stages, the child does not yet experience his body as
his own. It is, to begin with, bound up with the presence of the mother,
and the bodily functions which are not yet organized instinctively, still
require a long time of body and soul care by the mother. At stake are
time-giving inter-human rhythms which are, from the outset, not

grasped by autistic children. Therefore, these children are thrown back on to their own bodily existence quite early, which has not yet achieved an organized self-recognition.

In normal development the experience of the child's own body as a personal world, and the perception of the other human being as an independent person, occurs through the active grasping and taking hold of the world of things. This begins in the first year of life as a process leading to the objectifying of the world, and signifies a gradual alienation from the closed mother-child relationship. The archetypal reciprocity of encounter and the early connection of body experience and environment experience, as described above, undergoes a change. The world of things, of objects, transmitted by the senses of seeing, hearing, smelling and tasting, appears increasingly dominant in the child's consciousness, and consolidates the self-consciousness of the child *vis-à-vis* the world. The grasping and seeing of the world of things in the surroundings signifies a crossing point in the child's development. He experiences his body as an object among objects, and begins to construct his own world over and against his surroundings, and this remains then unmistakenly his own for all his life on earth. The normally developing child begins to be able to experience 'having a body and at the same time being a body'(see von Arnim in König 1966). Simultaneously with increased objectifying, perception of the surroundings begins to change from its original joint action to a pictorial recognition. The imitating joint action in the human world remains up to the seventh year. In this the ego seizes itself as a self *vis-à-vis* its surroundings. Rudolf Steiner described in detail this process of increasing individualization through increasing pictorial conceptions in the first year of life. Jean Piaget described in countless observations the change from the world of imitation to the world of images (Piaget 1962).

The non-achievement of objectifying in autistic children, makes the world of objects appear as belonging to their own bodies. The objects do not assume the character of a challenge to deal with actively; they do not become subjects of verbal references, nor do they engage the conceptual-pictorial activity of thinking. One can describe the gravity of this disorder as a limitation of the space of freedom, which normally, and in contrast to animals, consists in the manifold availability of the world of objects for action and play, for talking about them with somebody, and for forming mental images and memories.

Following the spiritual-scientific investigations of Rudolf Steiner (1970), we have to assume that the lack of objectifying of the world, has its roots in the disability of the autistic child to arrive at a conceptual judgement of perception in relation to the reality of the world of objects. This would normally express itself in consciousness as an acknowledgement that something *is,* relatively independent of myself, and yet in relation to myself and to other people as a common world reality. The fact that the classical natural scientific trend of thought equates the concept of reality with matter, shows that science has omitted to recognize this concept as a perceptual judgement. This has thereby caused the component of objectifying in child development to be overlooked, which we then meet in the autistic child as a disorder.

The role of the lower senses

In living with autistic children, it is clear that such a child does not discover the sphere of co-existence. Rarely is the gaze of such a child directed at another human being, his movements remain unrelated to the intentions of another person in gesture or expression, and the things of common use are not integrated into the same human space of relations and meaning; they are not objectified. We gain the impression that the autistic child, because of this primary disability, does not discover the world of images and pictorial memories, and cannot freely dispose of these within his soul. Instead, biographically irrelevant stereotypic forms of memory arise, often bound to space and locality.

The process of individualization, towards the seventh year of life, is only partially achieved, and therefore the bodily gestalt, facial expressions and movement patterns, remain almost unchanged up to the seventh year. Movement patterns and gestalt achieve some personal limited dynamic of habit, which consist in the manipulation of objects, and take place in space apart from human encounter.

For the autistic child things gain significance in space according to their position, size and form. The intentions of the child aim at creating compulsively, through rites and numbers, a closed space which renders him some security. This is quite different from the certainty of self-assuredness, brought about through recognized and remembered images, or through verbally transmitted contents which mediate the double experience of time, as past or as an opportunity for freely planning the future.

We can understand this closed space as one in the present; it is unhistoric and abstract, in as much as it is cut off from the fullness of possible human changes, especially of any involvement with, or an openness to, other people. It becomes a dead space without development. An autistic child is therefore adjusted to the spatial arrangements of things. These children try to establish a closed space which is perfect in the arrangement of things, simulating security, yet excluding inter-human intentions and meanings. Typical is the behaviour of one of our children who continuously places toy bricks in straight lines or circles. At mealtimes he suddenly jumps up and places his plate in front of a child at another table the moment that this child hands his plate to his group mother. The order of the circle has been disturbed, an opening has appeared, and the boy rushes to repair the circle with his own plate.

Any changes and additions, and sometimes even the intentional gaze of another person, can be experienced with horror and panic, as disturbances of this ordered environment. G. Bosch discussed the question of intersubjective objectification, which means that a thing can be seen differently through the eyes of another person. Bosch concludes correctly, that the autistic child mainly shows interests which do not require extensive objectification within a common world, or only to a small degree.

We also experience with the autistic child other characteristic ways of dealing with things. Synonymous with the concept of fixing or determining a position in space, there seems to be a special kind of sensory experience which produces an objectifying along the lines of classical physics. This reduces the world to identities of number and measure. Such data in space, that is, pseudo-facts, are taken as the starting point, which then excludes the element of reality. Autistic children deal similarly with the spoken word, which is reduced to a verbalization independent of any context, and which is then applied in all circumstances.

With this concept of fixing it should be made clear that this is a specific divergent structuring of the world of perceptions. We further notice that their manipulation of things, as well as their own body movements, shows a rhythm which, as in mechanisms, works as a closed system. The rhythmic movements of their own body-object can extend without transition to: the manipulation of light-switches or water taps; the compulsory opening and closing of doors; the continuous fitting together of shapes, such as in jigsaw puzzles; the piecing together and taking apart of mechanical, and often very complicated, items; repetitions of tunes; or the picking up again of the same activity, in which the repetition might take minutes or months. The attention of these children seems drawn into a magic circle of the relationships of size, number and weight, and the child seeks to make them real.

In this phenomenon too, we find the important rhythm of temporal-historic, inter-human relationships and ritualizations, games with objects, and the life rhythm of sleeping and waking, turned into something spatial. A kind of limited rhythm of self, which is non-pictorial and lacking history, replaces and annuls interpersonal communication. Generally, rhythmic happenings in the normal development of early childhood are shown as the phenomenon of encounter: in glancing and turning away, in grasping and letting loose, in taking possession of and yielding an object, and many other rhythmically bound and repetitive achievements. However, the reduction of the rhythmic circumference leads, on the one hand to movement and action stereotypes, and, on the other hand, to a compulsory getting fixed in sensory experiences and to the obsessive need to repeat. Later, in the development of these children, these repetitions become habitual. The discovery of such disturbances of rhythm seems important, and significant therapeutic consequences have followed with regard to shaping of the life-rhythms for these children.

A third phenomenon, which we observe time and again, refers to the relationships of balance. One of our children went through a phase in which he placed all kinds of objects along the edge of a table just preventing them from falling down, or, he placed toy bricks on top of each other to a height which no other child could have achieved!

We have also discovered the preference of these children for symmetry. One of our children, for many days, took all the shoes out of the wardrobe and separated the left ones from the right ones, put the right ones on one side of the passage, and the left shoes on the other side. The toes were placed exactly opposite each other! Such symmetric arrangements can also be found in the placing of toy bricks or colour-patterns, or in mirror patterns which, starting from the centre, are done with bricks or crayons. Another child, when asked to push in a drawer, pulled out all the other drawers to exactly the same extent, so that they agreed mathematically. In this instance, a spatial-geometric exact arrangement was obsessionally satisfied by sacrificing the functional meaning of a drawer, *i.e.* for pulling out or pushing in.

Finally, another behaviour should be mentioned which supplies further hints as to the kind of world an autistic child constructs, and which is linked with the sense of touch. Frequently we see autistic children observe objects such as a chair, from all sides. With their gaze they follow the structure of the chair exactly, along the back, around the seat; they turn the chair round, creep under it, as if they wanted to touch all its spatial dimensions — angles, lines, whether straight, round or diagonal — with their eyes. When one watches such a child intensively, one can experience how the sensory activity of seeing does what is otherwise done by the sense of touch. The sense of touch, however, only informs us of the boundary of our own body. The autistic child therefore misses out the image-experience and meaning of an object, and only recognises the spatial aspect in an autonomous, closed space.

When we consider these dimensions of the autistic world, we can conclude that this world is limited to the experience of the lower senses — the senses of balance, own-movement, life and touch. Throughout the first seven years of normal child development, these four senses provide the perception of our own body as self-world which comes into relationship with the world of things and the human environment. They thereby allow the self to become aware, as ego, within its bodily existence and within a differentiated world. However, in the autistic child, the self-world of the body is not individualized, but instead is fused unhealthily together with his perceptions of the environment. The autistic child distorts the experience of his own body as an intact self-experience, as well as his encounter with the environment. He is imprisoned in the world of the lower senses which invades the field of the middle senses — the senses for perceiving the environment — and does not allow these to unfold. Edmund Husserl maintains that experiences gained by solipsistic means are irreconcilable with experiences made by others. [SOLIPSISM: from the Latin *solus* (alone) and *ipse* (self). Originally used as a term for practical egoism, solipsism was used in the late nineteenth century from the theoretical view that only I and my experiences exist.] He pointed out that:

> Free from the need of confirmation through the other person
> and independent from inter-subjective objectification, are
> only such experiences which are objectified by logic-mathe-
> matical laws.

According to Husserl, only things based on measurement, number
and weight, justify themselves; that is, all logically, mathematically confirmed constitutions carry their objectification within themselves, and
are independent of place, time and human fellowship (Bosch 1962).

In comparing this with the behaviour of the autistic child, the following should be considered. The ability to think in abstract terms is usually only achieved at the end of the second seven-year period of
development, and is based on, and maintained by, a confirmed experience of the environment. This ability is not primarily present in the field
of sensory perception, but rests on the secondary formation of concepts
based on the matured lower senses: namely the senses of life, movement, balance and touch. In the autistic child, however, these secondary
forms of thinking become the content of primary world-structuring by
means of the lower senses. The autistic child actually seems to awaken
too early with regard to the environment, and is then unable to make the
step into the world of images and inter-human relationships.

Rudolf Steiner was the first person to point to the connection
between our body perception given through the lower senses and
mathematical-geometrical thinking. He described at length how geometrical activity, the rhythms of number sequences, the laws of conclusion and logical judgment in relation to the laws of space in
general, have evolved from the experiences made through the four
lower senses, which then appear as laws in the thinking consciousness.
In contrast, however, the perceptions of the lower senses remain
largely unconscious. Indeed they actually become unconscious during
the first year of life, in order to give the sense of sight, as well as the
other environment senses — sight, taste, smell and temperature — the
opportunity to construct the outer world and, in conjunction with the
higher senses, to also construct the social world with others.

We may then assume that the autistic child becomes too awake in
the lower senses whose primarily spatial qualities of recognition are
given scope among the environmental senses, especially in seeing.
Thereby the environment becomes a one-sided, spatial world which

cannot be communicated unless first turned into secondary mathematical or geometric concepts and conceptions.

A six and a half year old autistic girl impressively demonstrated her transition from a closed self-world towards the mutual co-existent world. At the age of four, this child still shows all the signs of a severe autistic contact disturbance, but she has slowly learned to enter the world of images and speech. These tender relationships to the co-existent world are still insufficiently developed, and the child still always makes her spatial security arrangements. For example, on the abacus she arranges the beads in different rows. The uppermost and longest she calls father, he is the tallest in the family; followed by granny in a slightly shorter row; then mother in the next row; followed by the older sister; then herself, and little brother. The human relationships here find expression according to size, which have, however, already taken on symbolical character representing the co-existent world. Here too, disturbances appear in the experience of time; that is, the age differences among the members of the family shown as spatial constructions.

Our observations serve to show that the autistic child fashions a closed spatial world for himself, to which the child alone belongs, and which alone promises security. This world represents a self-world that cannot be shared. This world is derived from the logical, mathematical form of thinking, underpinning a counting and calculating modern science, which today manifests itself increasingly as a determining factor in culture in the realm of technology. The intention behind it is perfection: a closed system, with the exclusion of any interference, of inter-subjective spaces of relationships; a world which functions and is tied, with the presumed and illusory expectation of security and complete control. It appears the more secure the more intensively it can be manipulated, without interfering with environmental intentions. This world has to be created for eternity, without making any inter-human claims; documenting the objectification of human self-forgetting. The appearance of autistic children in our present civilization therefore seems to us to mirror the culture stemming from the nineteenth century and reaching into our time, that of a natural scientific technological world view governed by logic and outer necessities.

Incomplete incarnation

Everyone who seeks lively contact with the autistic child asks the question: What brings such a child to live in a world closed to others, and how can we learn to understand the origin of his behaviour?

This question becomes ever more urgent, and the answers to date are contradictory and insufficient. At the present stage most of the presented theories attempting to recognize the causes, cannot be upheld. This disorder is neither genetically nor biologically inherited, nor, in the cases of most of the children can brain-organic disturbances be proved. More importantly, it is generally accepted that culturally and socially-determined characteristics of the parents, and related aspects of their mismanagement, while revealing a situation of destiny, cannot be the primary cause of it. Kanner and Eisenberg pointed to a frequent, yet not always present, parental pattern of behaviour which they characterized as: 'the mechanising of human relationships,' or the 'unconditional surrender to the principles of perfectionism.'

Such parents seem to take the 'obsessional sticking to rules and prescriptions' as a 'substitute for joy in life … Mother and child live in bodily proximity and yet move in different spheres' (Fischer 1965).

We have begun to assume that these children forgo the normal adjustment to the human, cultural co-existing world. Not only do parents receive their child but, and spiritual-science points to this, the newly born child is from the beginning actively engaged and seeks human connections in an intentionality which has its origin prenatally. The failure which seems specially important where the autistic child is concerned, is the lack of an intentional attitude. After birth, the child can recognize the pre-natal archetype of their human environment by way of remembering, and can open up to it. Rudolf Steiner exemplifies this attitude by pointing to the phenomenon of imitation:

> The child only continues, when entering through birth into physical existence, what he has experienced in the spiritual world before conception. As a human being one lives then within the beings of a higher order, and one does all the things which emanate as impulses from the beings of this higher order. One is then to a much higher degree an imita-

tor, because one is at-one with those beings whom one imitates. Then one is placed outside into the physical world.
This is, so to say, the first birth, and one continues the habit
to be at one with one's surrounding. This habit embraces the
beings who, as human beings, appear in the surrounding and
whom one imitates. It is a much greater blessing for the
child, the more he need not live in his own soul, but the more
he can live in the soul of the environment, in the soul of his
fellow human beings. (Steiner 1997)

This symbiosis can however go wrong, when the child omits, by
forgetting, the real intentions of imitating this living together. Subse-
quently the world of conceptual images, arising after the first objectification, although it may partially succeed, will also suffer mishap.
These conceptual images derive from pre-natal formative forces and
are not only a reflection of a physical-sensory, thought-out world
(Steiner 1996).

When we consider this primary failure we are then forced to look
to the world of the autistic child, which is not composed of fellow
human relationships of confidence, hope and security, or constructed
as a cultural-historic world. Instead the child becomes unhealthily
awake in a field of earth forces, which the normal child dimly experiences through the lower senses. This field too is one of destiny, one
which is initially not conscious to the child but which influences his
development. The normal human child realizes its destiny through
action and trust, and through encountering a co-existent world (Poppelbaum 1959). The autistic child, however, fails to accept the world
of destiny of his own doings and actions, which the normal child does
through the guidance of spiritual powers, and instead constructs a
closed, spatially-bound world granting him pseudo-security. His destiny cannot unfold because he rigidifies within the wakefulness of his
lower senses in relation to measure, number and weight, what should
only be undertaken as tasks later on in the secondary life stage of free
formation of concepts.

These children therefore become awake in a reversal of consciousness of incarnation directions with regard to the sleeping intentions of
destiny working in the life of will, and omit the wakeful consciousness
of self within the sensory circumference of human fellowship.

H.E. Lauer, following the indications of Rudolf Steiner, has described how in the lower senses cosmic laws from pre-natal life reveal
themselves. In early childhood these experiences become bodily, and
thereby also unconscious, in order to re-appear later on as mathematical and geometric laws. The autistic child, instead of forgetting, seems
to remember these systems of laws and to construct a self-world which
falls prey to the laws of space. By failing to incarnate into human fellowship and relationships and forgetting himself, but instead remembering and awakening in cosmic pre-natal laws, the autistic child omits
to grasp his own body as bearer of action and destiny.

In order to become a self-conscious, active person, a dullness in the
lower senses has to develop, and an awakening at the hand of the
objects of the environment. In the normal development of early childhood, true self-motivated action and the distanciating from things only
appears after the accomplishment of objectification. Then the child
experiences himself as acting, and realizes that his body's manifestation in acting, takes place within a co-existent world which can see
and experience him. This means that also the body becomes an object
among others, when the objectification is achieved in the course of the
second year of life (see Piaget). The absence, more or less, of the
experience of the own body as existent, also for others, is shown in the
life with autistic children in impressive experiences. We notice how
vulnerable such a child can be when, through a sudden appearance, a
confrontation, a gaze, or touch by another person, the child feels
exposed; so that one can gain the impression that many of the behaviour patterns of the autistic child are geared not to be seen. To be seen
is, however, an essential phenomenon of fellow-human relationships,
by which the ego in its revelation through the body, has to prove itself
and becomes subject to correction. The child-individuality who
reveals himself in action, recognizes himself not only in the dull perception of the body senses, but also through the gaze and the relating
attitude of the other person. In the early childhood relationship to the
co-existent world a decisive role is played by the environment, by the
way in which it responds to the first revelations of his own child-like
motivation. When we succeed in awakening in the autistic child even
the smallest motivated action within an inter-human situation, then an
important step has been done for the first experience of his own path
of destiny, and for opening up his self-world which is hemmed in by

objects. Autistic children, in the first phase of therapy, often try for a long time to avoid the interest of another person in relationship to their own actions. The growing tolerance of the child to be taken seriously, as a being acting in space, presents an important process in relationship forming. Bettelheim, in his biographical-analytical monograph on autism, has been able to demonstrate just this process, at the hand of some children, very convincingly (1967).

In conclusion, a path to an understanding of autism has been shown, such that our grasp of this development in early childhood requires the insights available through the modern science of the spirit — anthroposophy. The aim of this attempt is to render the curative educational encounter with the autistic child in accordance with destiny; to deepen it, and foster a curative educational attitude, which, in the long course of development of these children, opens up a life in a human world which is common to us all.

13. The Curative Educational School: Observations and Aims

Part 1

Taken from a report to the first German Federal Council for Help for the Autistic Child, given in December 1972. It was revised and printed in the conference proceedings of the same council.

When, at the beginning of the fifties in the Camphill schools in Scotland, under the leadership of Dr Karl König, we began to occupy ourselves with autistic children, we still called them, in accord with a widely used Anglo-Saxon concept, pre-psychotic children. These pre-psychotic children formed a large group which in treatment, care and education, we tried to distinguish from the so-called psychotics; that is, those with early childhood schizophrenia. Since then we have learned to observe and progress with these children through curative education. A great number of specific therapies and teaching methods have been developed, yet one cannot say that a model therapy or curriculum has evolved which would be applicable for all such children. Nevertheless, since that time we have tried to admit children in our schools with early childhood autism, and to further them in every possible way.

From the beginning, we adopted the view that it is not necessarily the task of society or schools to educate these children according to fixed programmes. Rather we respect the reality that every single child has a special destiny in this world, to which his parents also belong. We have also had the opportunity to follow the progress of a number of these children into young adulthood, each in their own particular life-situation. They have learned as adults, to live together with other people, though in a way specific to each of them, and perhaps without being able to understand, or live in, the real diversity of human life. The goals which we set ourselves regarding curative education relate to three areas:

1. To make it possible for the autistic child to gain the experience of himself *vis-à-vis* the world.

2. To help the child to unfold some of his own initiatives which become understandable and acceptable within a meaningful human field of inter-action, in spite of fixed, stereotypical and sometimes obsessive patterns of behaviour.

3. To lead the autistic child towards what is generally called *symbolic understanding*. With this we mean the general comprehension of the significance of actions, of human expression and physiognomy, which a healthy child develops during early childhood, and essentially before the acquisition of language.

Early childhood autism is recognized as a syndrome displaying disturbances in different dimensions such as thinking, feeling, speaking and acting. Therefore it is necessary to get to know these three areas more precisely.

Firstly, the so-called cognitive deficits of autistic children have the consequence that they do not understand a word or action, and that they cannot grasp the time factor in changes within the environment of objects and things. Furthermore, they cannot relate an important life-event to themselves, or can only perceive a fragment of such an event. All of these deficits have to be taken into account when considering the relationship of these children to their human environment.

The second area is the cognitive one that relates to human relationships in the true sense. We believe however that the term cognitive is too narrow for this dimension, as especially in early childhood development one cannot separate the realm of the sensory-cognitive from that of the feeling life of the child, which is often termed the *emotional* or *affective*. In practice, therefore, it is a superfluous question as to whether a therapy aims at the cognitive level or at the feeling life of the child. In the therapeutic encounter with the young child, you cannot separate the *therapeutic attitude* from *curative educational practice*.

The third area of the treatment, is, according to our own estimate, the most important one. This relates to the *enhancement of will,* which means intentions, and the formation of the imaginative faculties and motives of the child, which also extend to the inter-human area of perception. We notice that many autistic children act particularly quickly, when engaged in activities. This is especially evident in school, where they perform everything asked of them as if they want to get it behind them as quickly as possible, as if they have no time. Furthermore, the autistic child shows a pattern of behaviour which does not include another person in the field of their activity. This situation is, in the true sense of the word, *autistic*, and it is difficult to change it. Ultimately the action-behaviour of the autistic child is significant which, in the classical descriptions, is termed *sameness*. This concept signifies that the autistic child is anxious to maintain the spatial arrangements in their surroundings and that they therefore resist any spatial change. We notice that this anxiety relates particularly to the child's own activity. For example, if the child is supposed to move from one room to another, they are likely to stop at the threshold, rock to and fro, or start to make stereotypical movements, and do not cross the threshold. We have experienced this in the most varied situations, where the child was meant to do something, yet felt unable, and made a number of peculiar movements of a ritualistic kind instead. As a therapist, if one has the necessary flexibility, one will not only observe such behaviour but engage oneself, and often it is enough to take the child by the hand and lead them across the threshold. Usually one meets with success if one's own intentionality is placed quietly and surely at the disposal of the child, and without interfering arguments.

Doing something and moving oneself are not mere simple motor phenomena to be explained by neurology, but are human activities and movements occurring in a *mutual space of intentionality and meaning,* one that is, to begin with, closed to the autistic child. Belonging to this space of meaning is quite essentially, the *permanent experience of one's own body as a reality.* We are of the opinion that the autistic child, when asked to do something but feeling unable to do so, such as crossing the threshold from one room into another, is frightened of being lost. Normally a child overcomes this anxiety by relating everything he does, including his own movements in space, to certain perceptions which he holds on to and with which he identifies: *primarily the experience of his own body.* This seems to be disturbed in autistic children and they feel anxiety about losing themselves when they make a movement in action or speech.

This also appears to us to be the reason that autistic children, in the life with their parents, fix on certain recurring habits of behaviour, expecting always the same reaction to the same actions. Therein actually lies the difficulty in handling autistic children. Not only do the children demand the wrong self-assurance, through the behaviour pattern of the parents, but the parents too, generally expect normal and familiar reactions from the child. As a result, a vicious circle can develop which severely disturbs the family and which tends to become obsessional, leaving no opportunity for free decisions. The exclusive behaviour of autistic children also makes it hard for parents to enter into, and participate in, the closed circle of their child's activities. This situation, which can generally be termed the *autistic situation,* occurs mostly between the third and seventh year of life, when it is most necessary to give insight and advice to the parents.

There are a number of schools whose policy is to promote intimate body contact of the child with their parents, at the earliest stages of childhood in autistic children. This bodily rhythm plays a decisive part in the earliest, natural contact between a mother and her child, and is seen as preceding linguistic-symbolic behaviour. With many autistic children, soon after birth, a disturbance appears in the rhythm and soul interaction between mother and child. For example, a child might not lift his arms when one tries to help him into his jacket, or he does not respond to a smile, or respond when spoken to. These patterns reveal the basic lack of inter-human relationship.

The parents should be considered carefully to see how much they are capable of contributing to a therapeutic process and see it through. In many cases the parents cannot be productively involvd in the educational process with the autistic child from the start. Together with their child, they find themselves in a vicious circle of behaviour patterns, and it is helpful therefore if the a child, for a certain time, is away from home in order to break this circle and to allow everyone some respite from the autistic situation. In any event, every single case should, of course, be considered with reference to the situation of the parents and the parent-child relationship, when deciding which particular therapeutic and educational course to follow. During the time the child is in a residential school, regular contact with, and reports from, the co-workers give parents the opportunity to get to know their child anew.

From the beginning we have thought it best that the autistic child should be cared for in a special school. However, time and again objections are raised, and care in a special school is deemed inappropriate, because of the relatively high IQ evident in some of these children. Our experience shows, however, that it is important to realize that we are dealing with a syndrome, and that the emotional and will-disturbances, understood as *intentionality*, play a decisive role in the life of the child. The problem which arises, relates to what kind of school is actually most beneficial for autistic children.

From the very start, we decided not to found a school admitting only autistic children. We were guided by the fact that human life, especially in its unconscious dimension, is based on a wide range of encounters and experiences within the social field. For the conscious part of the human being it may appear differently, and a specialized training programme for autistic children may seem of importance. However, one should not underrate the subconscious factor of the child's participation in their environment. This is paramount for the autistic child. After having taken our lead from this, it became evident that within groups as well as in the class situation, children can help each other. Other children who do not show the same behaviour pattern, but are marked by their openness in dealing with the world, as is the case with the child with Downs syndrome, can especially help the autistic ones. They are able to break through the closed circle of the autistic child. Such a child just takes an autistic friend by the arm, takes him for a walk or looks at something together with him, or even does something with him which might not have been achieved by the group leader or the teacher! The communality among retarded children is an important aspect of a school class or a group. The special blessing of such a therapeutic community, according to our experience, is shown particularly after the seventh year of life when even the normal child seeks contact with children of their own age.

If this proves successful, one might have the first clue to understanding why many autistic children between the ages of eight and nine years become relatively normal, and manage to enter into an ordered human environment, whereas before that time they displayed considerable inter-human disorders. The world of early childhood and relationships starts to objectify, and the child is able to have new experiences and encounters with new kinds of people. We should give this opportunity to the autistic child, so that the child gains experiences of new social groupings.

We do not consider the special school only as an academic institution, but as part of the framework of a therapeutic community where we also work with the children in curative educationally-oriented groups, and in home groups of five to six children. Therefore, specific therapeutic and curative educational approaches are integrated into our special school programme, together signified by the term, *curative educational school.*

An autistic child joining a school class at the age of six or seven years adjusts quite quickly, according to our experience, provided that some essentials of the learning process are taken into consideration. The autistic child gains more from the lessons than they are able to show and it is possible, with the repetition of well-structured tasks, to give the child the possibility of a true assimilation of the subject if sufficient time is granted. To this end it is important that the main subject lessons are presented in block periods, and one then experiences that after three to four weeks, the child has made a part of what was offered to him, his own. Any form of learning pressure is avoided.

From investigations concerning long and short-term memory, it is quite clear that there is a great danger in training the autistic child for particular academic successes, which are then reproduced in a stereotyped manner, since their long-term memory, which is also a biographical one, is only insufficiently, or not at all, developed. It is up to the teacher to avoid such a training process, as otherwise the child might be hindered altogether from learning anything new. The autistic child places the highest demands on the therapeutic imagination and patience of the teacher.

Furthermore, a number of sensory exercises are included in the education of these children, designed specifically to enhance their own body perception through the so-called lower senses. These are the sense of balance, movement, life and touch (König 1986). For example, a child can be encouraged to learn to draw shapes or letters with his finger in sand without using his eyes, and to recognize them by touching. Thereby a letter or word read by touching becomes real.

Movement exercises and movement games are especially valuable. In our schools a special form of movement, called *eurythmy*, is available, which we use for autistic children. In this approach one can present the word tree to the child in its sound formation, by first demonstrating the sequence of sounds in eurythmy movements, and then letting the child repeat each letter. The first step is to make a word perceptible in its phonetic gestalt. When this is achieved one can proceed to the symbolic meaning of the words.

In the realm of music we have introduced other exercises. A note is sounded on an instrument and the child is asked to sound the same tone in response. In this way small tone sequences or melodies arise. Especially during the early stages of this exercise inter-personal contact can be much improved.

At a later stage, we attempt play therapy whereby we offer an opportunity for the autistic pupil to come into play contact with younger children, playing with dolls, or all kinds of objects.

We know that the autistic child, confronted with a jigsaw puzzle, quickly places the correct pieces without even looking at the picture. Here, too, it is noticeable that other people are completely excluded from the child's field of action. However, in a therapeutic situation the therapist sits, to begin with, next to or behind the child, and only later opposite the child, and tries as much as possible to gain a reciprocal relationship. For example, by handing a brick to the child, who then hands it back to the therapist, so that gradually they build something *together*.

The therapeutic aim is directed to making it clear to the child; what I do, you can see; what I do, you can do; what you do, I can do; what you do, I can see. Such simple attitudes and therapeutic experiments, often in a very short time, unlock the closed play orbit of the child and change it to togetherness in play. The chances for this are best when the autistic child is still young, before the seventh year of life.

We also engage the child in *warming* therapy, founded on the observation that, when autistic children are ill with a raised temperature, they appear to be almost normal. The stereotypes recede, the eye contact becomes clearer and, in such situations, one succeeds with ease in playing with the children. Sometimes even speech disturbance is lessened. As a result, we administer carefully monitored hot baths, and it is surprising to see how the child reacts to these in a relaxed way

(Klimm 1965). Simultaneously there arises a noticeable openness to interpersonal contact, although to begin with this only lasts for a short time. Following this *hyper-warming,* the therapist plays and speaks with the child.

All these therapeutic measures are integrated with teaching and socializing in the group, within the setting of the curative educational school. With regard to the socialising process in general, we want to give the autistic child the possibility of living within a human universe. However, the autistic child, like the normal child, becomes more distant from the world between the ninth and twelfth year of life. This distancing, which in autism already presented a pathological phenomenon in early childhood, is now more accepted and integrated by the child and others. It is noticeable that autistic children prefer to use any kind of medium in their dealing with the world rather than being confronted. Sometimes they learn more quickly to write with a pencil, some even with a typewriter, rather than speak. There are children who find their approach to speaking via spelling and reading. Normal steps of learning often come in the reverse, so that speaking is linked to reading. With older children especially, the therapeutic approach is directed at the person and not the symptoms, therefore also respecting and accepting a certain distance, through an enhanced paedagogic consciousness.

The destiny of the autistic child maturing into an adolescent, varies considerably according to the individual. There are those who, after dramatic developments in early childhood, slowly grow into a reassured life situation and create an environment for themselves within which they can exist. These children clearly show what they want and, when one responds positively, they can maintain this habit, which however remains limited. If accepted, an important satisfaction is evident in the child. On the other hand there are also children who, in spite of all efforts, remain searching for their own identity, who are in a kind of limbo and never feel at home in this world. These children are the most difficult and they frequently develop symptoms similar to psychosis, around their thirteenth, fourteenth and fifteenth year.

The socially integrated autistic children repeatedly present us with two characteristics. Firstly, a certain objectivity in their judgment *vis-à-vis* the world and other people, which is not very flexible, but gives the adolescent a kind of unerring character. Secondly, an unusual measure of self-recognition and also self-limitation, once they have reached their eighteenth/nineteenth year of life. This signifies a raised consciousness concerning their own actions, and limited insight in relation to the wide range of human needs and experiences. Such children do not enter certain situations if insight tells them that they could not cope.

In conclusion, based on the present extent of our experience, in practice as well as in theory, our point of departure is the assumption that every autistic child who comes to us is searching for their own individual destiny in life. There is not much sense in hastily devising teaching models or therapeutic plans with the promise of general significance. The early diagnosis of autistic children is of particular importance and allows us to discuss the situation with parents before the obsessional circle of the autistic situation arises. More institutions ought to be established which would make it possible for autistic children to have opportunities out of their accustomed settings. Finally, we consider it urgently necessary that every autistic child receives special schooling and therapy. The school should be established on the line of a curative educational school, where there is the possibility to give children a wide variety of therapeutic and social activities.

I believe the autistic child will find his place in society if we are prepared to accept that we are always dealing with a special child with his own individual destiny, not only the autistic syndrome. Such an insight is an effective therapeutic precondition for all curative educational activity.

Part 2

Taken from a lecture to special needs educators at the Paedagogical Institute, Düsseldorf, under the title 'Special Educational Aspects for the Development of Autistic Children.' First published in the papers of the Paedagogical Institute, Düsseldorf, Volume 35, November 1977.

Even after a relatively long experience we are still actively engaged in finding new curative educational approaches for autistic children. We have been fortunate in being able to accompany a great number of autistic children for a fairly long period of time, and to follow their path through school. Some areas will now be highlighted where it is important to recognize the specific disturbances of the autistic child if one wants to help them by means of curative education.

We are unanimous here in understanding that the symptoms shown by autistic children are linked with perceptual disturbances, and with the co-ordination and processing of different fields of perception. It is generally assumed that a person absorbs all kinds of sensory impressions which are then built up into perceptions, by an essentially hidden mechanism localized in the brain. Here we find a subtle working together of activities of will, experiences of feeling and cognitive structuring. Inasmuch as they connect with every sensory perception, these activities need to facilitate a meaningful interpretation of the world. This is of great significance for the teacher, who must not overlook that perceptions by the senses are active achievements. We cannot assume that we are passively conditioned through sensory experiences, but rather that we ourselves have to actively connect the sense perceptions as relational experiences with each other. This active relating of sensory perceptual fields through the ego and its organization, appears to be disturbed or limited in autistic children. The establishing of interrelationships is dependent on perceptual judgments, so we should ask which sensory fields are in question here?

Firstly, there is the field of seeing (sight). Other sensory perceptions such as smelling, tasting and, indirectly, hearing also belong to this middle field. We also have a second sensory field, which plays an especially important role in the treatment and education of autistic children. It relates to our balance and our movement, whereby we contend with the earth's forces of gravity. We are dealing here with the ability to sense movement. With autistic children we find an obvious severe disturbance in this whole field of own body experience which has to do with the four lower or body senses (touch, life, movement and balance). Following from this, we also find in the autistic child severe disturbances of what can be called the experience of the child's own identity with the body. This arrives early on in the case of the normal child, who builds up body schemata from experiencing through the senses of movement and balance.

There is also a third field of perception, which is not acknowledged by present-day science as a primary sensory realm. This is particularly regrettable because it presents an obstacle for the understanding of autistic children. This is the field where the attention of man is directed to the soul-spiritual nature of another human being; to their speaking, thinking and behaviour or, more precisely, to the intentions evident in their behaviour. If you observe the disorders in speech perception in these children you will discover that their problems of communication, imitation and non-perception of the social environment, are based on the autistic child's difficulty in developing this higher sensory field.

If our understanding of speech is limited to a secondary or symbolical processing of perceptions, then we will be limited in what we can do to help autistic children. Indeed, we may well produce the opposite results from what we actually hope to achieve! If our concept of speech fails to include the speaker and their intentions as part of the investigations of speech, we will be equally limited.

We have autistic children who treat speech like an object, they listen and repeat what they hear but do not relate the spoken word to the person of the speaker. This means that they have a severe disorder with regard to understanding through speech what is revealed about another human being.

The normal young child exercises abilities of direct perception in regard to the being, speech, and thought of the other person. If these inter-human fields of perception are not sufficiently available, as is the case with the autistic child, then the child also suffers a continuous collapse, or lack of development, in terms of his own experience of identity. Robbed of his own sense of identity, the autistic child has to invent all kinds of things — maintenance of sameness in their spatial surroundings, etc. — in order to achieve at least one aspect of security, one semblance of security, in the world.

From a paedagogical point of view it is essential that we educate in the three fields of lower, middle and higher senses. Motor-sensory training alone might be of some help, but its application is still far from fully addressing the real problem of the interaction of the three sensory fields in which the whole personality is involved, not only the functioning of the brain.

For example, an autistic child is piecing together a jigsaw puzzle, and you address that child. You may have the impression the child is deaf. You might experience a similar situation if you are intensely absorbed in something and somebody talks to you. In this instance, what is seen in an extreme form in the autistic child is not dissimilar to our normal experience.

In order to perceive the world normally, through our senses, we have to be able to perform active transformation; we have to wrest ourselves away from our field of action and turn towards the perceptual space available for listening and speech, in order to perceive the other human being. Otherwise we cannot understand.

The ability to change from one sensory field to another is not yet developed at birth. In fact the child gains this transformational ability, to combine the three sensory fields, around the third year of life. With autistic children we must exercise these transformative powers and so make possible the co-ordination of the sensory fields. The result of this co-ordination is signified essentially by the child learning to say I with regard to self. With the autistic child, we can say that we have succeeded in awakening this co-ordination in the child, when he is able to relate the words, I am, to himself.

Teachers have observed that, when asked to follow a line or lines drawn on paper or engraved in wood, with a pencil, finger or eye control, autistic children do less well than a normal child. However, the moment an autistic child is given a pencil in his hand to follow the line or lines blindfolded, he shows extraordinary speed and skill in following the lines! This skill is superior to that of normal children used to accompanying their activity with information gained by sight. However, the autistic child has a much reduced latitude of freedom to modify his movements and to experience himself as a self in his activity. From this example we can see how co-ordination from the lower sensory field, the sense of movement, is not sufficient here to accompany information from the sense of sight, belonging to the middle field. This presents a lack of perceptual rhythm between two different fields, a rhythm which is available to normal children, giving them the basis for self-consciousness in their activities.

An autistic child can do a jigsaw puzzle with extraordinary speed which is unobtainable for a normal child. The picture outline does not contribute to the process because the autistic child does not succeed in co-ordinating movement and seeing. The autistic child is riveted only to spatial patterns of his activity. We are dealing here not with a deficit in a single sensory field, but with a co-ordination disorder. The picture of the jigsaw puzzle is quite irrelevant for the autistic child; only the shapes are relevant and how they fit together. Inner mobility between two sensory fields (what above we have called transformation), is disturbed in a particular and specific way. This has considerable consequences for the special educational treatment of these children. If you fail to bring about the relationship of movement to sight, you do not actually help the child, and exercises and skills then remain exterior to the personality development of the child.

We know that a person gets dizzy if they turn round very quickly. When the movement stops they get a *post-rotational nystagmus;* the eyes continue moving, even though the body has stopped. This proves that, generally speaking, eye movement is linked with the movements of the entire organism. If one places an autistic child on a rotating chair and turns it fast, the autistic child will either not have a post-rotational nystagmus, or, will experience a much shorter one than a normal child. It appears as if these children are only turned from the outside and the own body, equilibrium experience, plays no part. The proof that this equilibrium experience is absent is shown in the non-occurrence of the dizziness; the body was merely an object that was turned round. We observe something similar with blind children.

The autistic child is subject to spatial determining factors with regard to their movement organism, without being able to co-ordinate their experiences with other sensory fields. There is even the danger that the other realms of the senses only relate symbiotically to the outer world of space. We can see this particularly in the fascination with mechanical-technical movements and programmed sequences in gadgets. The autistic child has the tendency to merge in fascination with these movements and, again and again, starts to perform these outer movements. All these external movements have nothing to do with the child's own body experience of movement, through which the body experience of the motile world is constituted as perceptual judgement, but with external laws of physics. In consequence the child becomes passive and finally resigns from all self-initiative to move.

Something else we can see in this connection is the decrease of motor achievements when a child is asked to do something. One can observe the dwindling or disintegration of stereotypical activities and one notices that, to begin with, all is well. However, soon the movements turn into only mechanical-stereotypical sequences of activity, which lack the transformation brought about through the optic field and through the perception of the other human being.

Something else, which is again connected with the co-ordination of the sensory fields, can be observed in the word-understanding of autistic children, connected with the third field of sensory perceptions, namely, the higher senses. The autistic child runs the risk of building up a certain space of activity around himself, which another person cannot easily penetrate or enter into. This can arise at school as a problem of communication. The difficulty for the autistic child is to establish a link between these two spaces of activity, to relate the space of activity of the other person and his own space of activity with each other.

This is one of the great difficulties at school: the fundamental problem of making contact. The autistic child does everything in a closed off space of activity and, when the teacher does something, it is alien to the child. The autistic child is obviously not able to build up a mutual space of activity with another human being. When, however, such disorders show themselves in the very young child, then we have to therapeutically build some common, mutual space of activity. I believe there are various ways to do this, but it should not take the form of sitting opposite the child and demanding certain tasks. One has to allow the child to accept something. For example, the child looks at an object, moves it and places it somewhere, and then allows their therapeutic partner to take the same object and do something with it. Within such a rhythm of encounter, which you can also call play or a game, there comes about via the objects a meeting place of a rhythmical nature between child and therapist.

All learning has to relate to a mutual common world, as the basis for relationships. If that is not the case, learning, imitation, acceptance and participation is not possible, and life consists of merely unrelated items. I see the establishment of a mutual world, as an essential therapeutic task. Whether to establish this meeting space with a purpose-designed play therapy, or how otherwise to bring it about, should be left to the ingenuity of the therapist or teacher. However, it is quite obvious that one-to-one therapy sessions are necessary.

Although autistic children seemingly have no difficulty in perceiving an object, even being able to recognize and sometimes name it, they have not yet learned to realize that this object is there simultaneously for another person, and that it is an object within the field of communication. This poses an important and central question in teaching and therapy, and much depends on how we think about it.

In order to awaken the communicative activity in the autistic child a curative teacher has to turn the child towards inter-human sensory perceptions. If a child does not understand the intentions of another person and you speak with this child and raise your voice, then the child might retreat further still! This is not because they cannot understand what is spoken, but because the intentions inherent in speech, or the intentions inherent in the actions of other people, are alien to them, or appear distorted or threatening. Every culture of any language is bound up with situations and spoken words which can only be understood when the intentions of the other person are perceived. I form within myself understanding for speech, in the moment when I turn towards the speech of the other person, and I listen.

This fact has extraordinary consequences for lessons. It is not enough to speak to the autistic child loudly and with good articulation, you also have to see that there is simplicity in your linguistic expression, and that you lead the child to listen actively in order to meet the intentions permeating your speech. You might have to whisper. What is at stake is the therapeutic attitude. This begins with teaching how to listen. What matters in this connection is that the teacher and therapist themselves have to undergo training to develop the right attitude and correct insights regarding these higher sensory fields.

We have to change our thinking in regard to these questions. We have to recognize that normally in a young child, a direct perception of the speech, thought and ego of another person takes place. Through our therapeutic attitude, we have to cultivate this activity of the higher senses of the autistic child in relation to the sense of movement, as one of the lower senses. It is important that one helps the child, through certain exercises, to experience their own body. Every action of ours is a gesture, a symbolic presentation to which we give shape through our body. Gestures come about only when I am able to make free use, as a human being, of my body as an instrument. My ego finds expression through my body. The severe disorders of autistic children in this area are well-known: their inability to make use of the body as a means of giving expression to soul and spirit. Even if an autistic child learns to write, we do not have the impression that it is a gesture in which the child is present. In such cases, we do therapeutic exercises in writing with the children. We try to dissolve the rigidity in their writing by letting them give shape to the same word or sentence in different forms. So we let them write from right to left, or from above to below, or in a different style, or with different colours or materials, so that children slowly begin to experience joy in expression. What we call motivation for our actions does not only arise from being able to achieve something, such as writing a word or saying something, but also depends on how far we can inwardly experience something through our sense of life.

A child at play is not concerned with ruling the world, or aiming at achievement. What are at stake are expressions, gestures. Play is kept going through the experience of their own movement. This experience, and the motivation related to it, is lacking in the autistic child. We should, then, take care that the child learns to experience joy, with which the ability to play is closely related. The sense of movement is linked to joy, as a body-soul quality. I have observed how autistic children, for the first time, jump freely in their surroundings, whereas before they darted to an object as if pulled by a string, or walked close to a wall with the most bizarre stereotypical movements. We give certain exercises, simple movements and balance exercises in eurythmy, with the aim that the child should slowly inwardly perceive their own movements.

The phenomenon of joy and smiling is not dependent on complicated psychological mechanisms but rather, and especially with the small child, simply on the unfolding of the sense of movement and the related ability to move freely and playfully. From this, we can see how great a store of sensory experiences, reaching into the soul existence, is transmitted to the human being from the realm of lower or body senses (König 1986).

During the course of the educational development of the autistic child, their symptoms not only change, but they also undergo development like any other child. The symptoms we find in autistic children are disturbances that prevent their personalities from sufficiently revealing themselves. Our task is to see the fixed pattern of activity and perception of the autistic child as a symptom, and to try to help the child so that his personality can unfold more freely.

Autistic children need many years of education, extending into adulthood, during which they can learn continuously. The suffering of autistic children is usually greatest during the first seven years of life. During the second seven years, many autistic children gain certain thinking abilities and learn gradually to cope with their discrepancies from the norm. They do not become normal, but they can learn to master their handicap. You can, for example, observe an autistic child of nine or ten years old who still has an obsession but, with curative education, learns to build up inter-human connections and gains some distance from his obsessions. Perhaps even a humorous attitude might develop. The child still has to run around the table before sitting down, but you have the impression that this is no longer a completely dominant ritual: the child could almost dispense with it. An intimate tendency of inner liberation from obsession becomes evident. Such observations are important because they show starting points for further educational and therapeutic progress.

During the third seven years of life, if the autistic youngster is cared for in a curative education setting, quite important developmental steps can still occur, especially in the domain of human-relationships. In supporting these children, much patience is required. One should not count on quick success. Above all, we have to consider the time factor in the development of a personality. In connection with this we should be aware of the maturing of the three sensory fields, discussed before, which the teacher needs to be particularly aware of.

In conclusion, reference should be made to the intelligence of autistic children. Comprehensive research has shown that these children have a special kind of intelligence in certain fields, which is generally considered to be visual-spatial. We have already said that the autistic child has an extraordinary, but pathological, affinity to the physical spatial world and its laws. All that belongs to formal logic we have extracted from the spatial conditions of the world by uniting ourselves with it during the first seven years of life through experiences of movement and balance (see Chapter 12). If we begin slowly to grasp this, then we are no longer astonished that the autistic child is able, quite early on, to develop formal conceptual structures, leading to abstract, yet impersonal, thought activity, which has arisen from the experiences of space and its laws. During the second seven year period you can follow this process step by step. You also see the severe lack of an imaginative kind of thinking, far less rigid and formalized than abstract thought, and which should come about through normal inter-human fellowship, and the ability to imitate. Linked to these imaginative conceptions in a normal child is also the ability to remember images, that is, a biographical long-term memory. This is disturbed in the autistic child with deep consequences.

In the autistic child we can see the premature intrusion and perception of the outer world of space, and a progression to conceptual, impersonal formulations, sometimes already during the first seven-year period. We notice that these children have the increasing tendency to translate everything into spatial terms, even in their verbal structures and expressions. They lack the time-related mobility of free creative thinking, and with it the ability to tune in with the direction of thoughts of another human being. Therefore we often have the impression that autistic children are very clever. This cleverness however pertains only to the area of formal structures, as developed by physical science. We find a kind of technical-formal intelligence which, in the normal child development, should only arise after imaginative thinking has developed, so that during the second and third seven-year periods the two can harmonize with each other.

We therefore have to educate autistic children early, and in the right way, because the age at which inter-human connections are formed is during the period of imitation, namely, the first seven years. The age at which technical intelligence emerges in a normal child, is around the age of fourteen, when they normally tackle the laws of physics and mechanics.

In the autistic child this development is reversed, because such children are bound to an exterior world which can only be put into context in a formal and logical manner. At the same time, they suffer a severe lack of speech and thought formation from their deficit of inter-human development. This discrepancy becomes a central problem at school. The formal thought structures of autistic children are obsessional, schematic and rigid, and serve to provide a pseudo-security of an impersonal kind. In contrast to the formal-logic, free thought image of an older, normally developed child, the thoughts of the autistic child are not free, but are a means to cope with the spatial world of perception. They are, therefore, bound up with many phobias.

The human being only becomes a secure personality through a balance between imaginative intelligence and formal intelligence. With a number of autistic children, engaging them creatively in the realm of crafts, and even in more general work activity, provides a great opportunity to foster and establish inter-human connections; especially when the autistic child has reached some degree of freedom in formal thinking. Nevertheless, their experience of the world remains still predominantly co-ordinated according to geometrical, mathematical and physical structures.

Lastly, our experiences in the curative educational field show how important it is with autistic children to work with small classes, and that it is necessary to have regular individualized therapies. A rhythm can be established between individual therapy and group teaching which then does justice to the special needs of each child.

14. Curative Educational Therapy: An Anthroposophical Approach

First published in German under the title 'Neue Aspekte der Förderung Autistischen Kinder,' in Autismus Heute *Volume 2, Verlag Modernes Lernen, Dortmund (1990).*

The exercises described in the following account are based on the recognition that the lower senses of touch, movement, life and balance not only play an essential role in the development of communication with the external world in early childhood, but are also the basis of the functional development of other senses, such as hearing and seeing.

During the first seven years, the child increasingly experiences his own body, which defines its limits *vis-à-vis* the environment and surrounding forces, and thereby he establishes a sense of ego-identity in space. During this stage the maturing lower body senses shape the child's experience of the child's own body form or body image. This dimension of a developing own world, disturbed in the autistic child, can be diagnosed in detail.

Inasmuch as the autistic child does not actively relate to the world through touching, experiencing gravity, or perceiving formative forces in the world around through the sense of life, the child cannot sufficiently develop his own body experience as the basis of communication. The body, therefore, is not available as an adequate locus for the processing of other sensory experiences, such as hearing and seeing. Normal development of an inner gestalt, or body schemata, is underdeveloped and impeded in the autistic child, and this is exemplified in the child's deficient ability to imitate. Disorders in the field of the four lower senses in the autistic child are evident in:

a. the relationship to organic substances (nutritional and digestive problems);

b. the relationship of own movement patterns to the environment
(on the one hand stereotypical movements and, on the other
hand, a dependency on external prompts);

c. touching; the avoidance of experiences through touch and
exploration; and:

d. the realm of gravity: the retreat into stereotypes and rituals,
and compulsive dependency on spatial positioning.

With these patterns of behaviour, the autistic child is manifesting
the attempt — through ritualized and compulsive means — to uphold
his identity. Such attempts constitute behaviour that we term autistic,
and represent the phenomenology of failed communication.

The following exercises, initiated mainly by a partner, have proved
effective in practical work with autistic children at the residential special school of Brachenreuthe. [A Camphill residential school in Southern Germany. Ed.]

The therapeutic task within the exercises is in the first place the
stimulation of the child's own will-activity (intentionality), however
basic it might appear, in order to provide a precondition for the gradual process of meaningful bodily experience which counters the
stereotypes, rituals and spatial compulsions.

Exercises in the realm of the four body senses

Resistance exercises

These stimulate the child coming to terms with the forces of gravity
and experiencing himself as independent, and able to stand on his own
feet. By means of such exercises the sense of balance in movement is
exercised by overcoming gravity in the environment, as this is done
(under normal circumstances), when the child learns to walk, but also
in grasping, moving or carrying objects.

Retarded interplay with the earth-gravity space is indicated by ritualistic movements, extremely lax muscle tone, walking on tiptoes, retarded explorative grasping (especially of heavy objects), as well as pathological movement patterns, and stereotypes in walking and running. Therefore we introduce a sense of gravity to the children by means of medicine ball games; exercises with hand weights; balancing; sometimes also using lead-weighted anklets in order to enhance resistance through gravity; carrying heavy objects; as well as carrying out partner resistance exercises to make the child aware of his own bodyweight. In the course of such planned daily exercises the following can soon be noticed: activating muscle tone; increasing surety of own body experience; decreasing spatial compulsions; as well as better grip and eye contact.

Through strengthening the child's body experience in this way he realizes: 'I can keep myself within the space in which I stand and walk. I remain always the same wherever I am in space and, with this experience, I judge the spatial situation of the world and of things.'

General movement exercises

We know that the autistic child fails in imitating; that already early on in the development of body movement, the transition from reflexes to imitation fails to take place sufficiently. This results in stereotypical movements with or without objects, and sometimes weak muscle tone. Own movement impulses cannot be implemented, nor can they be planned. The movements of these children are dependent on alien movements within the movement-space, and with which the autistic child likes to identify, and also with being passively moved.

We endeavour therapeutically to build up self-experience in movement via the sense of movement. To begin with, meaningful movements in eurythmy are undertaken which correspond to the sounds of speech. We do this together with the child at first, possibly from behind, until they begin to relate and, eventually, start to imitate spontaneously. The child learns to sense extension and contraction, fast as opposed to slow movement, and resistance, and gradually learns through elementary eurythmy to acquire the full scale of human movement. Through such exercises, joy often appears, sometimes for the first time expressing a sense of own movement within the world, but also often for the first time, expressing the experience of: 'I can achieve something in the world.' In curative eurythmy, special exercises are prescribed by a medical doctor, which work on the bodily formative processes, including the functioning of organs. Through such exercises the autistic child can gain own body experiences. These experiences can also be achieved by exercising left and right, up and down, behind and in front, and different types of walking. The connection of eurythmy exercises with the sounds of speech, stimulates the formation of the inner gestalt which underlies speech, and opens up new possibilities of response through imitation (Klimm 1981).

Many autistic children have problems with the development of dominance. This manifests not only in stereotypical symmetrical movement, but also in disturbed walking. Target exercises with bow and arrow, fencing in its traditional form, as well as exercises such as catching and throwing a rod with one hand, have proved useful. These exercises promote the asymmetry of the movement organization against the symmetrical tendency in the structure and function of the head and central nervous system.

The Sense of Life

A disturbed sense of life in the child requires special attention and manifests in a number of noticeable symptoms such as the refusal to eat, disturbed meal rhythms, or compulsive preferences for food with a particular appearance or consistency, as well as metabolic and body-building problems which are often of a chronic nature. Besides medical treatment of digestive activity, attention should be given especially to a regular daily rhythm of eating, as well as the soul shelter required in the eating environment. The child should learn, in due course, to accept all different kinds of food. Application of certain ointments, and baths with plant supplements, can also help. Children are often helped by a slight shading of the dining room as well as by a dark red basic wall colouring. Small, even tiny, portions are an essential initial help with eating difficulties, in order to stimulate the child's self-activity, which is important with all measures taken at the level of the body senses.

Touch exercises

We let the children look for an object in warmed sand or discriminate between several objects in sand by touching. We also exercise the explorative touching, without eye contact, with two-dimensional shapes, which can be made of plywood, as a pre-exercise for visual exploration of letters and other forms. We also use the same forms for the child to walk, or draw with his feet in sand, in order that one and the same phenomenon becomes reality for the child in different sensory media. The child's touching of parts of his own body and also that of the therapist, exercises, primarily, the demarcation experience of one's own body as distinct from another.

Such touch exercises are important because the earliest boundary experience of one's own body *vis-à-vis* the material world, is gained through touching. This normal development is, however, delayed or disturbed in the autistic child, and only when made possible through the sense of touch can communicative and active exploration of the environment take place, and touch-oversensitivity retreat. Then the personal body integrates into the existential substance of the world and the child experiences other bodies as objects in their own right.

The curative educator has every opportunity to discover new exercises within the parameters described here. Further exercises are described in *Sensory Integration and the Child* by A.J. Ayres (see Bibliography), whose remarks regarding the autistic child are of help, and partly supplement what has been stated here.

Which particular exercises to do with an individual autistic child is always a new discovery and does not require a specialist therapist. However, situations must be created where, in daily contact with the child, one can work on a one-to-one basis in a quiet room.

Play and imitation

Play can be based on sensory exercises or it can supplement them, according to the developmental stage of the child. The aim is to further the child's imitation in dealing with objects in partnership. Firstly, we position ourselves at a table with playthings, behind or next to the child, and encourage him to respond using mobile objects, such as marbles. Soon the child joins in playing, using his own initiative. Then the therapist can move to sit opposite the child. Instead of mobile objects, others are now introduced, such as toy bricks, and in partnership some construction is undertaken, a tower or a bridge. Rhythm is very important, and the therapist should say 'I place a brick, you place a brick, I place a brick,' until the tower is built. This mutual play initiative is accompanied by speech and, in turn, challenges the own activity of the child. It is important that the child can experience that objects can stand together in space in different positions — next to, above, beneath, behind, in front — and that the child can be guided to establish these different and changing spatial positions with the same objects. The aim of these exercises is to see that the object remains the same, in various spatial situations, never mind whether it is moved by the child or therapist. This realization is a preliminary to forming concepts. The mutual and alternating handing on of objects with which to play, and the child's acceptance of this reciprocal action is often a necessary preliminary exercise to playing. The fundamental aim is to set imitation in motion and to establish a mutual world of objects.

Exercises in the listening space

These exercises aim to enhance in the child a more wakeful ability to perceive the elements of tone. Diagnostically, the problems of these children within the acoustic field are shown in delayed participation in group singing and, especially, in the detailed and rigid rendering of once-heard rhythms and melodies, which can take on a compulsive character, and be used by these children as a defence strategy in stressful situations.

This shows the child's inability to synchronize perception and memory of what has been heard, because the autistic child in his movement organization (muscle tone) is not sufficiently able to accept musical experience directly. Tone eurythmy has particularly shown its worth, as the heard musical elements (pitch, duration, rhythm) are performed by the child through movement within the directions of space.

The child can thereby learn to experience himself in tone eurythmical movement; actively reaching to overcome the dependencies and fixations which are shown by many of these children. These exercises have proved particularly positive for children and adolescents during and after puberty, as has country dancing.

We conduct these exercises in the frame of tone eurythmy group lessons, but also as tone curative eurythmy single lessons. By uniting the heard music with movement, frozen musical memories can be released, and the perceptive ability and openness of the child's movement organism for music is refreshed and developed. With another therapy exercise, also done individually, we have good results with autistic children with slack muscle tone and whose over-sensitivity to tone and noise is a noticeable sympton of their handicap. In tone eurythmy the child learns movement gestures for the intensity of tones, to counter the strong musical tones produced, for example, by a trumpet. It is important for autistic children that, within the sensory field of hearing and rhythm, balance is achieved between under- and over-sensitivity. It becomes evident that this relationship is essentially dependent on the movement organization and related muscle tone condition. In listening space therapy, we try to harmonize the interrelationship between listening and moving. This is an essential pre-exercise for furthering the autistic child's interest in the sounds of speech.

Another exercise in this field is improvised musical conversations, where the therapist speaks to the child with tone phrases on the lyre, and the child is encouraged to answer freely on his instrument. Such tone conversations have the power to undo the pathological habit, in some autistic children, of talking to themselves, which prevents spontaneous communication owing to the preponderance of rigid memories.

When, in earliest childhood, autistic symptoms begin to show, the lyre (a string instrument) has proved effective. The young child accepts instrumental music which is tuned in with the rhythmic organization, more easily than speech. One can also here accompany the sounding of tones with movement impulses. (Not passive moving but stimulating the child's own movement-intentions, through gentle muscular massage or touching.)

All these exercises are directed at further developing the connection between listening and movement organization, as the basis of perceptual interest and processing of hearing perceptions. Stereotyped fixation of movement and slack muscle tone, are outer signs of a disturbed relationship which can lead to a high degree of aversion or avoidance within the acoustic realm, including speech. Such avoidances in the auditory field have similar cause and effect as the avoidance of eye contact in the visual. These children are unable to engage exploratively in aspects of time or sequence, of what was seen or heard. Therefore they are often diagnosed as hearing impaired.

Warmth therapies

Among the curative therapies which we have successfully applied are controlled temperature baths, or pyrogenic baths. These stimulate the warmth organization of the autistic child and have proved successful in other institutions (Klimm 1981). Physically, the autistic child is, by nature, a cold child. We apply oil dispersion baths or simple temperature-increase baths with an increase of one or two degrees centigrade above the child's body temperature. During and after such applications the children make better eye contact and, in speaking children, their speech is activated, and they can communicate better with simple games and imitation. Similar effects can also be seen with warm foot baths in the morning, followed by rubbing until the feet become pink. Such foot baths in the evening help children who have problems in falling asleep.

Through regular therapy of this kind, continued for some months, the ego of the child can learn to establish itself within the peripheral warmth organization, and thereby lay the foundation for soul expressions.

However all measures described here, can only become effective with autistic children and adolescents when seen within the framework of other social, curative educational, and special educational approaches. A constitutional medical therapy also belongs here, using potentized medicines on the basis of an anthroposophically extended art of healing.

Appendix

1. Additional anthroposophical background

Rudolf Steiner and anthroposophy

Steiner described in detail how to embark on this *Path of Knowledge,* both in his fundamental books (Steiner 1973, 1989 & 1993) and in various lecture cycles (Steiner 1969a, 1978 & 1990a). It is clear from these that the conscientious study of anthroposophy constitutes the first, essential step on this path towards *higher* knowledge.

In 1925, from the viewpoint of the spiritual investigator, he wrote:

> The subject-matter of his exposition, namely the realities of the world of spirit, will be cast into forms of thought which the prevailing consciousness of our time — scientifically thoughtful and wide-awake, though unable to see into the spiritual world — can understand. (Steiner 1989, 8)

Environmental factors

In anthroposophy, the profound formative importance given to early imitation has not been lessened by current views which fail to see this capacity as a key feature of child development (Sylva & Lunt 1982). However, it has to be understood that with regard to imitation Steiner did not simply mean the mere copying of the behaviour of others. He pointed to a very subtle process of active internalization which works covertly into the finer organic constitution of the child.

> ... the human being during the first period of life inwardly reproduces all that is happening around him. (Steiner 1988, 50)

Steiner said that everything in the way of movement and gesture is inwardly reproduced by the young child, and it is precisely because infants literally sleep and dream their way into earthly life, that they are such natural imitators and mimics. In early consciousness they are effectively at one with all that is around them.

> When a child enters physical existence he only continues the experiences he had in the spiritual world prior to conception. ... There we are imitators to a much higher degree because we are united with the (spiritual) beings we imitate. ... Benefit for a child is all the greater

the more he is able to live not in his own soul but in those within his environment. (Steiner 1969b, 13)

If Steiner is indeed correct we must therefore see in imitation that power which already leads us, as infants, instinctively into the realm of inter-human relationships and social reciprocity.

The first three years of life

From what has been written about Child Development (see Chapter 8) it is clear that anthroposophy sees the infant's experiential world as very different in quality from the adult's in the areas of consciousness, perception and conception. Unlike adults, during the first life period, (from birth to the seventh year), the ego of the child is intensively involved in constructing its individualized physical body. According to Steiner, during the first two and a half years this wisdom-filled ego activity is especially directed towards the refinement of the brain.

> The ego has to elaborate the brain into a more delicately complicated structure, in order that later on the human being will be able to think. During the first years of life the ego is very active. (Steiner 1976a, 87)

Moreover, anthroposophical research discovered that it is precisely through the activity of the ego that the three monumental milestones of child development — walking, talking and thinking — are achieved. These occur during the first three years while the child is functioning perceptually like a unified sense organ, and very differently from an adult. Indeed, the child's very essence is of a perceptive and 'imitative susceptibility' (Kügelgen 1975), through which they are intimately aware of, and sensitive to, their human environment. Therefore, in contrast to later adult awareness, we can perceive the infant's consciousness as wide and peripheral; expansive and universal (Weihs 1984; König 1994). This enables a direct *living into* the souls of others, without the limitations imposed by the individual self-centredness of later childhood.

The sensory organization

In order to appreciate the developmental role of perception more fully and exactly, we first have to look at anthroposophy's knowledge of the Twelve Senses as described by Steiner (1981 & 1990b), and later by other anthroposophical authors (Soesman 1990; Aeppli 1993; Childs 1996). It is only through the functioning of our complicated multi-sensory organization that as adults we can integrate ourselves experientially into daily life. If any one of our senses is impaired or lacking, we will suffer from some degree of sensory deprivation. According to Steiner (1990b), we have access to these distinct realms through our twelvefold sense organism; namely, there are three distinct orientations accessible via our complete sense organism:

— our own corporeality;
— our natural environment;
— our specifically human, social surroundings.

For each of these three realms or fields of perception, a group of four senses is normally available. The Twelve Senses divide into three groups, as follows:

1. Four *body* or *lower* senses of touch, life, movement and balance to perceive our own corporeality (our body).
2. Four *soul* or *middle* senses of smell, taste, sight and warmth, to perceive our natural environment.
3. Four *spiritual* or *higher* senses of hearing, word, thought and ego, to perceive our human, social surroundings.

This threefold ordering of the twelve senses can also be seen in relationship to the three soul forces of thinking, feeling, and willing, as shown in Table 15.

Whereas the higher senses function on the level of *awake* conscious cognition, the lower senses, in polar contrast, belong to the level of the *sleeping*, unconscious will processes. In between, the middle senses function on the level of *dreaming* feelings (Aeppli 1993). Therefore, we can also call the four higher senses the *cognitive* senses, and the four lower senses, the *will* senses.

It would need a specific research volume in order to comprehensively describe the physiology, functioning, genesis and development of these twelve senses. Yet, even without this, it is clear that Steiner's extension of the

Soul Force	Sense Group
Thinking	Spiritual or higher senses
Feeling	Soul or middle senses
Willing	Body or lower senses

Table 15. Relationships of the three soul forces and the three sense groups.

sense organism, beyond the customary five senses, is of great significance for any holistic understanding of the human being and for developmental psychology.

Early motor and sensory developments

We are now in a position to consider normal sensory and motor developments which occur during the first three years of life, so that we can recognize incisive steps of incarnation which result in the child becoming both self-conscious and socially interactive.

The four lower senses unfold and function during the first year of life (Aeppli 1993, 45). It is likely that the *sense of touch* operates even before birth, and is afterwards stimulated by the caregiving and hands-on bodily contact which takes place, especially with the mother, and also through continual contact with immediate physical surroundings.

The *sense of life* is developed through the repeated rhythms of feeding, sleeping, changing, and the vital processes of life, such as breathing, digestion, excretion, warming etc.

The *senses of movement and balance* develop as the infant learns to co-ordinate, order and control his initially chaotic, movement organism. Weihs (1984) called this 'the descent of motor control,' beginning with the co-ordination of the eyes, head and neck, and extending via shoulders and arms into the trunk and lower limbs. In this way the child quite literally *grows* down, head first, into its earthly body. Having passed through the stages of reaching out, sitting and crawling, this descent leads to the child pulling himself into an upright position, firstly with the aid of some object. He is at last able to stand unsupported and soon after launches into his first steps.

However, according to anthroposophy, babies and infants have not yet gained a centred self-consciousness, though their initially diffuse, peripheric awareness — consisting of merging sense perceptions and feelings — is increasingly *lit up* as the world becomes differentiated from their bodily self-experience.

> The upright posture alone causes the abyss to open between self and world, and this leads to the further acquisition of speech and thought. (König 1984, 19)

Babbling, as a precursor to proper speech, begins some time after the sixth month, reaching its peak by nine to ten months. It has been found to be universal in infants the world over (see Sylva & Lunt 1982).

At the end of the first year, together with uprightness and walking, the *sense of word* begins to function, and language can be perceived. According to König (1984), the development of this higher sense is a necessary prerequisite for speaking. As long as children babble they have not yet developed *word sense.* At around eighteen months, an important new developmental step is made.

> Suddenly and quite spontaneously, the child grasps the connection of things through names ... An immediate understanding for the word itself and its meaning is present....
>
> This new understanding of the meaning of words is due to the emergence of the sense of thought. Concepts are now perceived and grasped.
>
> Thus a small child does not think the meaning of words he acquires, but perceives it through his senses. (König 1984, 38–98)

A striking example of the first functioning of the sense of thought is shown in the remarkable case of Helen Keller, who was both blind and deaf. When, at the age of seven, this sense awakened in her, she perceived with joy and excitement that:

> Everything had a name, and each name gave birth to a new thought. (Meadows 1986, 121)

Although children in their second year are typically walking, talking, human beings, they do not yet think consciously.

Self-consciousness

The normal acquisition of self-consciousness enables all experiences in a child's life — perceptions, thoughts, feelings and deeds — to be referred to this newly gained *self-hood,* to his own soul centre.

> But now, the moment we use the word 'I,' we have become inhabitants of the earth. This moment is a critical point in human development, and so is one of the most difficult events in a child's life, a crossroads at which many children falter and perish. Many autistic and psychopathic children break down at this particular point. (König 1994, 104)

Why should it be a 'most difficult' event? Precisely because, until this moment in time, children are living in a dream-like consciousness in which they are still closely connected to their spiritual, pre-birth existence where they had dwelt with, (and in), more highly evolved spiritual beings. This is best expressed by Steiner:

> Whereas what we call the child's aura hovers around it during its earliest years like a wonderful human and superhuman power and, being really the higher part of the child, is continued on into the spiritual world, at the moment to which memory goes back, this aura sinks

> more into the inner being of the child. ... Henceforward the con-
> sciousness is at every point brought into connection with the external
> world. This is not the case with a very young child, to whom things
> appear only as a surrounding world of dreams. (Steiner 1970a, 6–7)

This 'world of dreams' is not in any way qualitatively inferior for the young child than their newly acquired earthly self-consciousness, but rather it reflects the soul's closeness to its spiritual origins. As we have already seen, the state of dreaming consciousness belongs to the feeling realm of the soul, and lies between *awake thinking* and the *sleeping unconscious* processes of the will. In this sense, the experience of acquiring self-consciousness is, quite literally, an *awakening* from a previous dream state.

Thinking and the Sense of Ego

In recent years, much has been written about the young child's thinking processes (Donaldson 1978; Wood 1988; Meadows 1983 & 1993). It is now considered that the pre-school child is much more cognitively able than was previously believed (Piaget 1982).

An anthroposophical understanding sees that the awakening to self-consciousness in the child, during the third year, and the awakening to thinking as a real cognitive activity go hand in hand (König 1984; Lievegoed 1987). This is quite distinct from the functioning of the sense of thought at around eighteen months. Both stem from the encounter of the dreaming child with something of his own true being. Then, with the *new age of defiance* that emerges strongly in the child after the birth of individual self-consciousness and thinking, the sense of ego can also begin to function.

This special sense of the ego as the inner essence of another person, grows in its perceptive capacity until, at around the ninth or tenth year, it reaches a certain maturity. At this age too, the child will once again meet something of his own spiritual being, and, in consequence and contrast, achieve a strengthened earthly self-consciousness. This existential experience is often accompanied by feelings of undefined loneliness and separation from the child's spiritual origins, as the incarnation process continues further and deeper into the physical bodily organization (Koepke 1989).

The social context

Early child development takes place through interaction with others.

> Children are born into a complex social world: from infancy on, they
> are active participants in a world of other people - adults and chil-
> dren, familiar and not-so-familiar others. (Dunn 1988, 2)

Moreover, it has been observed that:

> During the first few months of life, the baby is fascinated by the world of people. (Karmiloff-Smith 1994, 202)

There are, therefore, clear early indicators that a child is destined to become a social being; to become both a recipient of, and a contributor to, the human community. However, children come to this social context already bearing certain seeds and intentions for the future which, given favourable conditions, germinate and unfold over the course of time. Foremost amongst these necessary conditions will be the development of reciprocal relationships and interactions.

> These gifts and potentials can only be awakened when the surrounding world turns towards the child ... because a child will become nothing without the world of human beings. (König 1994, 91)

The neonate, infant, and young child must be able to establish active contact and communication with his social human surroundings so that developmental processes, involving metamorphosis and transformation on different levels, can underpin his successful incarnation.

Two key concepts

Through new earthly incarnations, separated by intervening periods of intense activity spent in supersensible worlds of soul and spirit, the human being receives many opportunities by which to evolve to higher levels of development (Steiner 1973). This anthroposophical perspective is clearly the complete antithesis of any materialistic, evolutionary viewpoint which regards death as the end of individual consciousness and existence. However, it is also very different from any religious viewpoint that regards an afterlife (whether in heaven or hell) as the final destination and resting place of individual souls.

In particular, it is only through incarnation and ego-integration that each person can become a more moral and unselfish being, who carries co-responsibility for the progress of the world. This moral path of evolution can, however, only be exercised and gradually realized in the company of other people — in the active social milieu, not in individual solitude and isolation.

2. Specific therapies and medical treatments

Listening space therapy

The aim is to harmonize the interrelationship between listening and moving. Several children can be taken together in a room where visual stimuli are reduced; for example, there is dimmed lighting. The children move when music is played on a lyre, flute, and/or recorder. At first the music is composed of short, swift notes, and the children are encouraged to make quick forward steps in time to the music. Then some long notes are also played and the children shall move backwards slowly. Gradually, during the course of the session, the long, slow notes and the backward walking predominate, and this brings the children to greater peace, and an increased listening capacity. In the second part of the therapy, the children sit and listen whilst music is played behind them. This therapy is particularly helpful for restless and hyperactive children, and autistic pupils can also benefit from this therapy.

Trumpet therapy

In this a number of children are guided to perform walking, and eurythmy arm movements, while tones are sounded. A trumpet is used to produce tones of increasing intensity. Autistic children can benefit because the therapy calls upon their own ego-forces to counter the strong trumpet sounds. This can also help to overcome any hypo-or hyper-sensitivity in hearing, due to a lack of ego-integration.

Music therapy

Autistic children are often very receptive to music, and therefore they can receive particular support and help through this medium. This has been clearly acknowledged in curative education:

> Music therapy is of particular value in the treatment of autistic children. Very severely autistic children who completely refuse to make use of language are often very musical and able to sing. Such children may sometimes be coaxed into a first kind of conversation on the basis of the duet. The therapist hums the first bars of a melody which the child may continue and thus, without looking at one

another, they can sometimes establish a to and fro in a purely musical realm. (Weihs 1984, 96)

While such simple musical conversations may well be used by curative educators, it will additionally require the expertise of a music therapist to apply this field in a much more precise way, such that:

> ... melodies, intervals, single tones, pitch, harmony, rhythm and metre, are elements used therapeutically to work deeply into the living processes of specific organs and can aid ego-integration of a growing individual, as well as work on the emotional life. (Hansmann 1992, 138)

Riding therapy

According to Hansmann (1992), horse riding therapy, as developed in curative education, is helpful for a broad spectrum of pupils including those who are autistically withdrawn. A certain relationship with music therapy exists, since the horse walks at a 4/4 rhythm, trots in a 2/2 rhythm, and canters in a 3/4 rhythm. Riding helps to regulate a child's breathing rhythm and thus supports the flow of speech.

The special relationship which the autistic child can form with the horse, is therapeutic in itself, and fosters inner security and confidence. If the autistic child can actually learn to direct the horse in a good walking rhythm, this will bear witness to their increased ego-control and integration. Other significant benefits have also been clearly described (see Hansmann 1992).

Curative eurythmy

Of all the therapies in the field of curative education, this is probably the most important. It must be applied by a trained curative eurythmist working under the advice of an anthroposophical doctor, and done with each child individually. Special eurythmy movements, based on speech sounds and musical tones, are used according to the individual diagnosis. These movements work deeply into the etheric formative forces and organs in the child's body (Kirchner-Bockholt 1992). When prescribed for a particular autistic child, the therapist first needs to gain the child's trust and co-operation, in order to lead them into active participation in the exercises.

Play therapy

The autistic child has little or no ability to play creatively or spontaneously. Therefore this therapy, guided by the therapist's empathetic understanding, can be especially helpful:

> The child can be led from a set, inflexible way of being, into a future with new possibilities of expression and experience. (Hansmann 1992, 146)

The therapist is called upon to create an inner soul space in themselves which can receive and accept the child as he is, and also recognize the difficulties which confront the child's real being. This interrelationship with the child calls upon the therapist's own creative and imaginative potentials, and can employ a wide range of materials. A moving and classic account of the value of play therapy, in psychotherapy with an emotionally withdrawn child, is found in the book *Dibs in search of self* by Virginia Axline (1985).

While not confined to play therapy, the use of a puppet theatre for autistic children can be included here. The very indirectness and non-commitment involved with a puppet show can bring relief and pleasure to the autistic child.

> The most severely withdrawn child will become indistinguishable from other normal healthy children in his reaction to a puppet performance, for he can enjoy and participate in a great variety of dramatic human situations without committing himself. (Weihs 1984, 97)

Art therapy

Art therapists will usually be able to offer painting, modelling, and drawing, to meet the child's needs. The therapy, in whichever medium, aims to harmonize the threefold nature of the child (see Chapter 8), by working especially on the rhythmic system and the feeling life. By strengthening this middle sphere of breathing and blood circulation, a dynamic balance can be developed within the human threefoldness, both for body and soul.

Painting, for example, makes use of the differential qualities of colours, and their relationships and gestures (Hauschka 1985). Painting and colours work particularly on the child's astral nature. Modelling strengthens the etheric body. Form or dynamic drawing stimulates the lower senses. Ego-integration through the middle senses of sight, warmth, smell and taste, can be cultivated through anthroposophical art therapy, and an autistic child can benefit greatly from this, when using the medium best suited to meet his individual needs.

Coloured light therapy

This therapy is still in its early stages of development (Luxford 1994, 83). It unites eurythmy, colour and music, and aims to harmonize the breathing process in children. Overall, it has a quietening and calming effect.

A group of children sit on one side of a large, semi-transparent screen, and watch the play of beautiful coloured shadows created from the movements performed by a eurythmist on the opposite side of the screen. The coloured light comes from daylight passing through coloured windows or celluloids, and the actual combination of colours can be controlled and varied during the therapy. This is accompanied by music, usually from a lyre.

Chirophonetics

In this therapy the therapist phonates a sound while simultaneously stroking a corresponding shape on to the child's back. This massage stroke represents the form of a breath in the mouth during articulation.

Originally, this therapy was meant for children in whom speech failed to develop at the appropriate age. However, today chirophonetics is not used exclusively in stimulating the speech impulse, but more generally.

> ... particularly in the treatment of autism, with its many unsolved questions. An autistic child does not have recourse to the possibilities which his speech organs offer, he or she avoids confrontation with others through speech, most particularly when one wants to entice such a child to speak. ...
>
> However, as chirophonetics makes no active demands on the child, it was helpful in a number of cases, in stimulating the will to speak. (Baur 1993, xv)

This therapy can also stimulate the power of imitation which is impaired in young autistic children (Baur 1992).

Rhythmical massage

Massage must be rhythmical in order to strengthen the forces of the rhythmic middle system in the human threefoldness, which especially supports the feeling life of the soul (Evans & Rodger 2000). Moreover, it is through breathing, that the incarnation process takes place. Therefore this therapy can also be used to help an autistic child to achieve better ego-integration, provided the child will tolerate direct touching.

In this massage treatment special oils are used, as indicated by the doctor, to enhance the curative effects.

3. Useful contact addresses

The National Autistic Society (NAS)
393 City Road
London EC1V 1NG
Tel. 020–7833 2299
Fax. 020–7833 9666
website:
http://www.oneworld.org/autism_uk/

**Allergy Induced Autism
Organization (AiA)**
210 Pineapple Road
Stirchley
Birmingham B30 2TY
Tel. 0121–444 6450
email: AiA@Kessick.demon.co.uk
website:
http://www.demon.co.uk/charities/AIA/aia.htm

The Autism Research Unit
School of Health Sciences
University of Sunderland
Sunderland SR2 7EE
email: aru@sunderland.ac.uk
website:
http://www.osiris.sunderland.ac.uk/autism/

Autism Independent UK
(previously known as Society for the
Autistically Handicapped or SFTAH.)
199–205 Blandford Avenue
Kettering NN16 9AT
Tel/Fax 01526–523 274
email: autism@rmplc.co.uk
website: http://www.autismuk.com

Association of Camphill Communities
Gawain House
56 Welham Road
Norton
York YO17 9DP
Tel. 01653–694 197
Fax 01653–600 001
email: info@camphill.org.uk
website: http://www.camphill.org.uk

**European Co-operation in
Anthroposophical Curative
Education and Social Therapy**
Duinweg 35
3737 LC Bosch en Duin
The Netherlands
Tel. +31–30–693 5213
Fax +31–30–693 5217

**International Council for
Anthroposophical Special
Education (Konferenz)**
Brosiweg 9
4143 Dornach
Switzerland
Tel. +41–61–701 8485
Fax +41–61–701 8104

**The National Autistic Society in
Wales (NASW)**
William Knox House
Britannic Way
Llandarcy SA10 6EL
Tel. 01792–815 915

The Scottish Society for Autism (SSA)
Hilton House
Alloa Business Park
Whins Road
Alloa FK10 3SA
Tel. 01259–720 044
Fax 01259–720 051
website:
http://www.autism-in-scotland.org.uk

Parents for the Early Intervention of Autism in Children (PEACH)
School of Education
Brunel University
300 St Margaret's Road
Twickenham TW1 1PT
Tel. 020–8891 0121 ext. 2348
Fax 020–8891 8209
email: peach@brunel.ac.uk
website: http://www.peach.uk.com

Autism Network for Dietary Intervention (ANDI)
(AiA's sister organization in the USA)
PO Box 17711
Rochester NY 14617–0711
website: http//www.AutismNDI.com

Autism Research Institute
4182 Adams Avenue
San Diego CA 92116
Fax (619) 563 6840
website: http://www.autism.com/aro
OR http://www.autism.org

Other websites:

Gluten Free Casein Free (GFCF)
American website produced by parents and professionals. Some British products listed. UK section to follow shortly.
website: http://www.gfcfdiet.com
website: http://www.AutismDiet.com

Local organizations:

Please note that there are other regional organizations in your local area who will also be able to help you. Check your local telephone directories, or contact your local library or Social Services for further details.

Bibliography

Aarons, M. and Gittens, T. 1992. *The Handbook of Autism: A Guide for Parents and Professionals.* London and New York: Routledge.

Aeppli, W. 1986. *Rudolf Steiner Education and the Developing Child.* New York: Anthroposophic Press.

—, 1993. *The Care and Development of the Human Senses.* Forest Row, Sussex: Steiner Schools Fellowship Publications.

Alvin, J. and Warwick, A. 1992. *Music Therapy for the Autistic Child.* Oxford University Press.

Arnim, G. von. 1986. Körperschema und Leibessinne. *In* König 1986.

Astington, J.W. 1994. *The Child's Discovery of the Mind.* London: Fontana.

Attwood, T. 1998. *Asperger's Syndrome, a Guide for Parents and Professionals.* London: Jessica Kingsley.

Autism Research Review. 1995. Vol. 9, No.4. San Diego: Autism Research Institute.

Autism Research Unit. 1991. *Therapeutic Approaches to Autism: Research and Practice.* London: National Autistic Society.

Axline, V.M. 1985. *Dibs in Search of Self.* Harmondsworth: Penguin Books.

Ayres, A.J. 1995. *Sensory Integration and the Child.* Los Angeles: Western Psychological Services.

Baron-Cohen, S. and Bolton, P. 1993. *Autism, the Facts.* New York: Oxford University Press.

Barron, J. and S. 1993. *There's a Boy in Here.* London: Chapmans.

Baur, A. 1992. Chirophonetics. In *Curative Education and Social Therapy* Issue 1. Easter 1992. 10–12.

—, 1993. *Healing Sounds: Fundamentals of Chirophonetics.* Sacramento: Rudolf Steiner College Press.

Beck, V. & Beck, G. 1998. *Unlocking the Potential of Secretin.* San Diego: Published on website http://www.osiris.sunderland.ac.uk/autism/sec.htm

Bettelheim, B. 1967. *The Empty Fortress.* New York: Free Press.

Biesantz, H and Klingborg, A. 1979. *The Goetheanum, Rudolf Steiner's architectural impulse.* London: Rudolf Steiner Press.

Bosch, G. 1962. *Der frühkindliche Autismus.* Berlin.

Bott, V. 1982. *Anthroposophical Medicine.* London: Rudolf Steiner Press.

Boucher, J. and Scarth, L. 1977. Research and the teaching of autistic children. in Furneaux, B. and Roberts, B. *Autistic Children.* London: Routledge & Kegan Paul.

Britz-Crecelius, H. 1979. *Children at Play, Preparation for Life.* Edinburgh: Floris Books.

Childs, G. 1991. *Steiner Education in Theory and Practice.* Edinburgh: Floris Books.

—, 1996. *Five + Seven = 12 senses. Rudolf Steiner's Contribution to the Psychology of Perception.* Stroud: Fir Tree Press.

Christie, N. 1989. *Beyond Loneliness and Institutions.* Norwegian University Press.

Connor, M. and Ferguson-Smith, M. 1977. *Medical Genetics,* Oxford: Blackwell Science.

Courchesne, E. 1991. Neuroanatomic imaging in autism. *Pediatrics* 87. Part 2. Supplement. 781–90.

Davy, J. (Ed). 1975. *Work Arising from the Life of Rudolf Steiner.* London: Rudolf Steiner Press.

Delacato, C.H. 1974. *The Ultimate Stranger, the Autistic Child.* California: Academic Therapy Publications.

Dohan. Cereals and schizophrenia: data and hypothesis. *Acta Psychiatr. Scand.* 42:125.

Donaldson, M. 1978. *Children's Minds.* London: Fontana.

—, 1992. New edition. Harmondsworth: Penguin Books.

Dunn, J. 1988. *The Beginnings of Social Understanding.* Oxford: Basil Blackwell.

Ekstein, R. 1973. *Grenzfallkinder.* Munich & Basel.

Elgar, S. and Wing, L. 1981. *Teaching Autistic Children, Guidelines for Teachers No.5.* London: National Autistic Society.

Elliot, A. 1990. Adolescence and early adulthood: the needs of the young adult with severe difficulties. In Ellis, K. (Ed) 1990. *Autism.*

Ellis, K. (Ed) 1990. *Autism, Professional Perspectives and Practice.* London: Chapman & Hall.

Engel, P. 1968. Movement patterns and behaviour. Unpublished lecture, given at Camphill British Regional Conference in Thornbury. Sheiling School Library.

Erikson, E.H. 1968. Die Ontogenese der Ritualisierung. *Psyche 7* (July).

Evans, M. and Rodger, I. 2000. *Healing for Body, Soul, and Spirit: an Introduction to Anthroposophical Medicine.* Edinburgh: Floris Books.

Farrants, W. 1988. *Camphill Villages.* Camphill Press.

Feuser, G. 1980. *Autistische Kinder.* Solms-Oberbiel.

Fischer, E. 1965. *Jahrbuch für Jugendpsychiatrie und ihre Grenzgebiete.* Vol. 4. Bern.

Flavell, J.H. 1985. *Cognitive Development.* Prentice-Hall.

Frankland, M. 1995. *Freddie the Weaver.* Sinclair-Stevenson.

Frith, U. 1989. *Autism, Explaining the Enigma.* Oxford: Basil Blackwell.

—, (Ed). 1991. *Autism and Asperger Syndrome.* New York: Cambridge University Press.

Furneaux, B. and Roberts, B. 1979. *Autistic Children, Teaching, Community and Research Approaches.* London: Routledge & Kegan Paul.

Garvey, C. 1991. *Play*. London: Fontana.

Glöckler, M. and Goebel, W. 1990. *A Guide to Child Health*. Edinburgh: Floris Books.

Grandin, T. and Scariano, M. 1986. *Emergence Labelled Autistic*. Ann Arbor Publishers Ltd.

Hansmann, H. 1992. *Education for Special Needs, Principles and Practice in Camphill Schools*. Edinburgh: Floris Books.

Happé, F. 1994. *Autism, an Introduction to Psychological Theory*. London: UCL Press Ltd.

Harris, J.C. 1995. *Developmental Neuropsychiatry*. Volume II. Oxford University Press.

Harris, P.L. 1991. *Children and Emotion*. Oxford: Basil Blackwell.

Harwood, A.C. 1975. Threefold man. In Davy, J. (Ed) *Work arising from the life of Rudolf Steiner.*

—, 1982. *The Recovery of Man in Childhood*. New York: Anthroposophic Press.

Hauschka, M. 1979. *Rhythmical Massage*. London: Rudolf Steiner Press.

—, 1985. *Fundamentals of Artistic Therapy: the Nature and Task of Painting Therapy*. London: Rudolf Steiner Press.

Heider, M. von. 1995. *Looking Forward*. Hawthorn Press

Hobson, R.P. 1993. *Autism and the Development of Mind*. Lawrence Erlbaum Associates.

Hocking, B. 1990. *Little Boy Lost*. London: Bloomsbury.

Holtzapfel, W. 1993. I drown in loneliness. In *Curative Education and Social Therapy*. Issue I. Easter 1993. 4–9.

—, 1995. *Children with a Difference*. East Grinstead: Lanthorn Press.

Horvath, K., Papadimitrou, J.C., Rabsztyn, A., Drachenberg, C., Tildon, J.T. Gastro-intestinal Abnormalities in Children with Autistic Disorder. *Journal of Pediatrics,* Volume 135(5) 559–563. November 1999.

Howlin, P. 1994. Facilitated communication and autism; are the claims for success justified? In *Communication*. Vol. 28. Issue 2. 10–12.

ICD-10 1993. *International Classification of Diseases*. Geneva : World Health Organization.

International Molecular Genetics Study of Autism Consortium. Newsletter Number 2. April 2000. www.well.ox.ac.uk/-maestrin/news2000.html

Jordan, R. *Autistic Spectrum Disorders*. David Fulton Publishers. 1999.

Jordan, R. and Powell, S. 1990. *The Special Curricular of Autistic Children: Learning and Thinking Skills*. London: The Association of Head Teachers of Autistic Children and Adults.

—, 1996. *Understanding and Teaching Children with Autism*. John Wiley & Sons.

Kanner, L. 1943. Autistic disturbances of affective contact. *Nervous Child 2*. 1943. 217–50.

Karmiloff-Smith, A. 1994. *Baby it's You*. London: Ebury Press.

Kaufman, B.N. 1976. *Son-rise*. New York: Warner Books.

Kehrer, H.E. 1978. *Kindlicher Autismus*. Basel, Munich: S. Karger.

Kirchner, H. 1977. *Dynamic Drawing: its Therapeutic Aspect*. New York: The Rudolf Steiner School.

Kirchner-Bockholt, M. 1992. *Fundamental Principles of Curative Eurythmy*. London: Temple Lodge.

Klimm, H. 1965. Über die heilpädagogische Behandlung von Kindern mit autistischen Erscheinungen. *Pro Infirmis*. June.

—, 1981. *Beobachtungen and Erwägungen beim Autimus, Der frühkindliche Autismus als Entwicklungsstörung*. Stuttgart: Freies Geistesleben.

Knivsberg, A.M., Reichelt, K.L., Nodland, M. 1999. Autism spectrum disorders in children in mainstream classes. A collection of papers from the conference held in the University of Durham. April 1999.

Koepke, H. 1989. *Encountering the Self, Transformation and Destiny in the Ninth Year*. New York: Anthroposophic Press.

Konferenz for Curative Education & Social Therapy, Secretariat of (Ed). 1995. *List of the Anthroposophical Homes, Schools, Workshops, and Village Communities for Curative Education and Social Therapy*. Dornach.

König, K. 1960. *The Autistic Child I & II*. English Translation in Sheiling School Library. (In German in Muller-Wiedemann *et al.* 1988.)

—, 1971. *Sinnesentwicklung und Leiberfahrung, Heilpädagogik aus anthroposophischer Menschenkunde – 5*. Stuttgart: Freies Geistesleben. (English Translation Sheiling School Library.)

—, 1984. *The First Three Years of the Child*. Edinburgh: Floris Books.

—, 1986. *Sinnesentwicklung und Leiberfahrung*. Stuttgart.

—, 1989. *Being Human: Diagnosis in Curative Education*. Camphill Press.

—, 1990. *Man as a Social Being, and the Mission of Conscience*. Camphill Press.

—, 1994. *Eternal Childhood*. TWT Publications Ltd., on behalf of the Camphill Movement.

König, K. *et al.* 1953. The treatment with Thalamus. Camphill in-house publication.

König, K., von Arnim, G., and Herberg. 1978. *Sprachverständnis und Sprachenbehandlung*. Stuttgart.

Kügelgen, H. von. (Ed). 1975. *Understanding Young Children, Extracts from Lectures by Rudolf Steiner compiled for the use of Kindergarten Teachers*. London: Rudolf Steiner Press.

Lauer, H.E. 1977. *Die zwölf Sinne des Menschen*. Schaffhausen.

Le Breton, M. 1996. *Diet Intervention and Autism*. London: Jessica Kindersley.

Lewis, L. 1998. *Understanding and Implementing Special Diets to Aid in the Treatment of Autism and Related Developmental Disorders*. Future Horizons Inc.

Lievegoed, B. 1987. *Phases of Childhood*. Edinburgh: Floris Books.

—, 1993. *Phases, the Spiritual Rhythms of Adult Life*. Bristol: Rudolf Steiner Press.

Lovell, A. 1978. *Simple Simon: the Story of an Autistic Boy.* Lion Publishing.

Lutz, C. 1968. In Müller-Wiedemann *et al* 1988. *Der frühkindliche Austismus.*

Luxford, M. 1994. *Children with Special Needs; Rudolf Steiner's Ideas in Practice.* Edinburgh: Floris Books.

Mahler, Margaret S. 1968. *On Human Symbiosis and the Vicissitudes of Individuation: Infantile Psychosis.* Connecticut. International Universities Press.

—, 1995. *Infantile Psychosis.* Volume 1 of *Selected Papers of Margaret S. Mahler.* New Jersey: Jason Aronson.

Meadows, S. 1983. *Developing Thinking: Approaches to Children's Cognitive Development.* London & New York: Methuen.

—, 1986. *Understanding Child Development.* London: Unwin Hyman.

—, 1993. *The Child as Thinker.* London & New York: Routledge.

Miedzanik, D. 1986. *My Autobiography.* University of Nottingham, Child Development Research Unit.

Müller-Wiedemann, H. 1966. Social development in handicapped children. In Pietzner, C. *Aspects of Curative Education*, Aberdeen University Press.

—, 1982. *Autism and Ego-Development.* Unpublished notes from three lectures given in Camphill, Scotland. 14–21 June 1982. Sheiling School Library.

—, 1990. Neue Aspekte der Förderung autistischer Kinder. In *Autismus Heute.* Vol. 2. Dortmund: Verlag Modernes Lernen.

Müller-Wiedemann, H., König, K., Weihs, T.J. *et al.* 1988. *Der frühkindliche Autismus als Entwicklungsstörung.* Stuttgart: Freies Geistesleben.

Niederhäuser, H.R. and Frohlich, M. 1974. *Form Drawing.* New York: Rudolf Steiner School.

Opie, I. & P. 1988. *The Singing Game.* Oxford University Press.

Park, C.C. 1983. *The Siege.* London: Hutchinson & Co Ltd.

Piaget, J. 1962. *Play, Dreams and Imitation in Childhood.* New York: W.W. Norton.

—, 1982. *The Child's Conception of the World.* London: Granada Publishing Ltd.

Pietzner, Carlo (Ed). 1966. *Aspects of Curative Education.* Aberdeen University Press.

Pietzner, Cornelius, (Ed). 1990. *A Candle on the Hill: Images of Camphill Life.* Edinburgh: Floris Books.

Poppelbaum, H. 1959. *Schicksalsrätsel.* Dornach.

Raffe, M. et al 1974. *Eurythmy and the Impulse of Dance.* London: Rudolf Steiner Press.

Richardson, P. and J. 1994. Auditory integration training: how it helped our son. In *Communication.* Vol. 28. Issue I. 9–12.

Rimland, B. 1996. *My 35 Years of Experience with Facilitated Communication.* San Diego: Autism Research Institute.

Roggenkamp, W. and Fischer, B. (Eds). 1974. *Healing Education Based on Anthroposophy's Image of Man.* Vereinigung der Heil und Erziehungs-Institute für Seelenpflege-bedürftige Kinder e.V. and Sozial-Therapeutische Werkgemeinschaft e.V.

Rutter, M. and Schopler E. (Eds.). 1978. *Autism: a Reappraisal of Concepts and Treatment.* New York, London.

Rutter, M. and Howlin, P. 1989. *Treatment of Autistic Children.* John Wiley & Sons.

Rutter, M. *et al.* 1994. Autism and known medical conditions: myth and substance. In *J. Child Psychology.* Vol. 35. No. 2. 311–22.

Sacks, O. 1994. An anthropologist on Mars. In *The New Yorker.* Dec 27, 1993/Jan 3, 1994. 106–25.

Sahlmann, L. 1969. Autism or Aphasia. In *Developmental Medicine and Child Neurology.* II: 443–48.

Sanderson, N. and Fraley, G. 1994. Exchange of views. In *Communication.* Vol. 28. Issue I: 22–25.

Sandler, A. and colleagues. 1999. Lack of benefit of a single dose of synthetic human secretin in the treatment of autism and pervasive developmental disorder. The *New England Journal of Medicine.* Volume 341. No. 24. 9 December 1999.

Schreibman, L. 1988. *Autism.* SAGE Publications.

Scotson, L. 1985. *Doran: Child of Courage.* London: Collins.

Seddon, R. 1988. *Rudolf Steiner, Essential Readings.* Crucible: The Aquarian Press.

Sellin, B. 1995. *In Dark Hours I Find My Way, Messages From An Autistic Child.* London: Victor Gollancz.

Shattock, P. and Whiteley, P. *The Sunderland Protocol.* Durham Conference Paper 2000. Published on website: http://osiris.sunderland.ac.uk/autism/durham2.htm

Sheridan, M.D. 1988. *From Birth to Five Years, Children's Developmental Progress.* NFER-Nelson.

Simons, J. and Oishi, S. 1987. *The Hidden Child, the Linwood Method for Reaching the Autistic Child.* Rockeville: Woodbine House.

Smith, T. 1995. *The Human Body.* London: Dorling Kindersley Limited.

Soesman, A. 1990. *The Twelve Senses.* Hawthorn Press.

Stehli, A. 1991. *The Sound of a Miracle, a Child's Triumph over Autism.* New York: Doubleday.

Steiner, R. 1959. *The Inner Nature of Man, and the Life between Death and a new Birth.* London: Anthroposophical Publishing Company.

—, 1967. *A Lecture on Eurythmy.* London: Rudolf Steiner Press.

—, 1969a. *True and False Paths in Spiritual Investigation.* London: Rudolf Steiner Press.

—, 1969b. *Education as a Social Problem.* New York: Anthroposophic Press.

—, 1969c. *The Manifestations of Karma.* London: Rudolf Steiner Press.

—, 1970. *The Case for Anthroposophy.* London: Rudolf Steiner Press.

—, 1970a. *The Spiritual Guidance of Man.* New York: Anthroposophic Press.

—, 1970b. *At the Gates of Spiritual Science.* London: Rudolf Steiner Press.

—, 1972. *Curative Education.* London. Rudolf Steiner Press .(New edition published as *Education for Special Needs* in 1998).

—, 1973. *Theosophy, an Introduction to the Supersensible Knowledge of the World and the Destination of Man.* London: Rudolf Steiner Press.

—, 1975. *Life between Death and Rebirth*. New York: Anthroposophical Press.

—, 1975a. *The Education of the Child in the Light of Anthroposophy*. London: Rudolf Steiner Press.

—, 1976a. The work of the ego in childhood. In *Anthroposophical Quarterly*. Vol. 21. No. 4. Winter. 86–92.

—, 1976b. *The Christ Impulse and the Development of Ego-Consciousness*. New York: Anthroposophic Press.

—, 1978. *The Effects of Spiritual Development*. London: Rudolf Steiner Press.

—, 1980. *Zur Sinneslehre*. Stuttgart.

—, 1981. *Man as a Being of Sense and Perception*. Vancouver: Steiner Book Centre.

—, 1982. *The Kingdom of Childhood*. London: Rudolf Steiner Press.

—, 1983. *Health and Illness*. Volume 2. New York: Anthroposophic Press.

—, 1986. *Soul Economy and Waldorf Education*. London: Rudolf Steiner Press.

—, 1988. *The Child's Changing Consciousness and Waldorf Education*. London: Rudolf Steiner Press.

—, 1989. *Occult Science — an Outline*. London: Rudolf Steiner Press.

—, 1990a. *Learning to See into the Spiritual World*. New York: Anthroposophic Press.

—, 1990b. *Study of Man*. London: Rudolf Steiner Press.

—, 1992. *The Philosophy of Spiritual Activity*. London: Rudolf Steiner Press.

—, 1993. *Knowledge of the Higher Worlds, How is it Achieved*? London: Rudolf Steiner Press.

—, 1996. *The Foundations of Human Experience*. New York: Anthroposophic Press.

—, 1997. (Lecture 9 August 1919) *Education as a Force for Social Change*. (GA 296) New York: Anthroposophic Press.

—, 1998. *Education for Special Needs*. London. Rudolf Steiner Press.

Steiner, R. and Wegman I. 1996. *Extending Practical Medicine*. London: Rudolf Steiner Press.

Stores, G. and Wiggs, L. 1998. Abnormal sleep patterns associated with Autism. *Autism*. Volume 2. Number 2. June 1998.

Sylva, K. and Lunt, I. 1982. *Child Development, a First Course*. Oxford: Basil Blackwell.

Taylor, B., Miller, E., Lingham, R., Simmons, A., and Stowe, J. 'Measles, Mumps and Rubella Vaccination and Bowel Problems or Developmental Regression in Children with Autism: population study.' *British Medical Journal*. 324:393–396. 16 February 2002.

Tinbergen, N. and E.A. 1983. *Autistic Children, New Hope for a Cure*. London: George Allen & Unwin.

Trevarthen, C., Aitken, K.J., Papoudi, D., and Robarts, J.Z. 1996. (second edition 1998). *Children with Autism, Diagnosis and Interventions to Meet their Needs*. London: Jessica Kingsley Publishers.

Tustin, F. 1992. *Autistic States in Children*. London & New York: Tavistock/ Routledge.

Verny, T. and Kelly, J. 1982. *The Secret Life of the Unborn Child*. London: Sphere Books.

Wachsmuth, G. 1937. *Reincarnation, as a Phenomenon of Metamorphosis*. Dornach: Philosophic-Anthroposophic Press.

Waring, R.H. 2000. Suphation in Autism. Lecture at Autism Europe Congress, May 2000.

Wakefield, A.J., Murch, S.H., Anthony, A., Linnell, J., Casson, D.M., Malik, M. *et al*. 1998. Ileal-lymphoid-nodular hyperplasma, non-specific colitis, and percusive developmental disorders in children. *The Lancet*. Volume 351. 1998.

Weihs, T.J. 1975. The handicapped child — curative education. In Davy, J. *Work arising from the life of Rudolf Steiner.*

—, 1984. *Children in Need of Special Care*. London: Souvenir Press.

Whiteley, P., Rodgers, J., Savery, D. and Shattock, P. 'A Gluten-free Diet as an Intervention for Autism and associated Spectrum Disorders: preliminary findings.' *Autism*. Volume 3. Number 1. March 1999.

Williams, D. 1992. *Nobody Nowhere, the Extraordinary Autobiography of an Autistic*. New York: Times Books.

—, 1994. *Somebody Somewhere*. Doubleday.

Wiltshire, S. 1991. *Floating Cities*. London: Michael Joseph.

Wing, L. 1990. What is autism? In Ellis, K. *Autism.*

—, 1993. *Autistic Continuum Disorders, an Aid to Diagnosis*. London: National Autistic Society.

—, 1996. *The Autistic Spectrum, a Guide for Parents and Professionals*. London: Constable.

Wood, D. 1988. *How Children Think and Learn*. Basil Blackwell.

Woodward, R.S. 1985. *Aspects of the Waldorf (Rudolf Steiner) School Curriculum as Offered in Schools for Normally Developing Children, and the Adaptation and Particular Contribution of this Curriculum for some Children with Special Educational Needs*. University of Bristol Library (unpublished Diploma dissertation).

Woodward, R.S. 1992. *Theory of Mind in the Light of Rudolf Steiner's Anthroposophy*. University of Bristol Library (unpublished M.Ed. Thesis).

Zeylmans van Emmichoven, F.W. 1982. *The Anthroposophical Understanding of the Soul*. New York: Anthroposophic Press.

Index

270   AUTISM: A HOLISTIC APPROACH